Pat Graham **Silent Pictures**

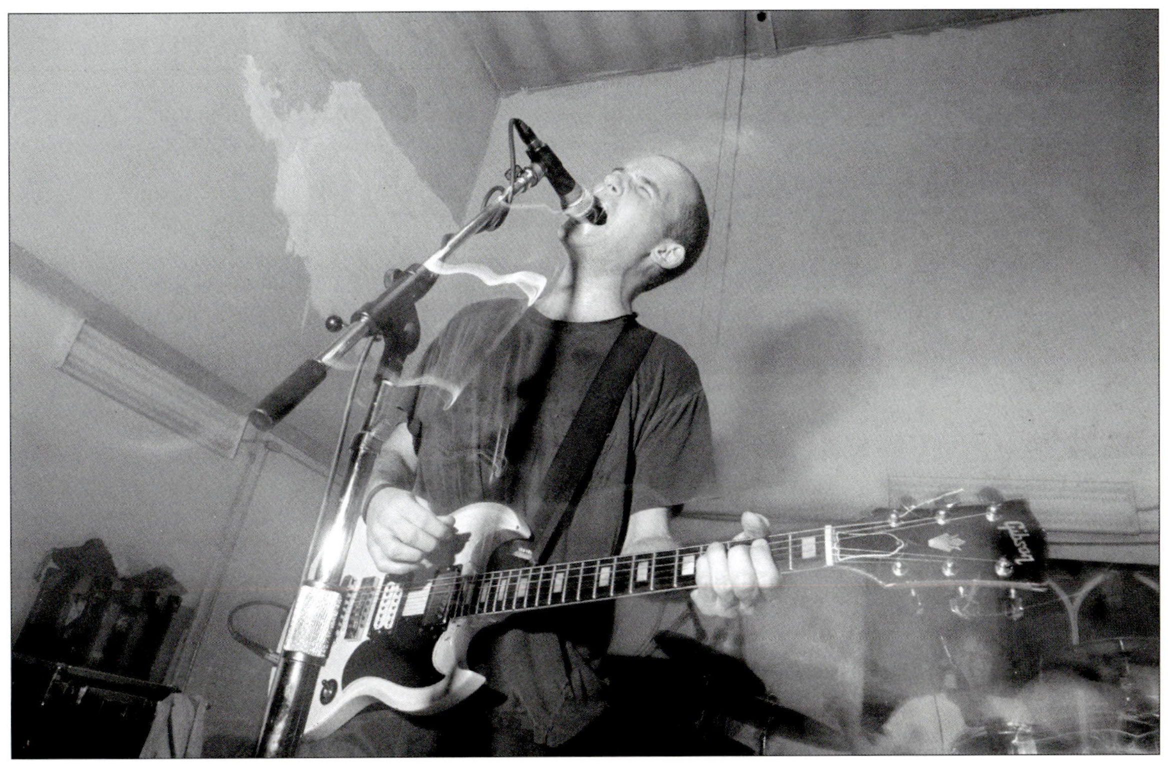

For Melanie, Honor, and Prue

Music can be so powerful and crowds so energetic that one needs only to stick a camera in the air at some shows to come away with something interesting to fans of a particular band or genre. History can make any picture relevant, but there is also a deeper language of photography that is able to communicate without the benefit of context. These are the pictures that draw people in and inspire them to engage and create.

In studying the images that Pat Graham has chosen for this collection, I am struck by how some of them are almost family photos for me, while others are of people I've never met, making music I've never heard. There are incidental views of communities that I'm intimate with, and loving studies of faraway scenes. There are photos of other people's experiences taken in a way that makes me feel as though I was there, but also a picture of my guitar (one that hung on my shoulders for over fifteen years) so intimate that I almost don't recognize it.

In Pat's eye they all find balance.

—Ian MacKaye

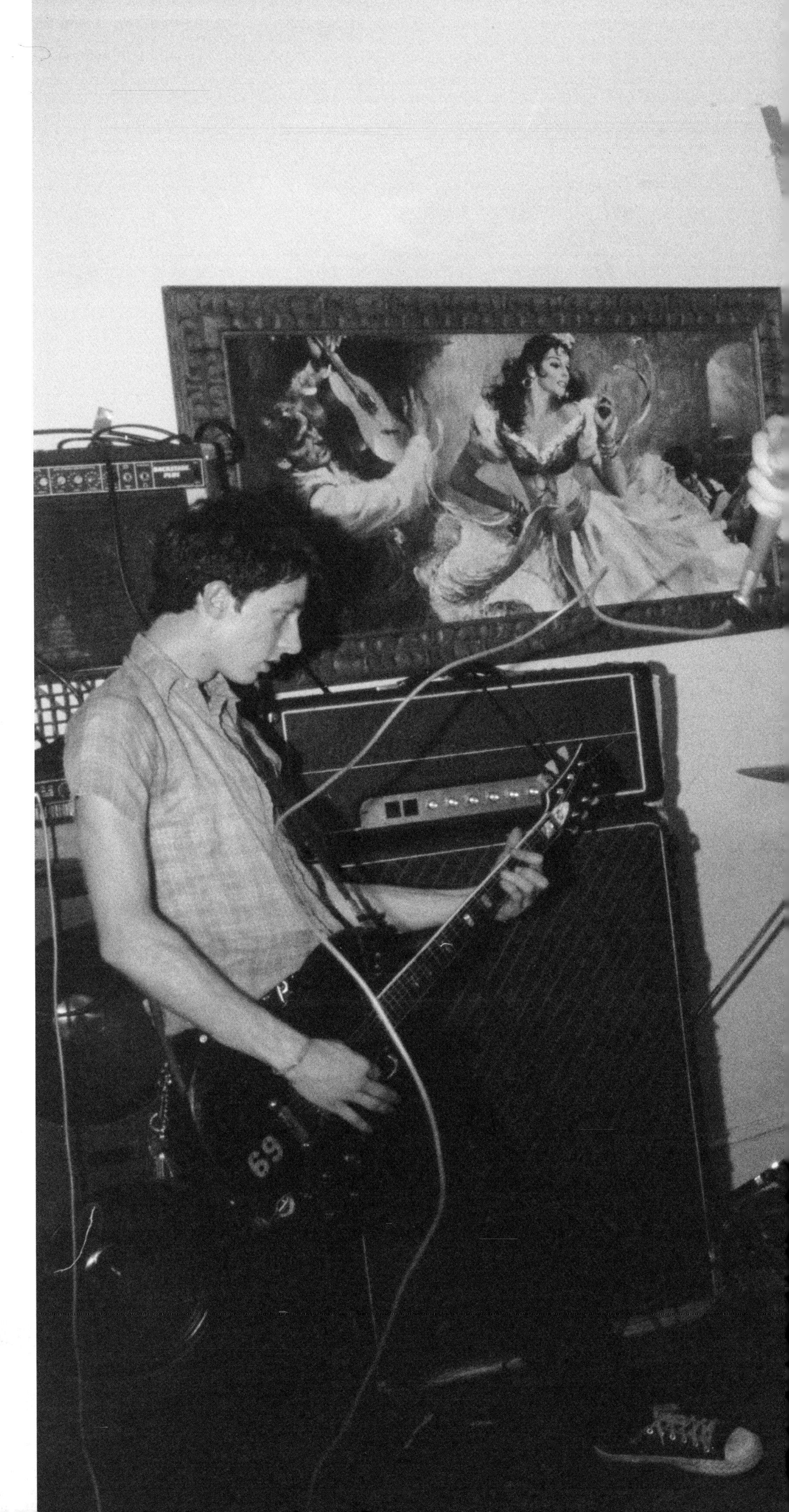

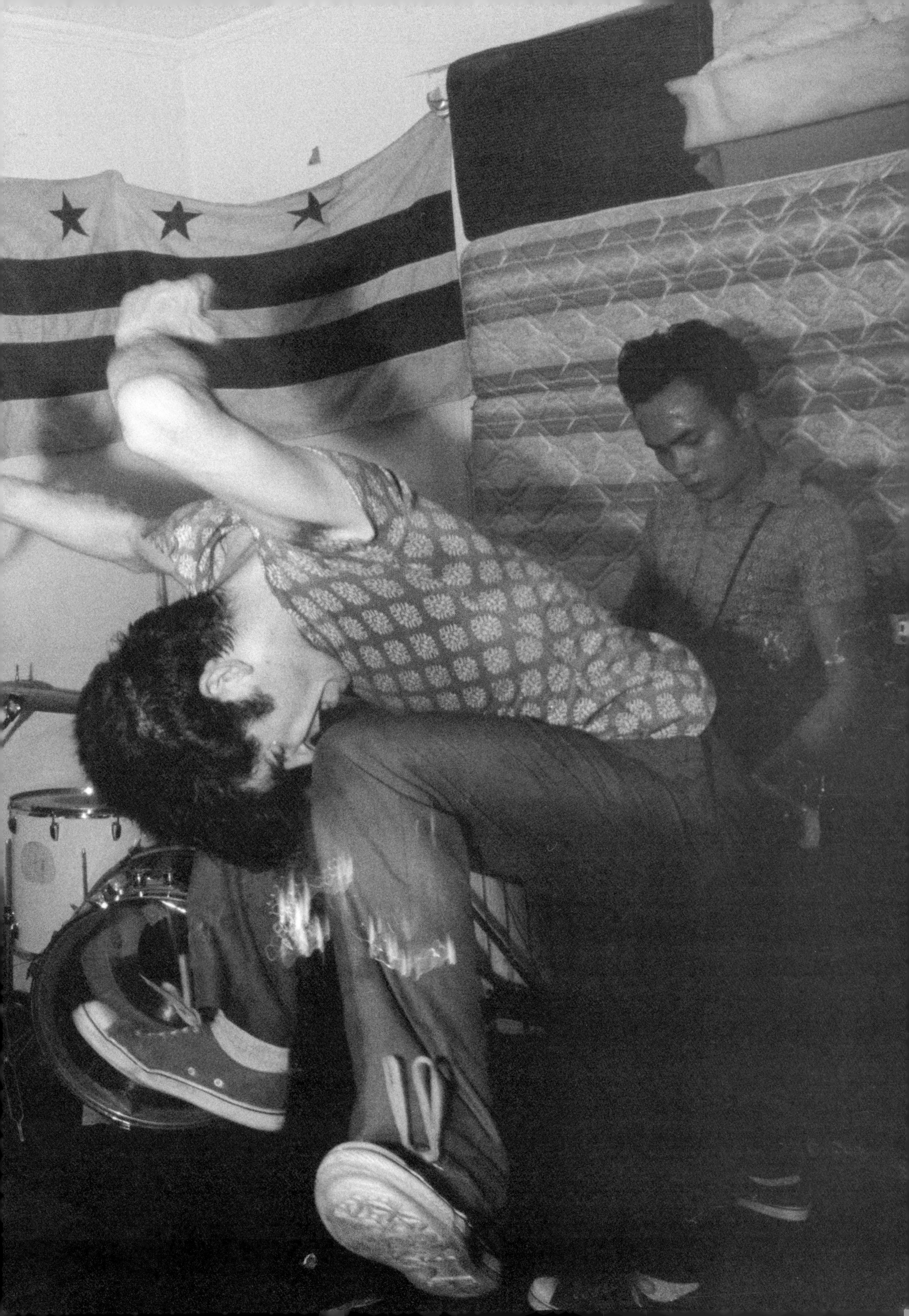

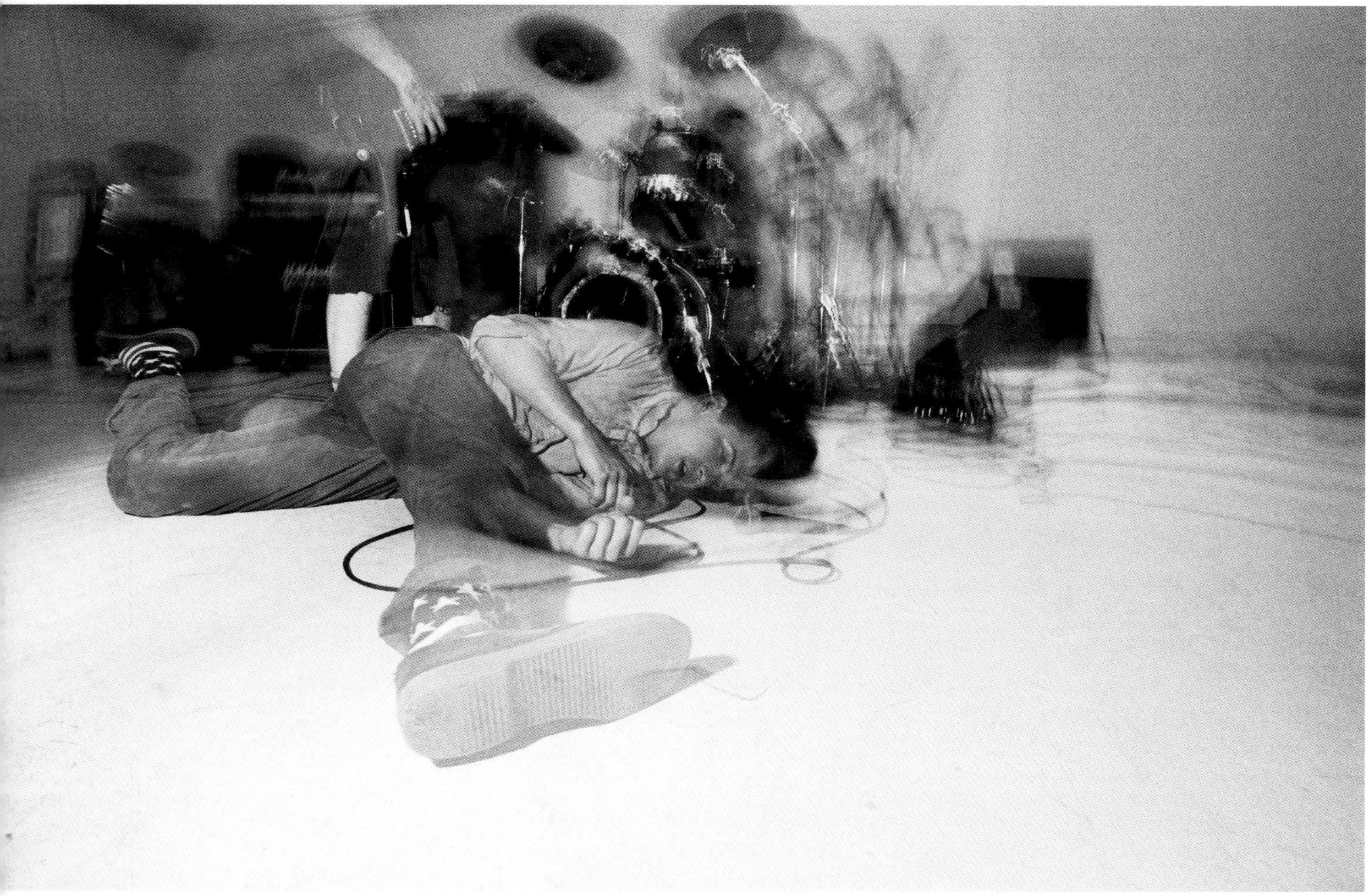

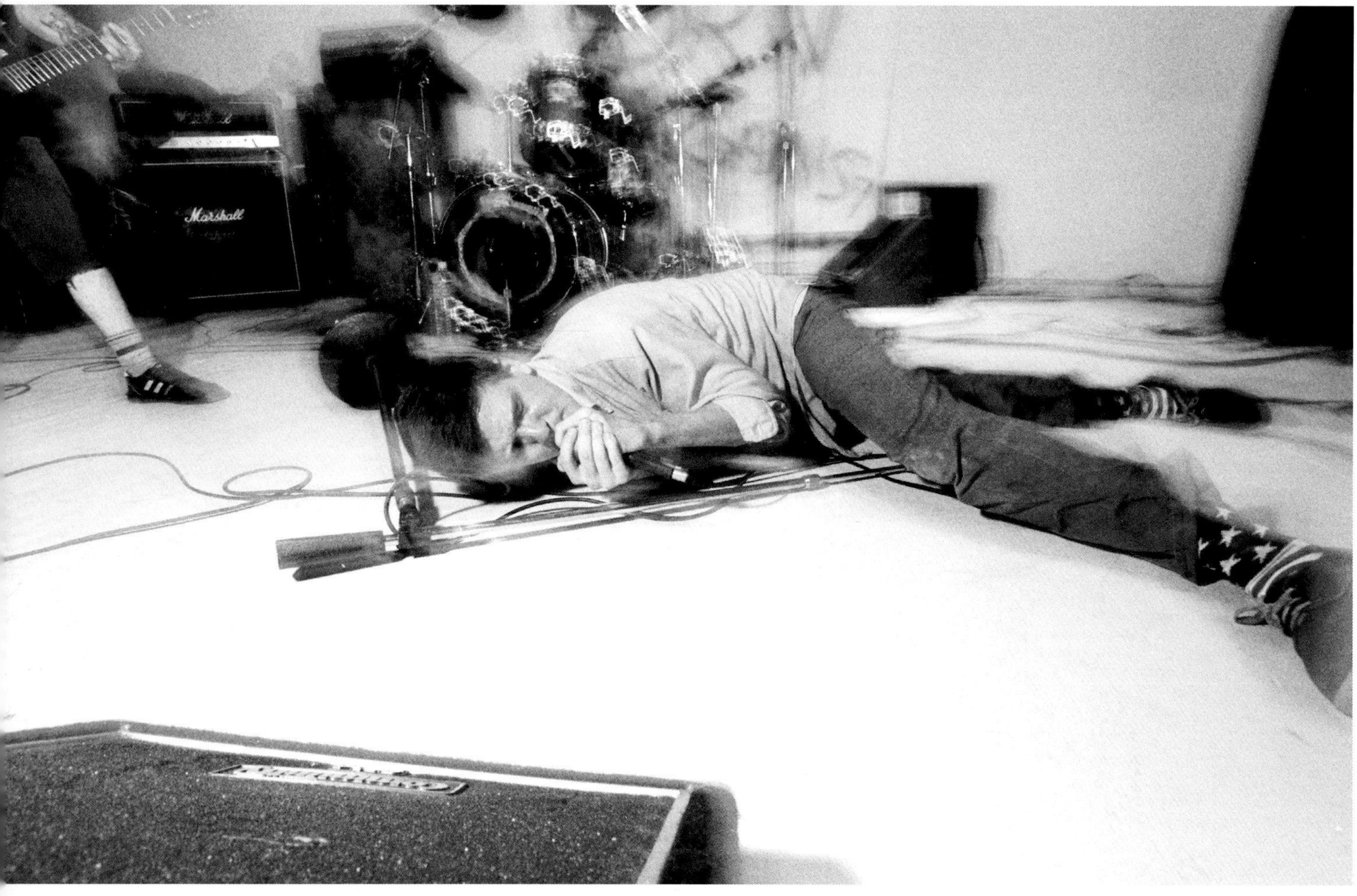

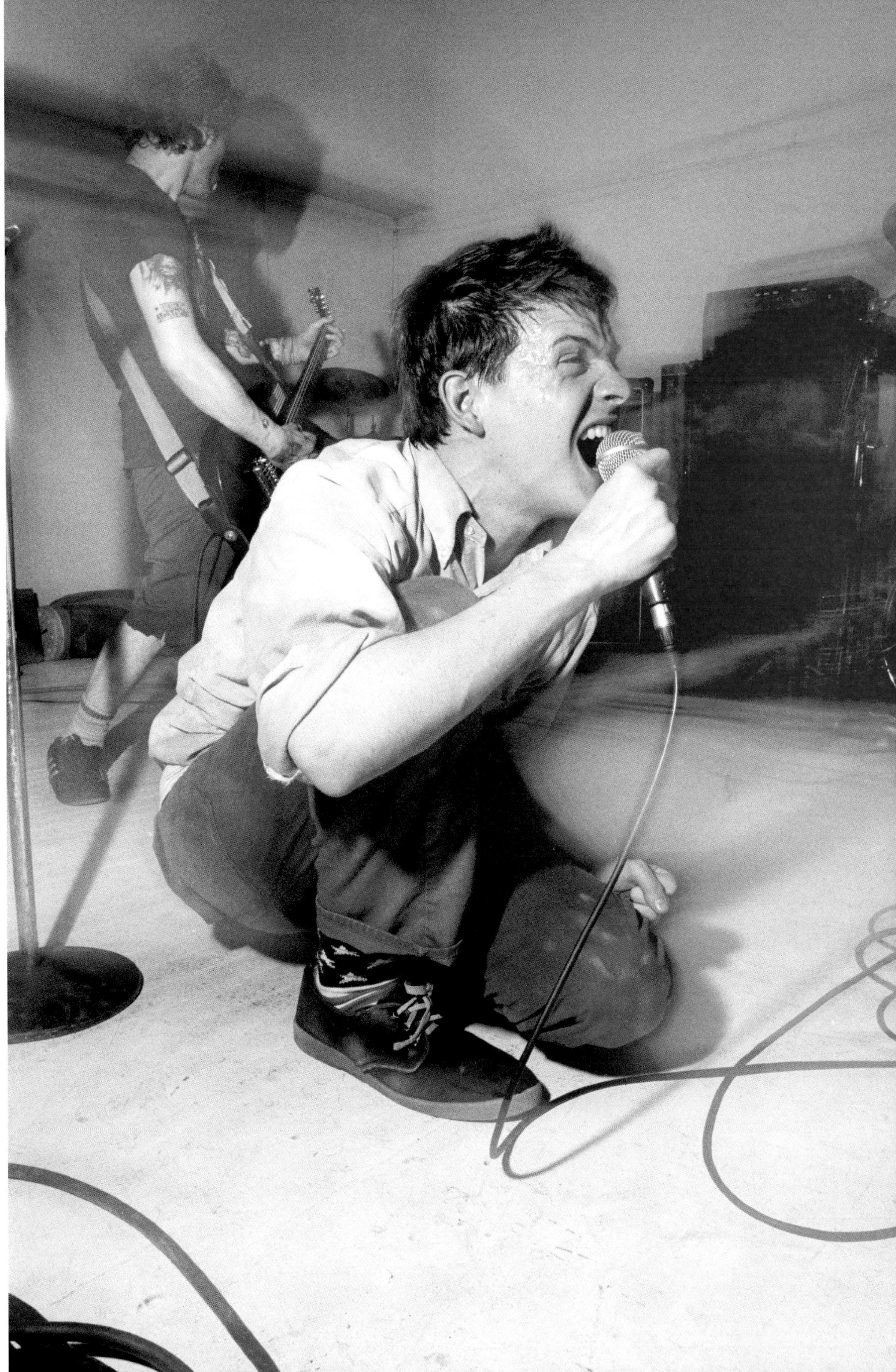

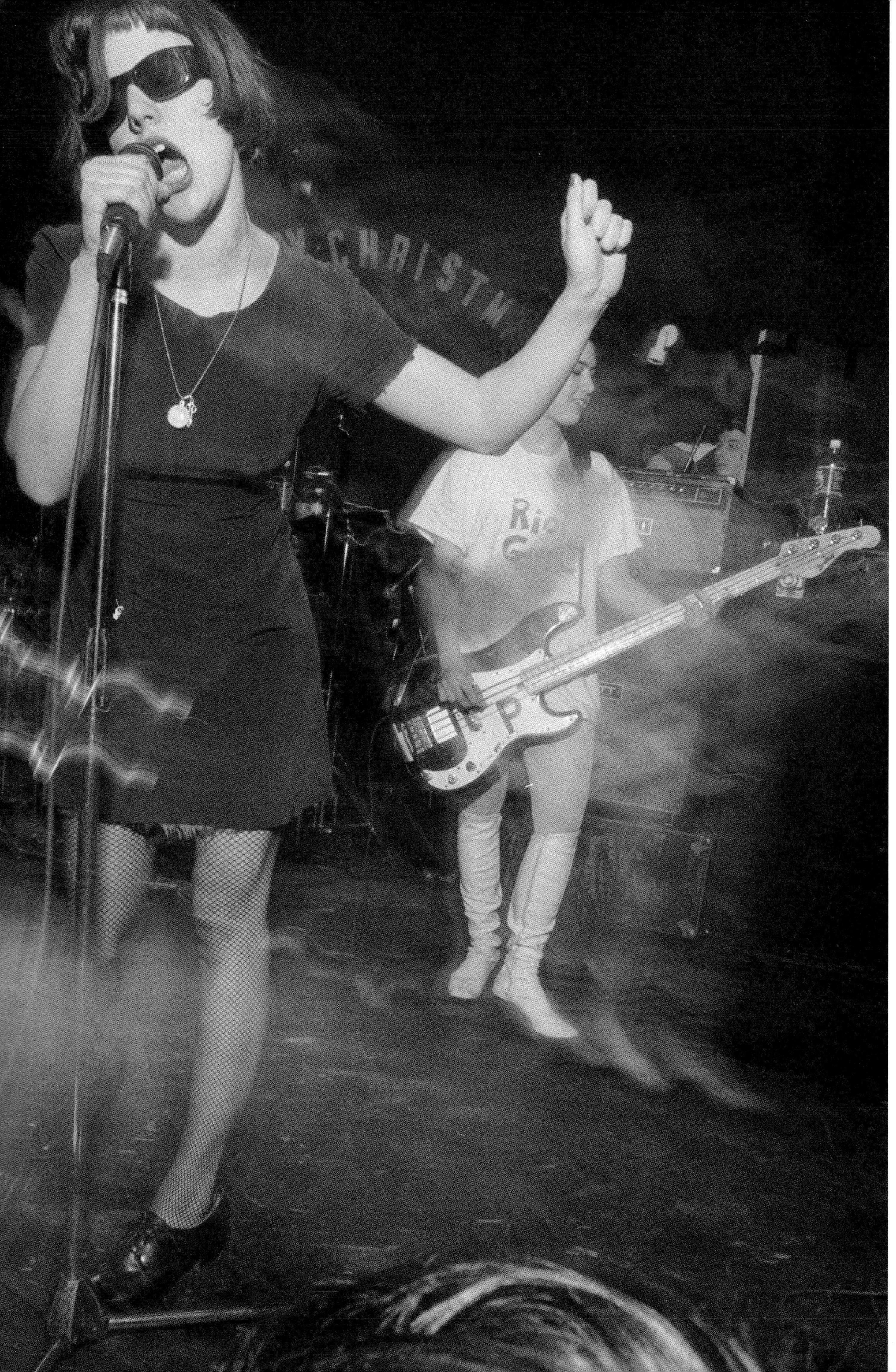

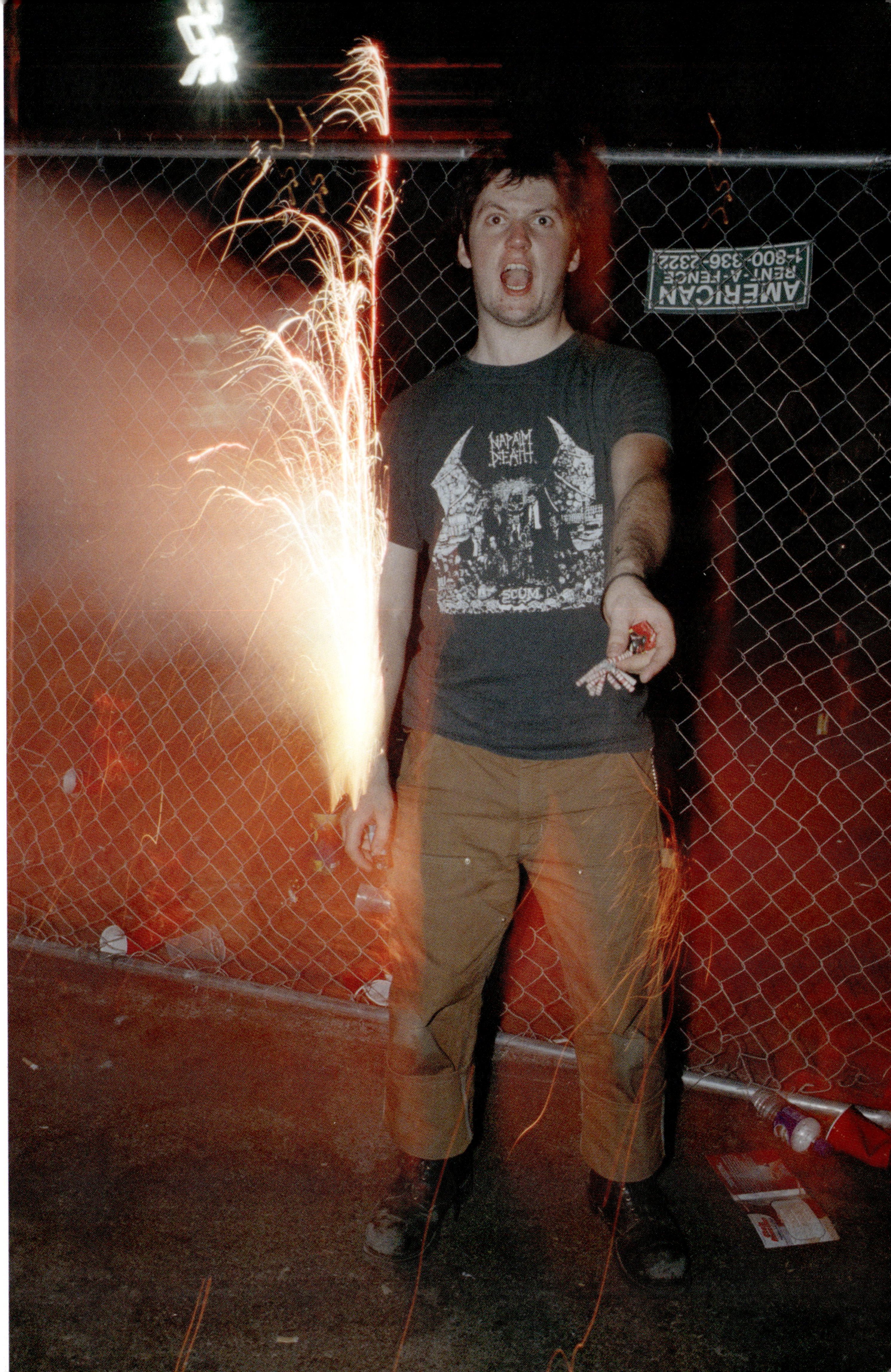
AMERICAN
RENT-A-FENCE
1-800-336-2322
NAPALM DEATH
SCUM

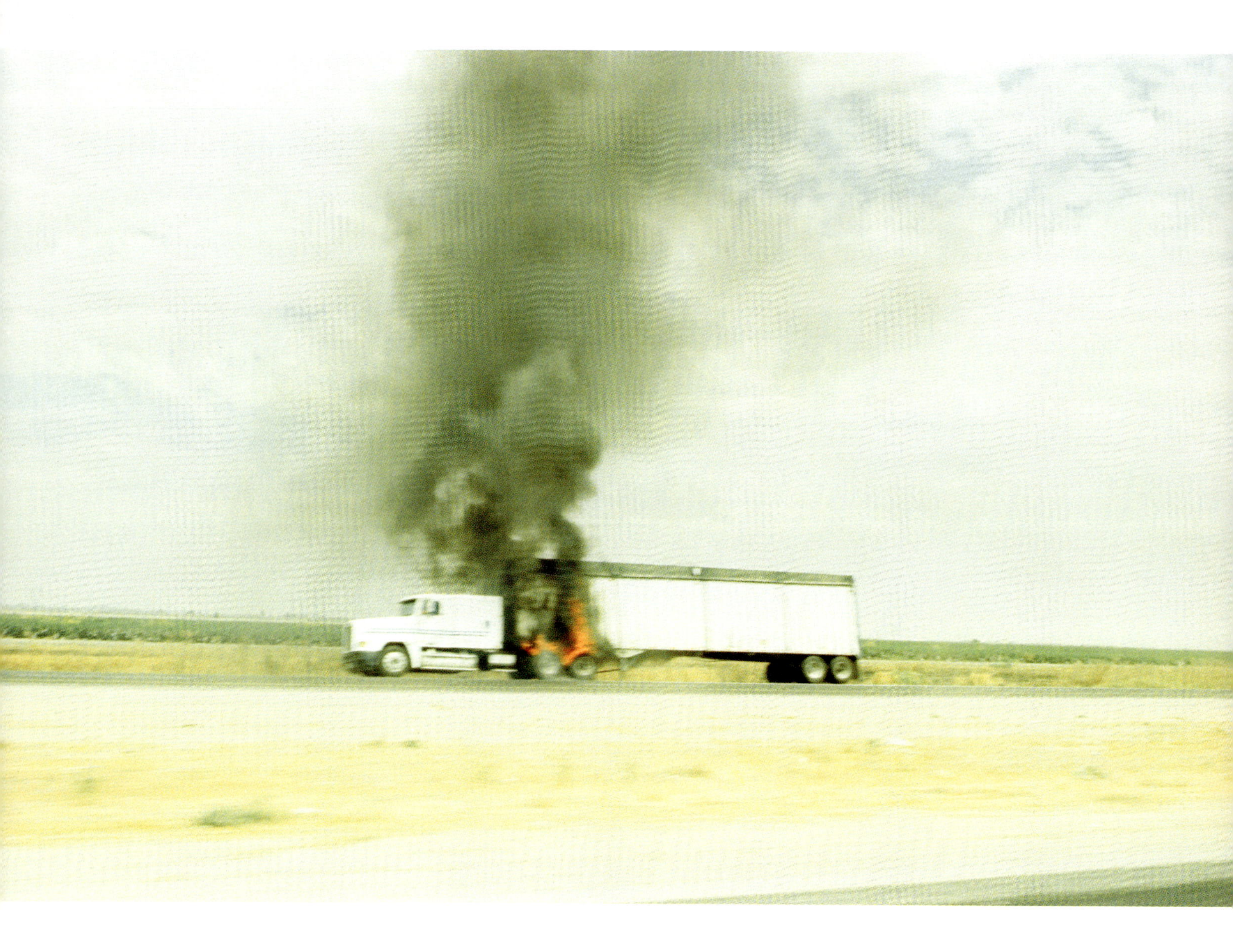

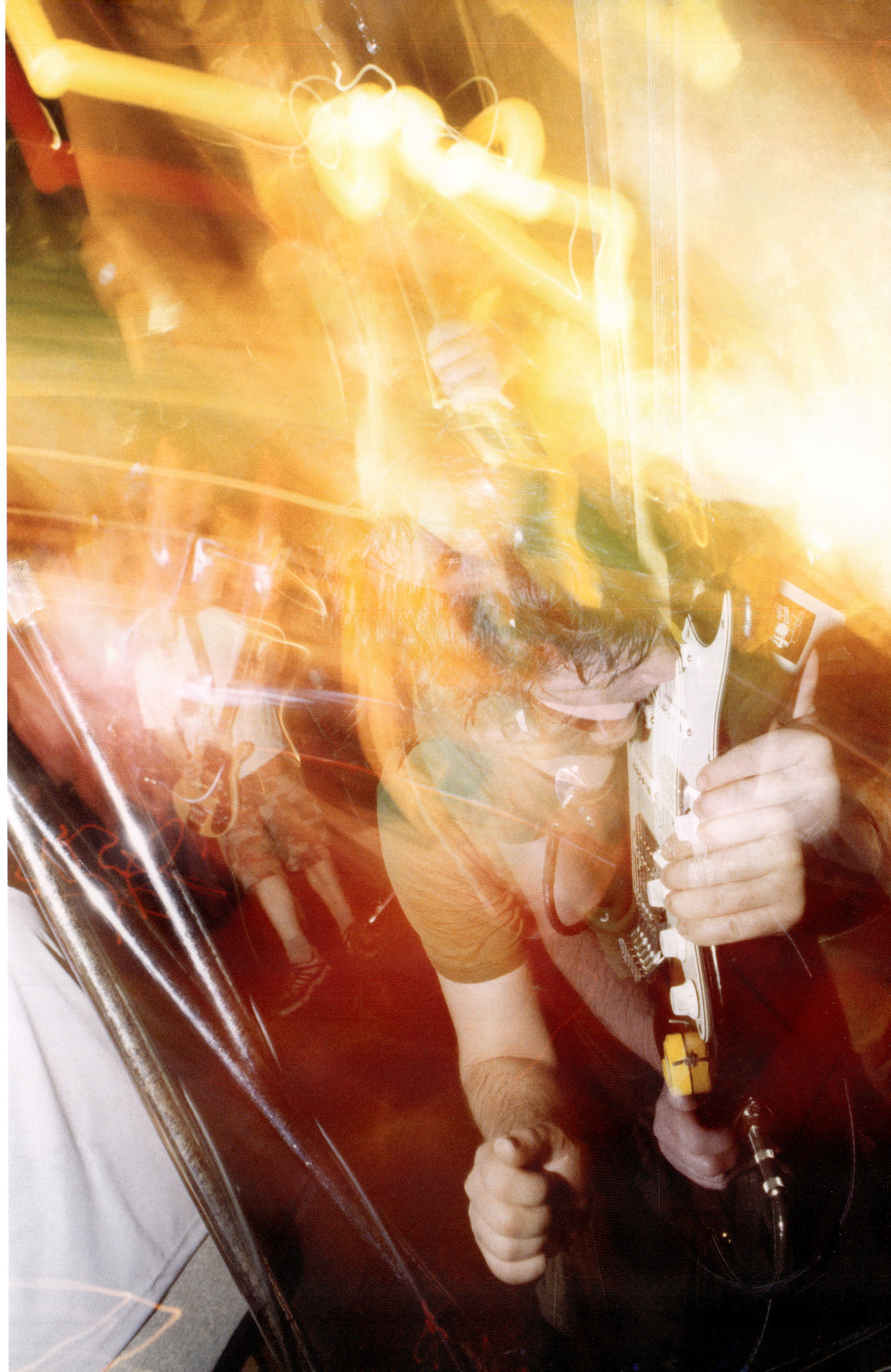

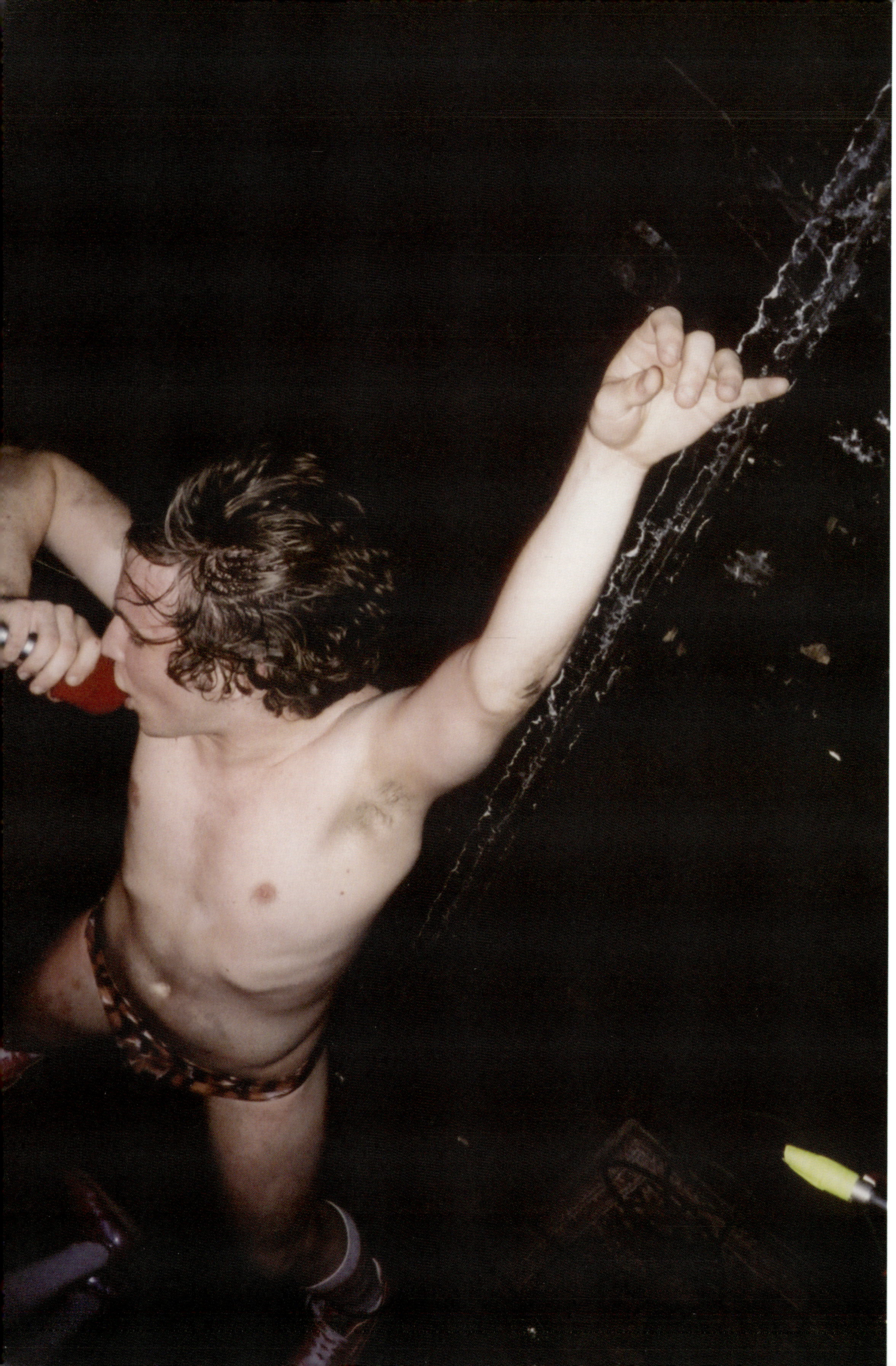

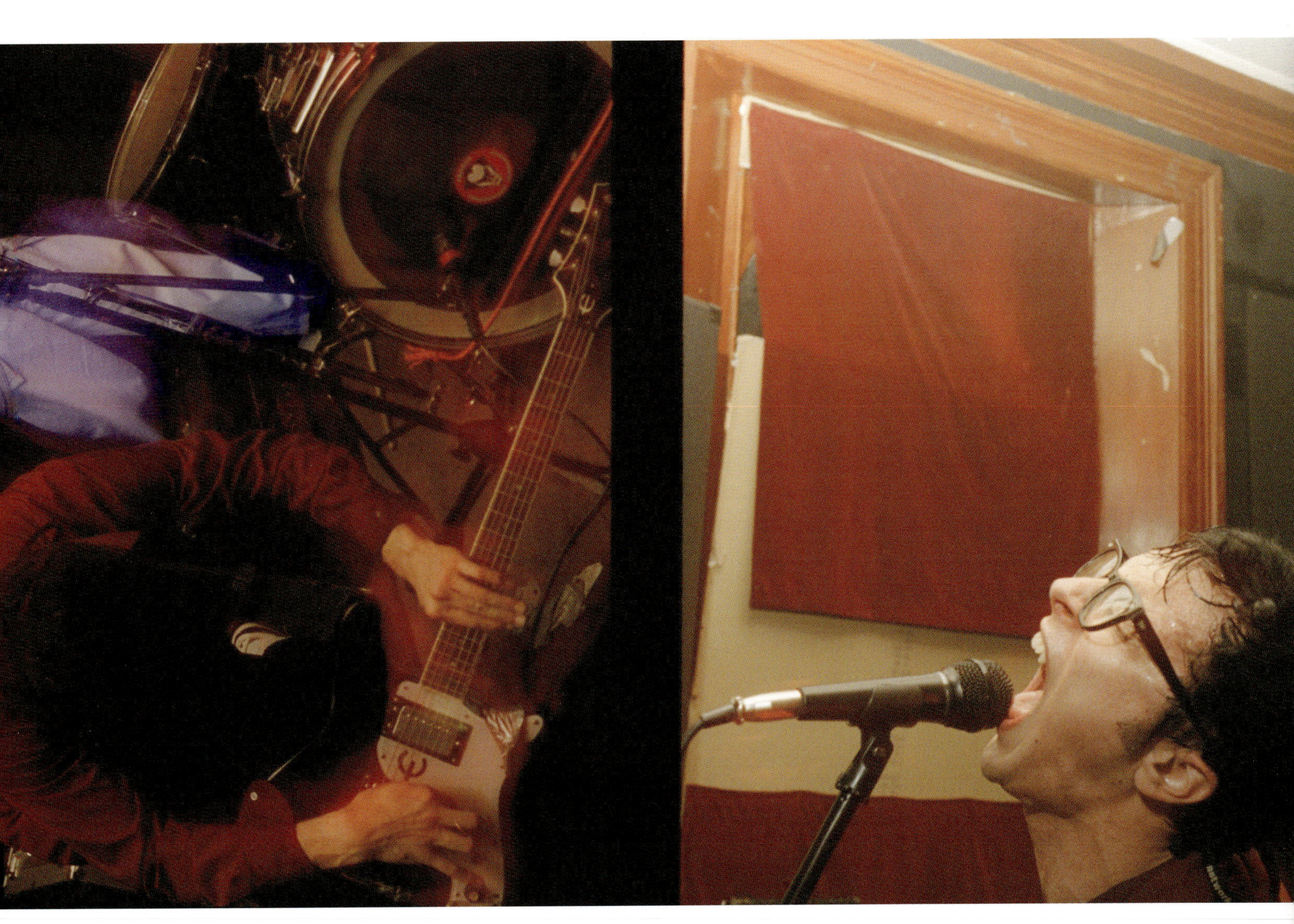

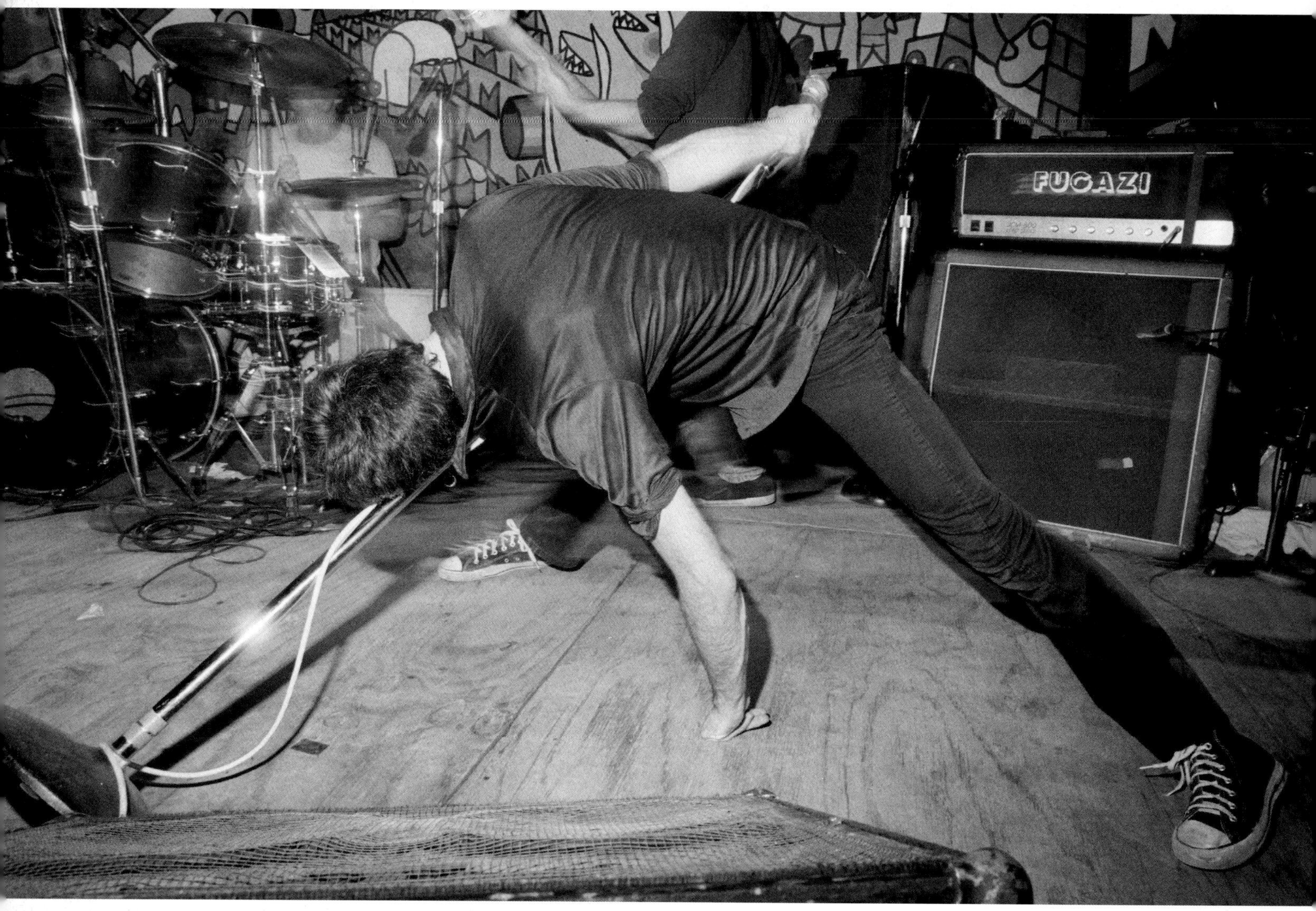

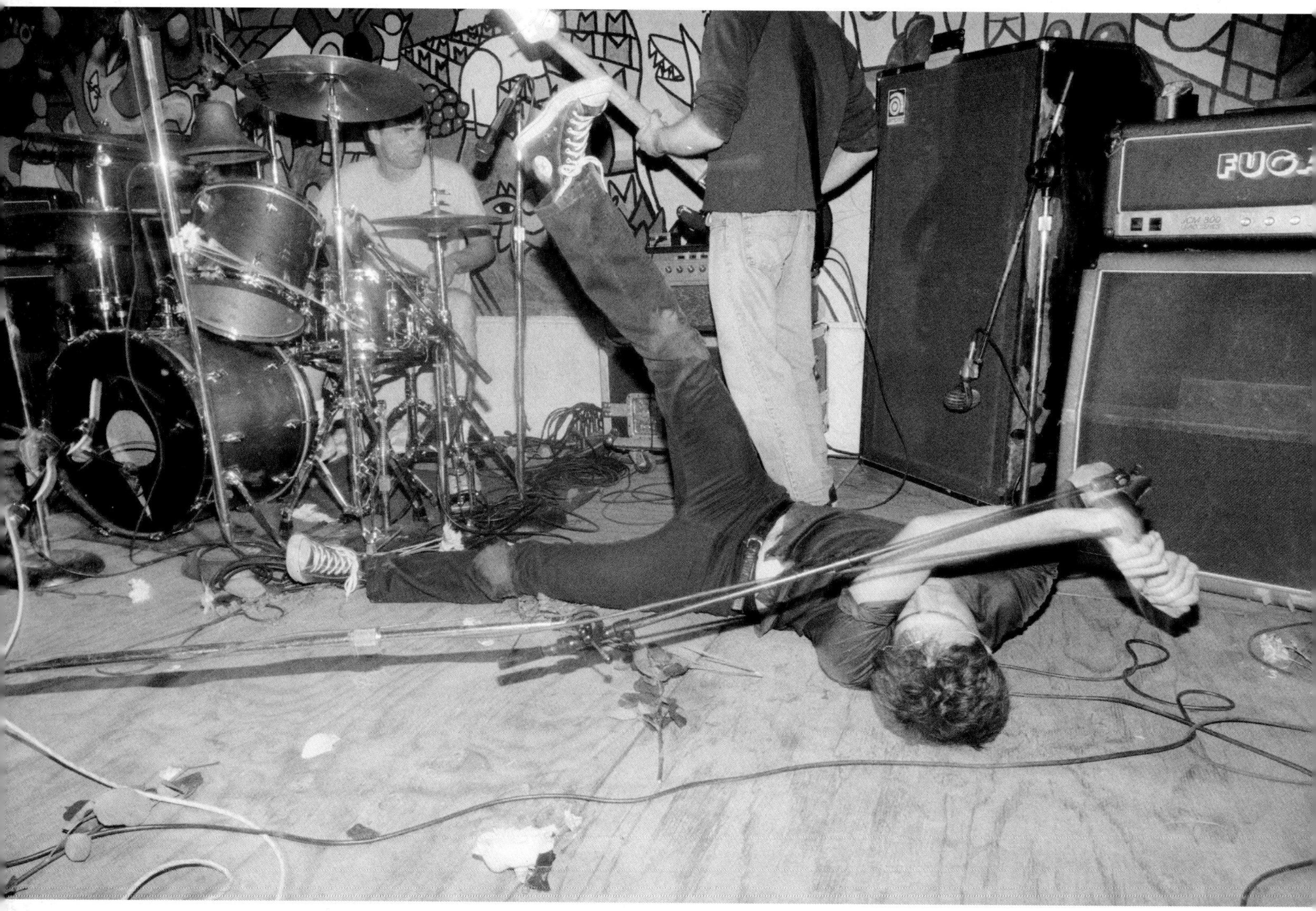

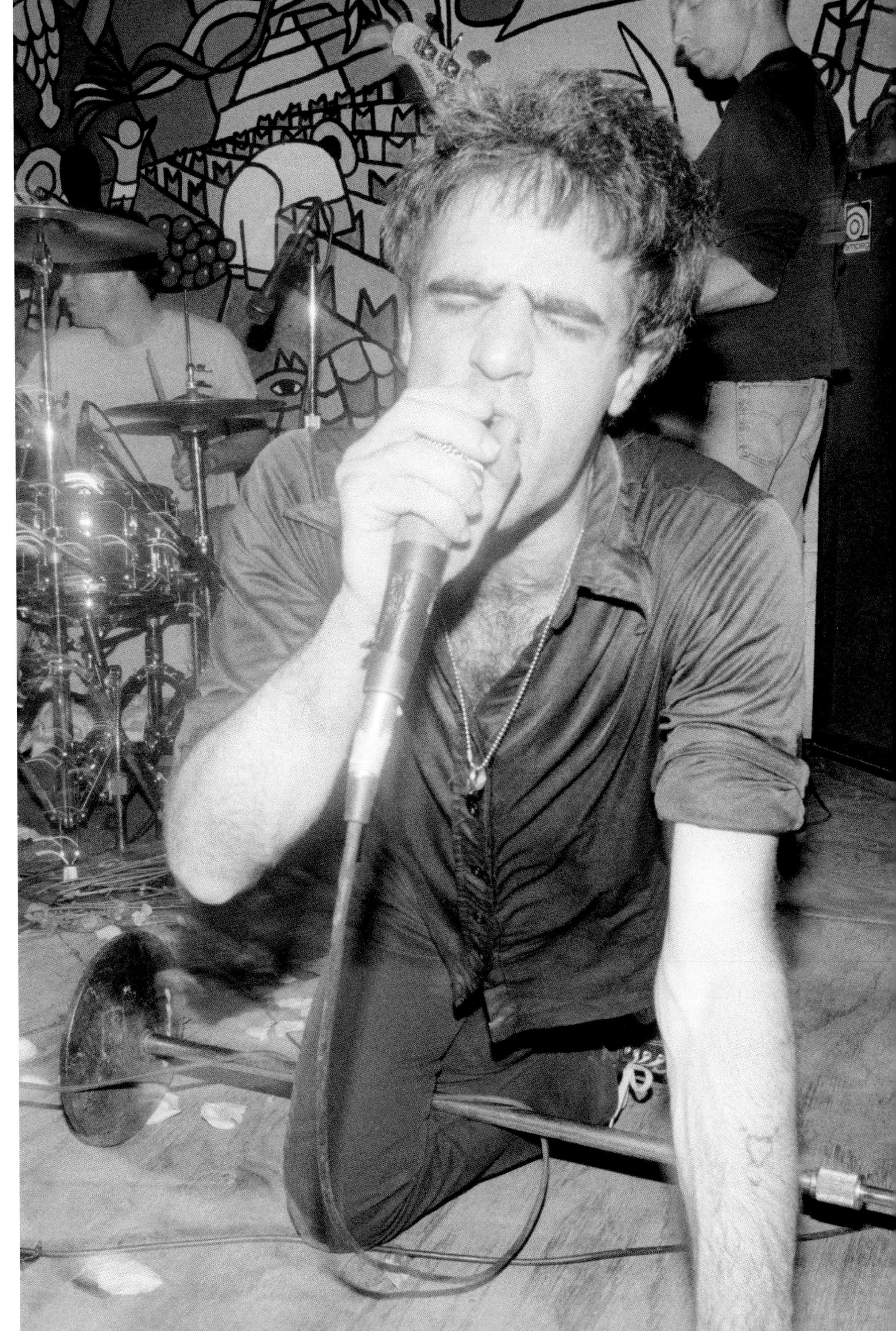

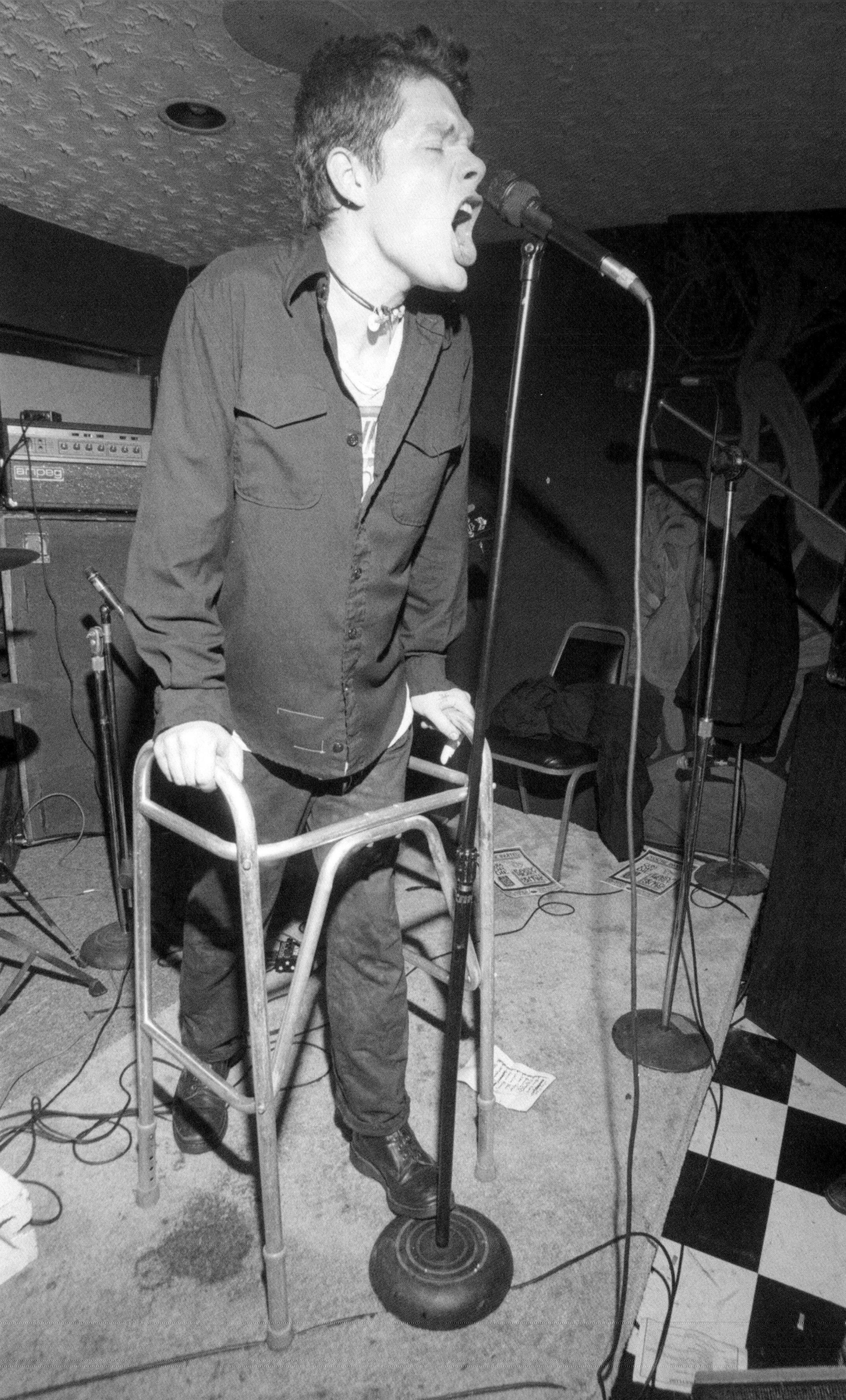
ampeg

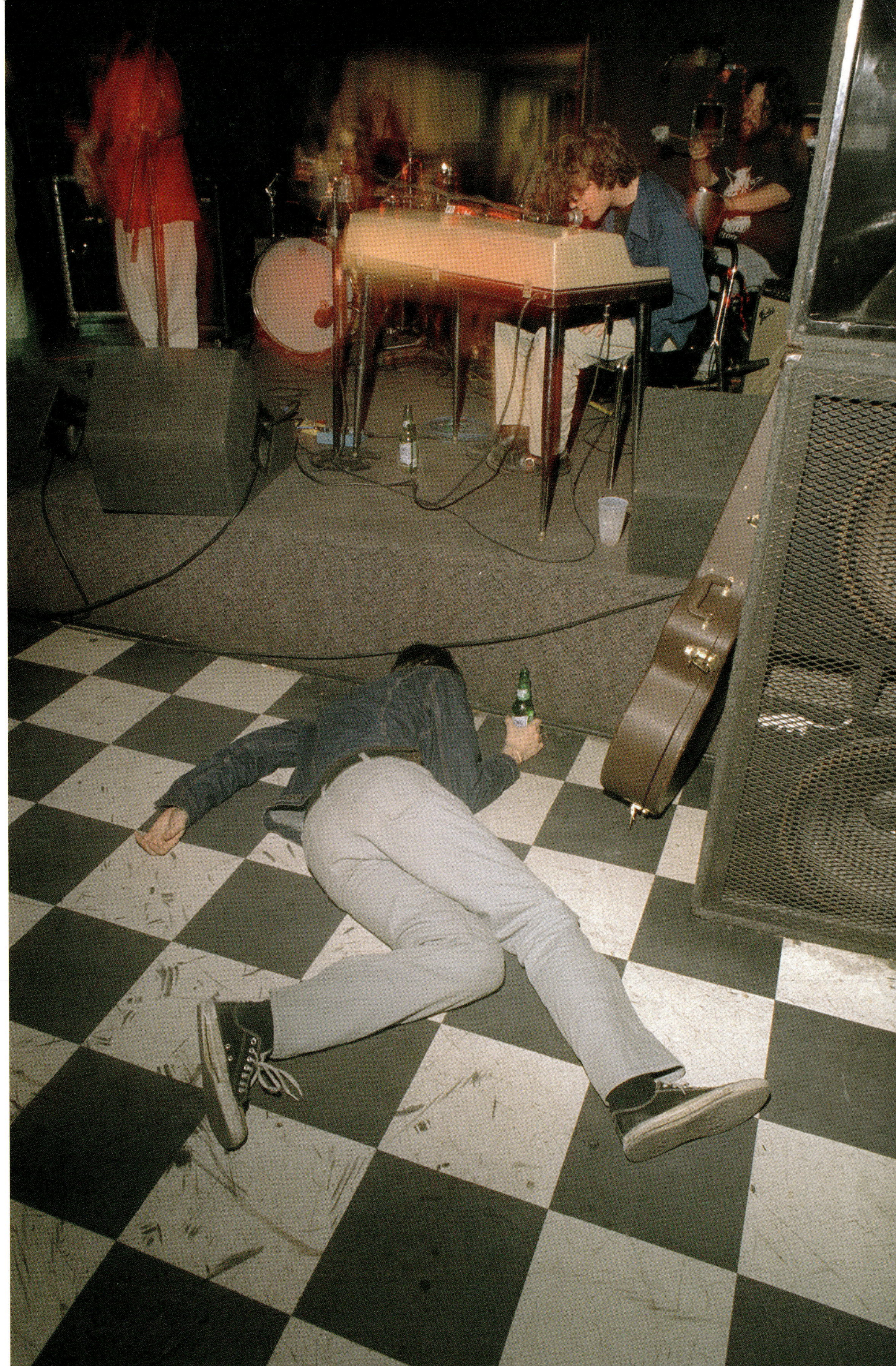

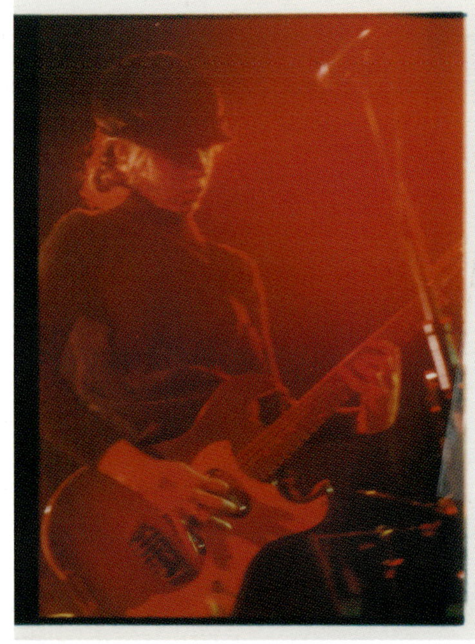

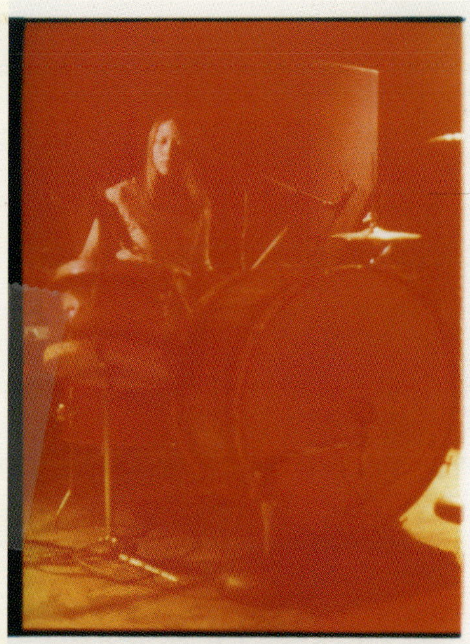
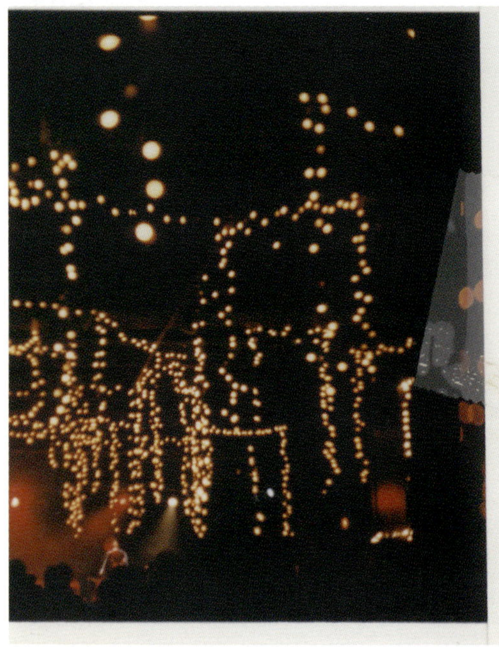
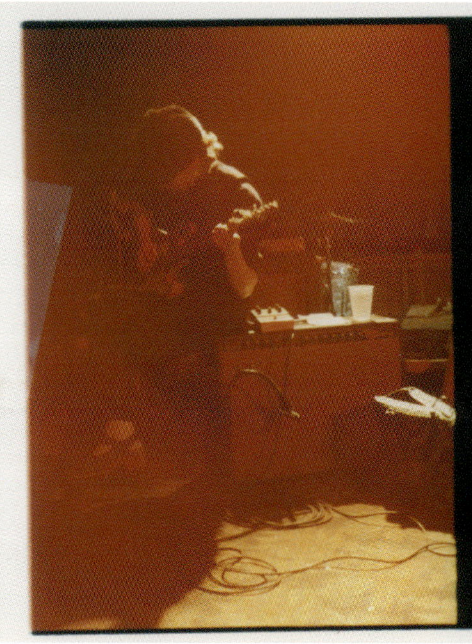
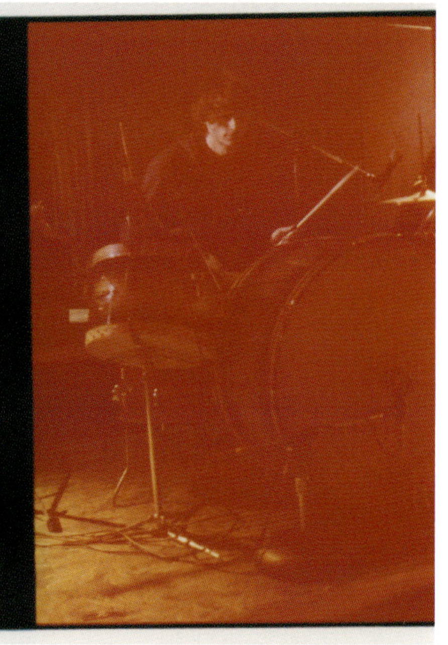
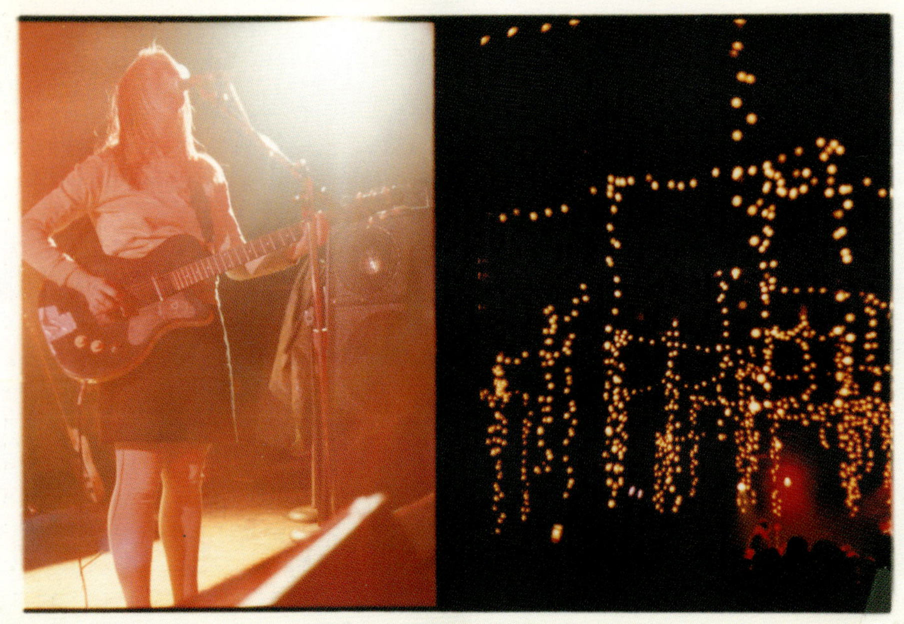
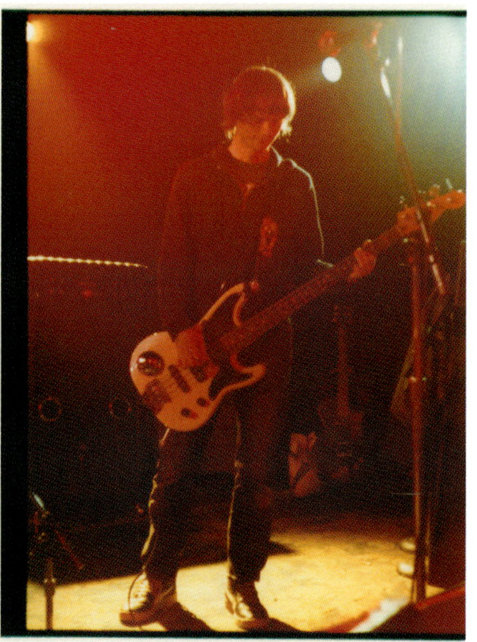

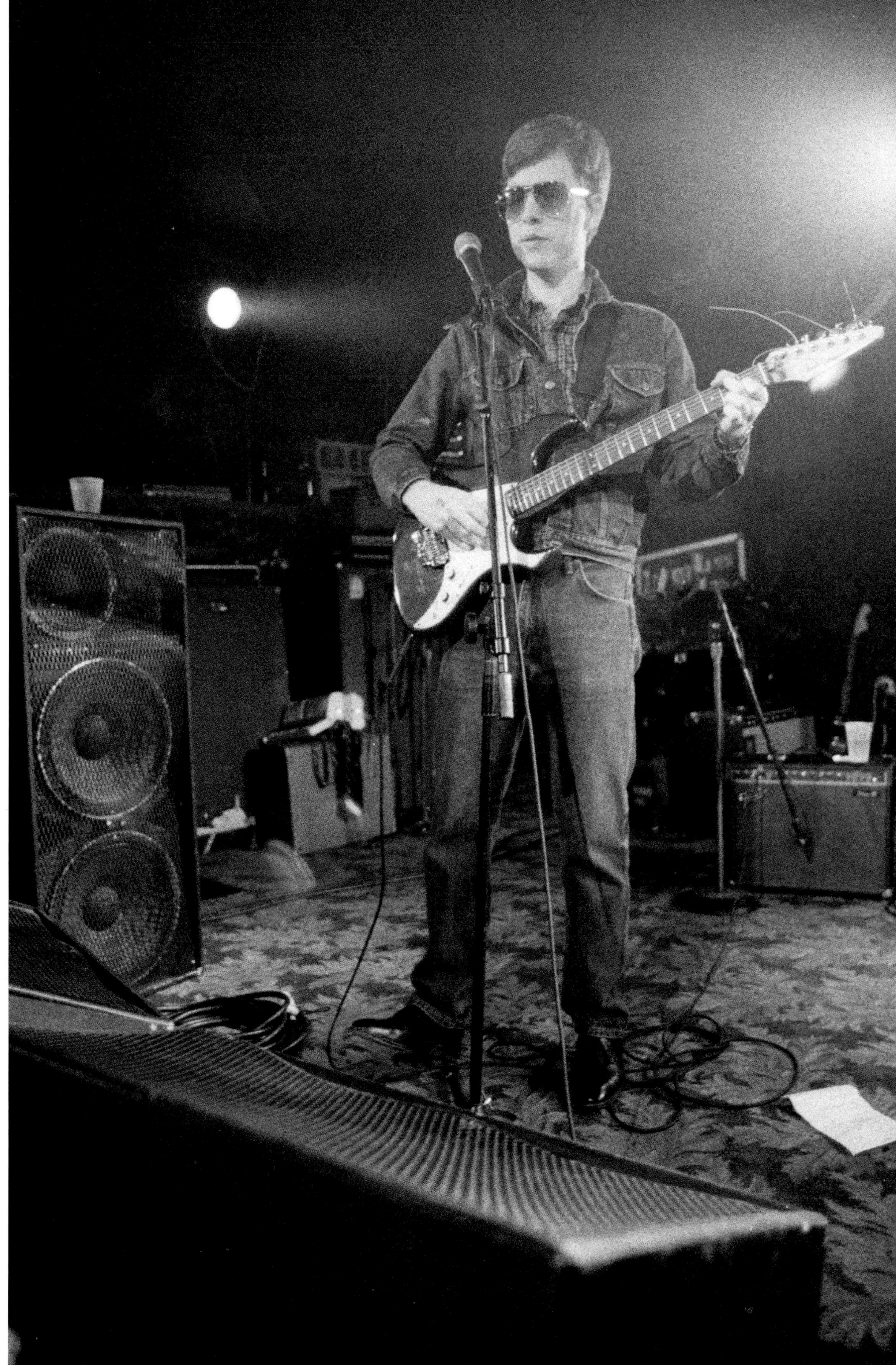

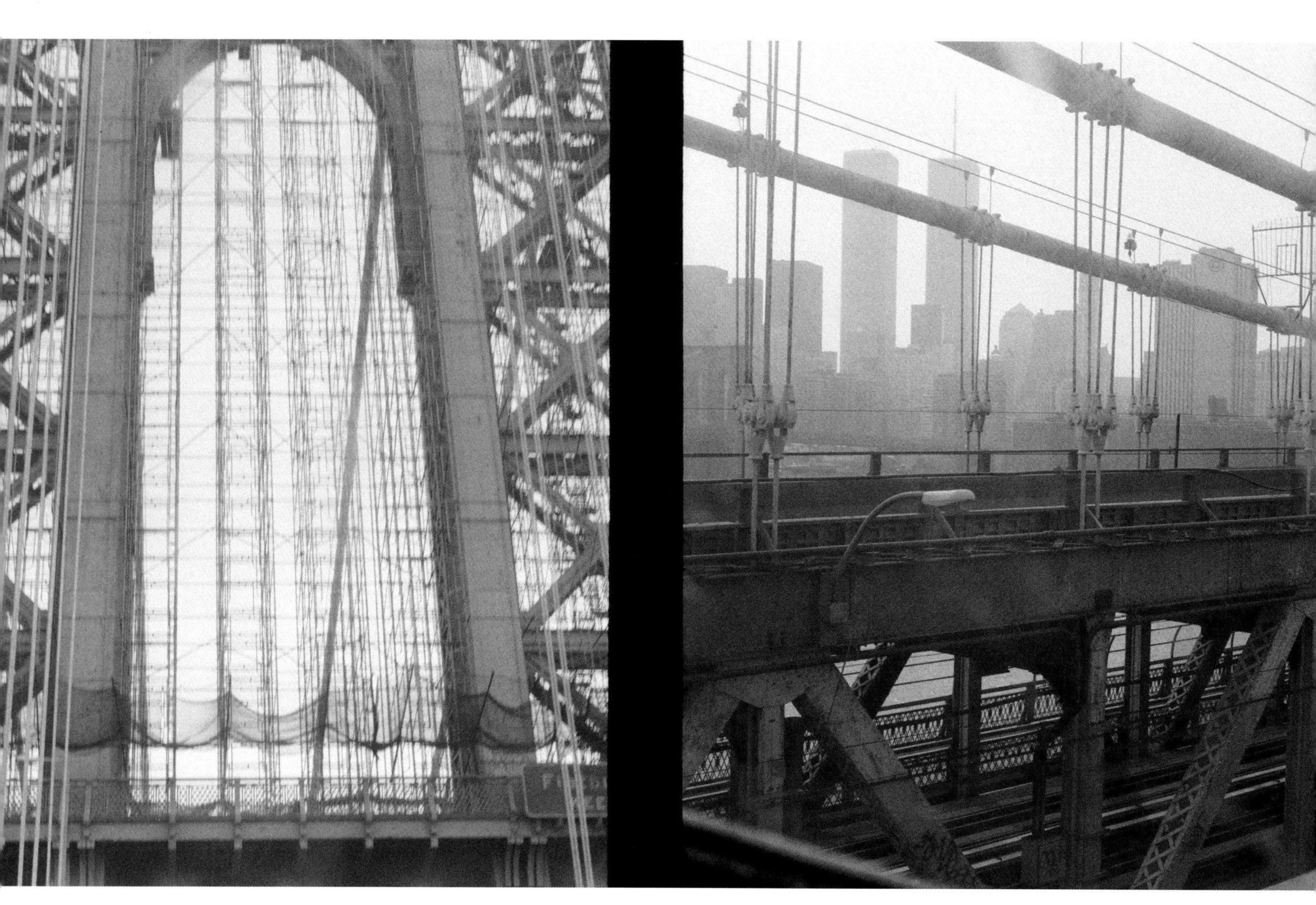

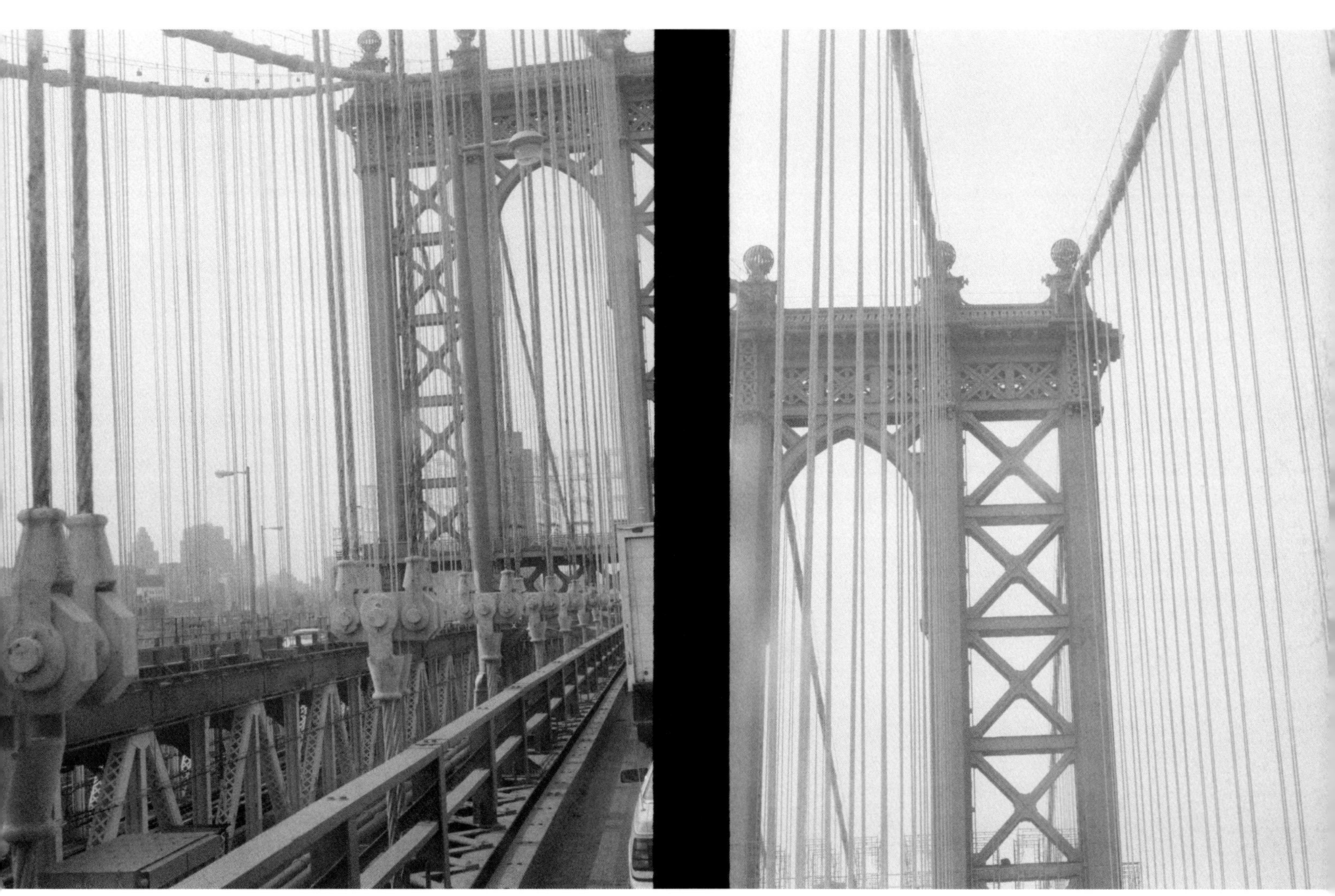

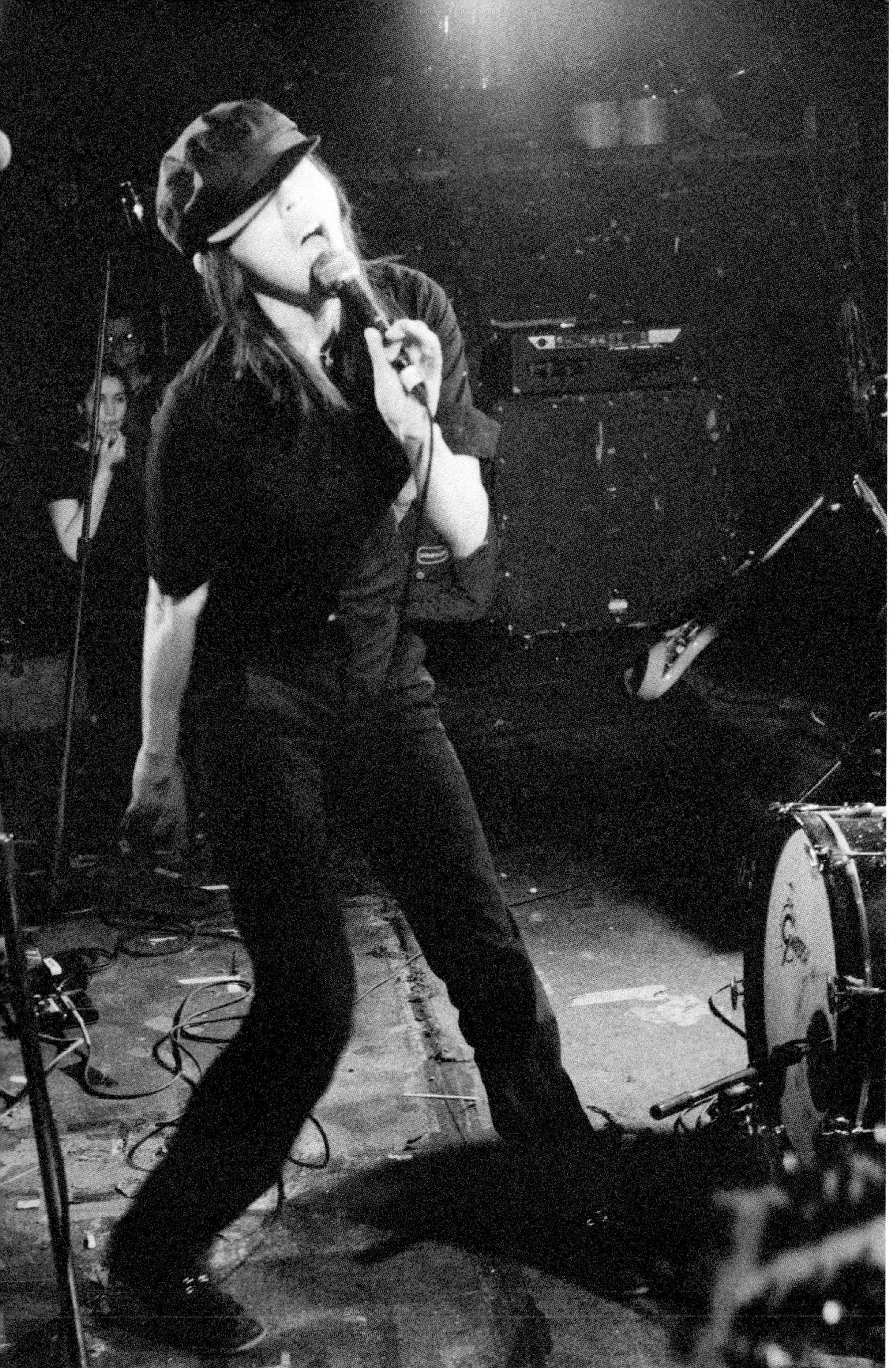

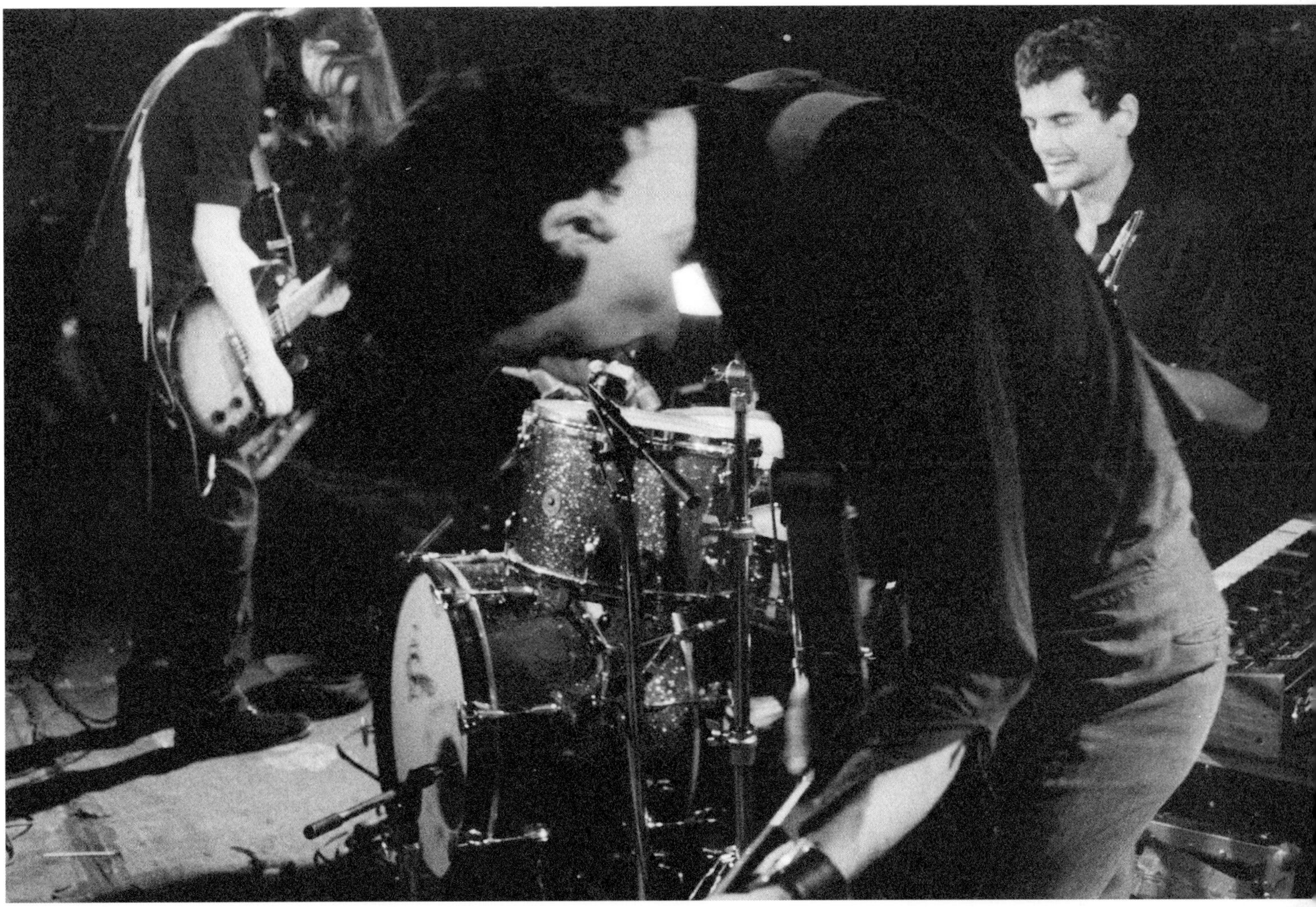

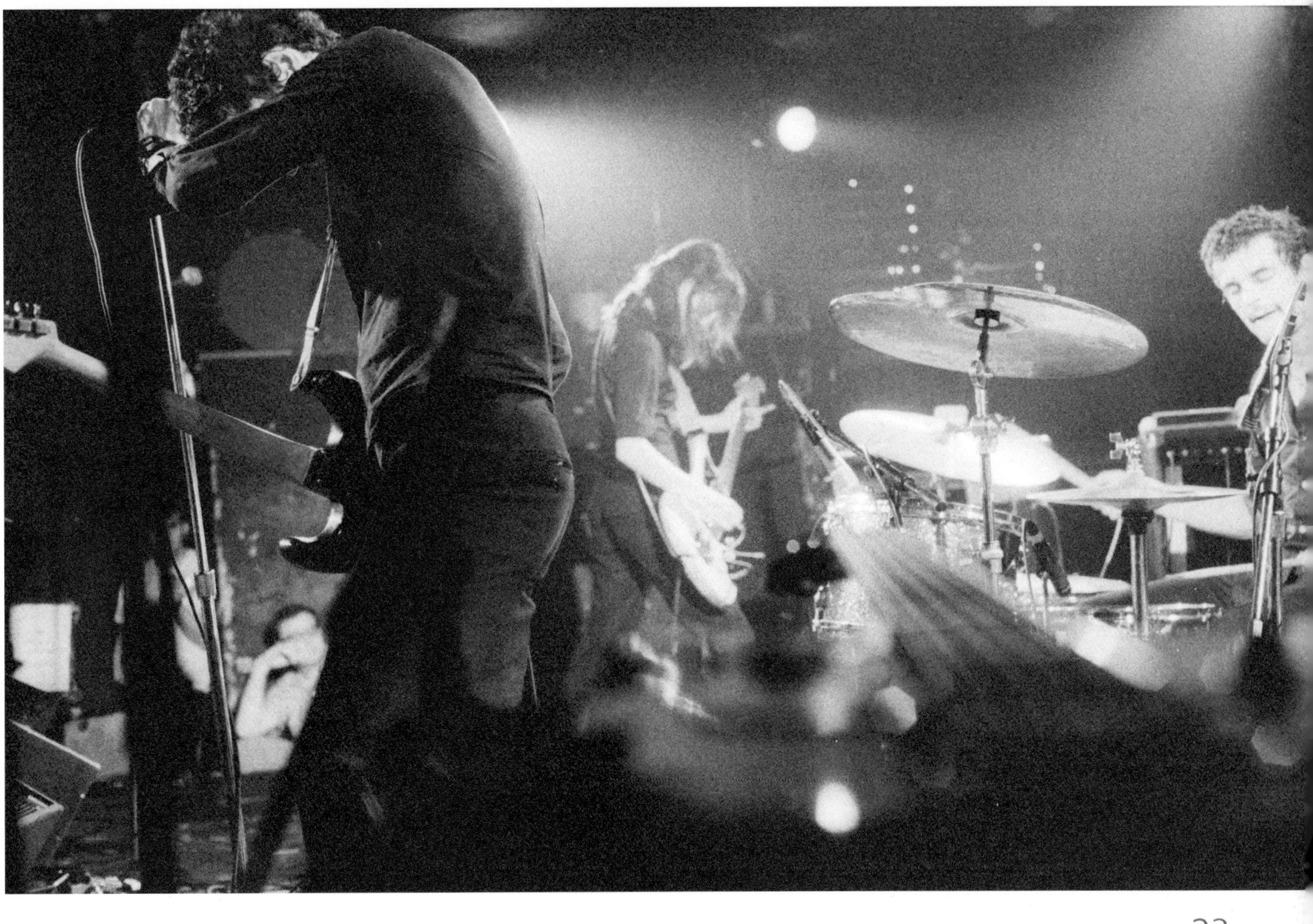

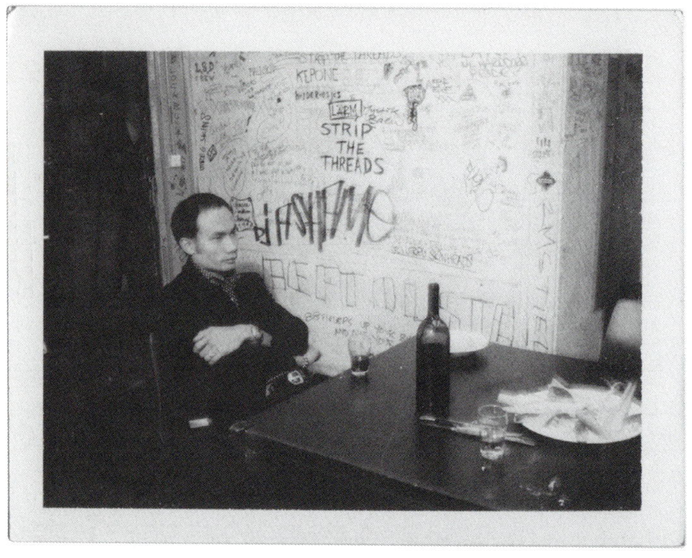
KEPONE
STRIP
THE
THREADS

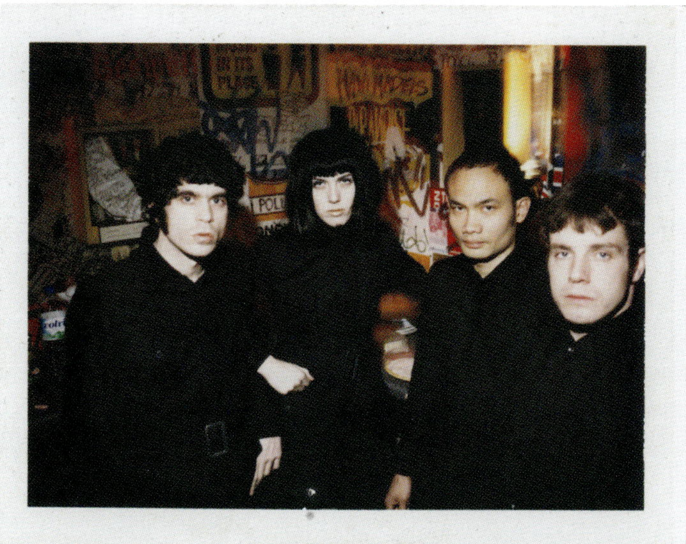

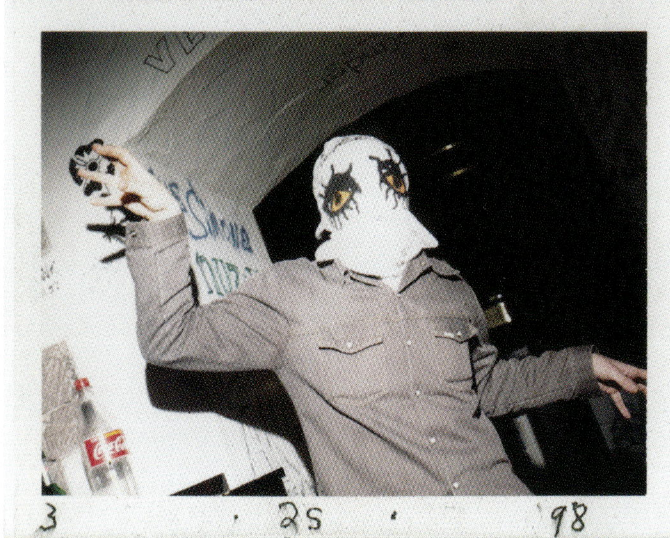
3 · 25 · 98

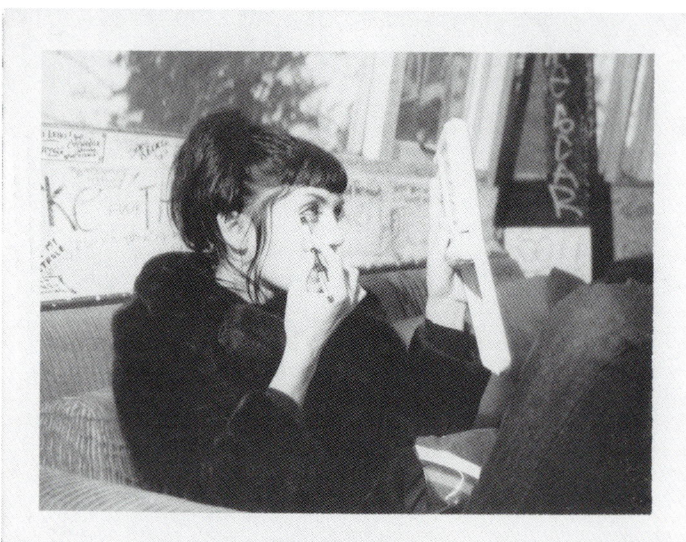

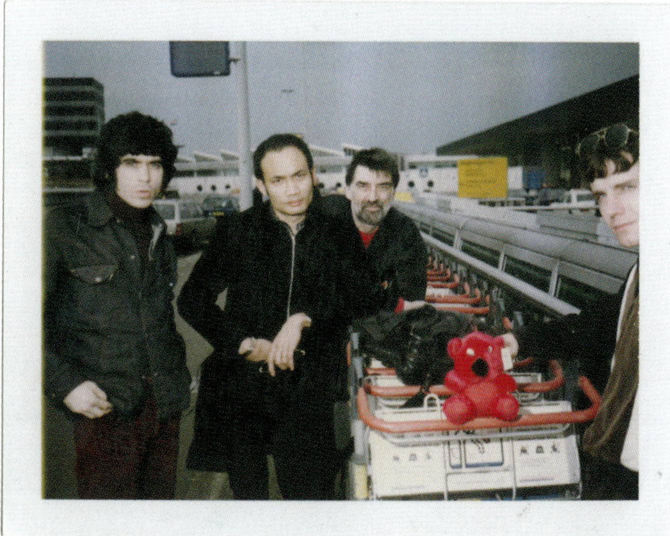

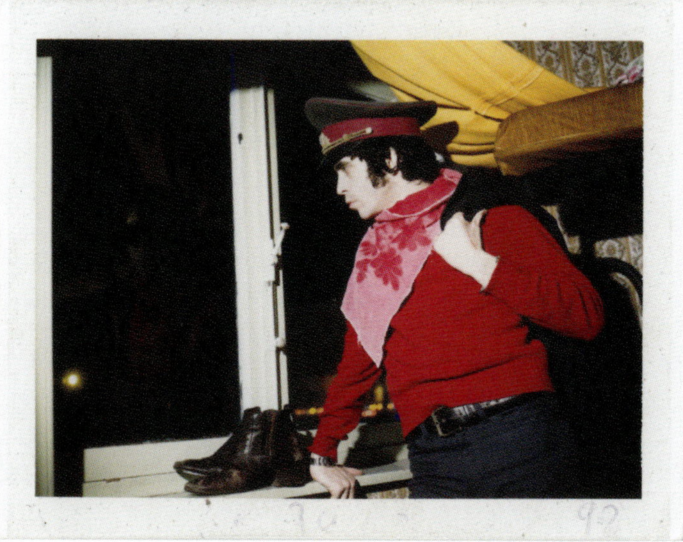

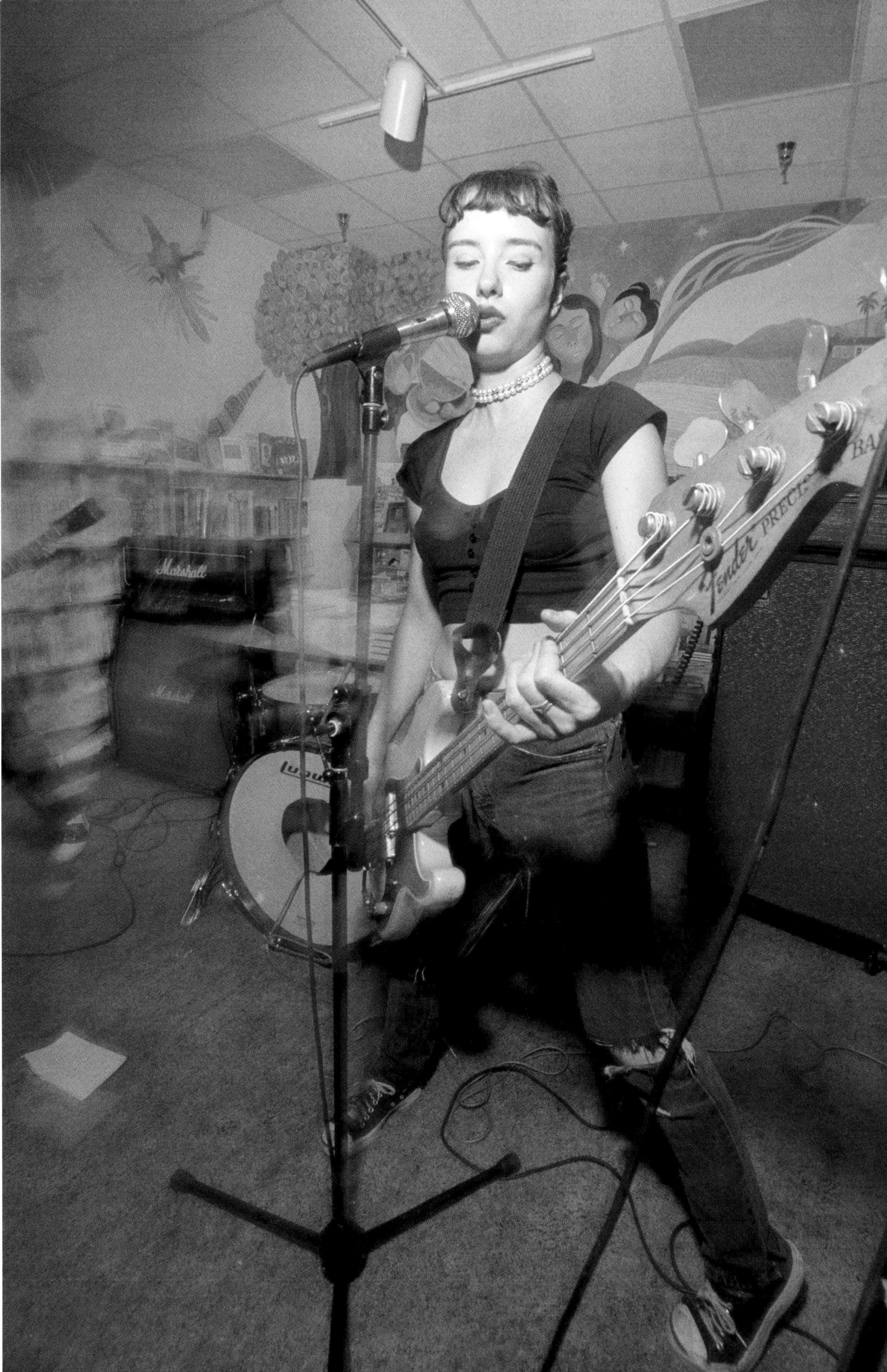
Marshall
Marshall
Fender

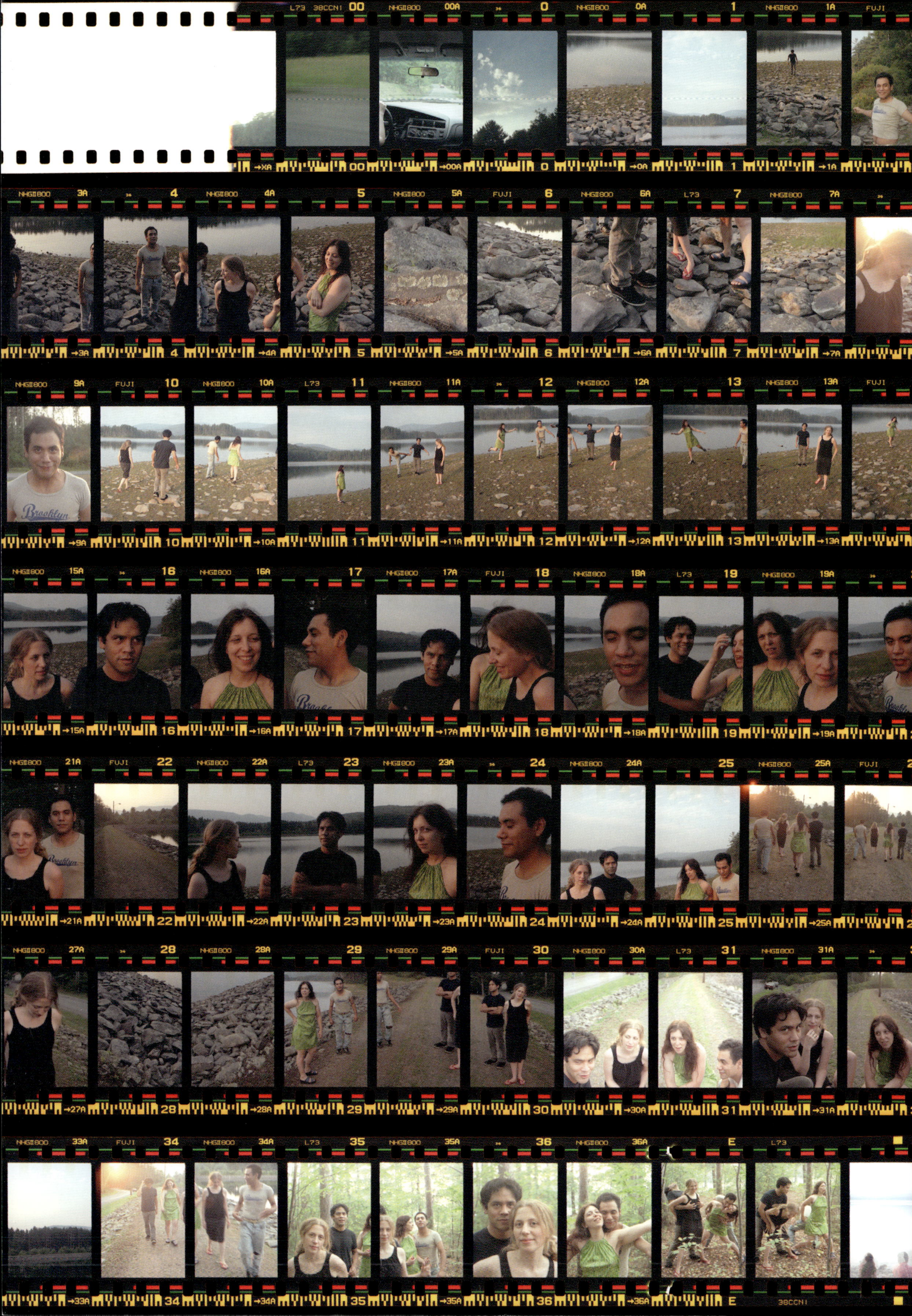

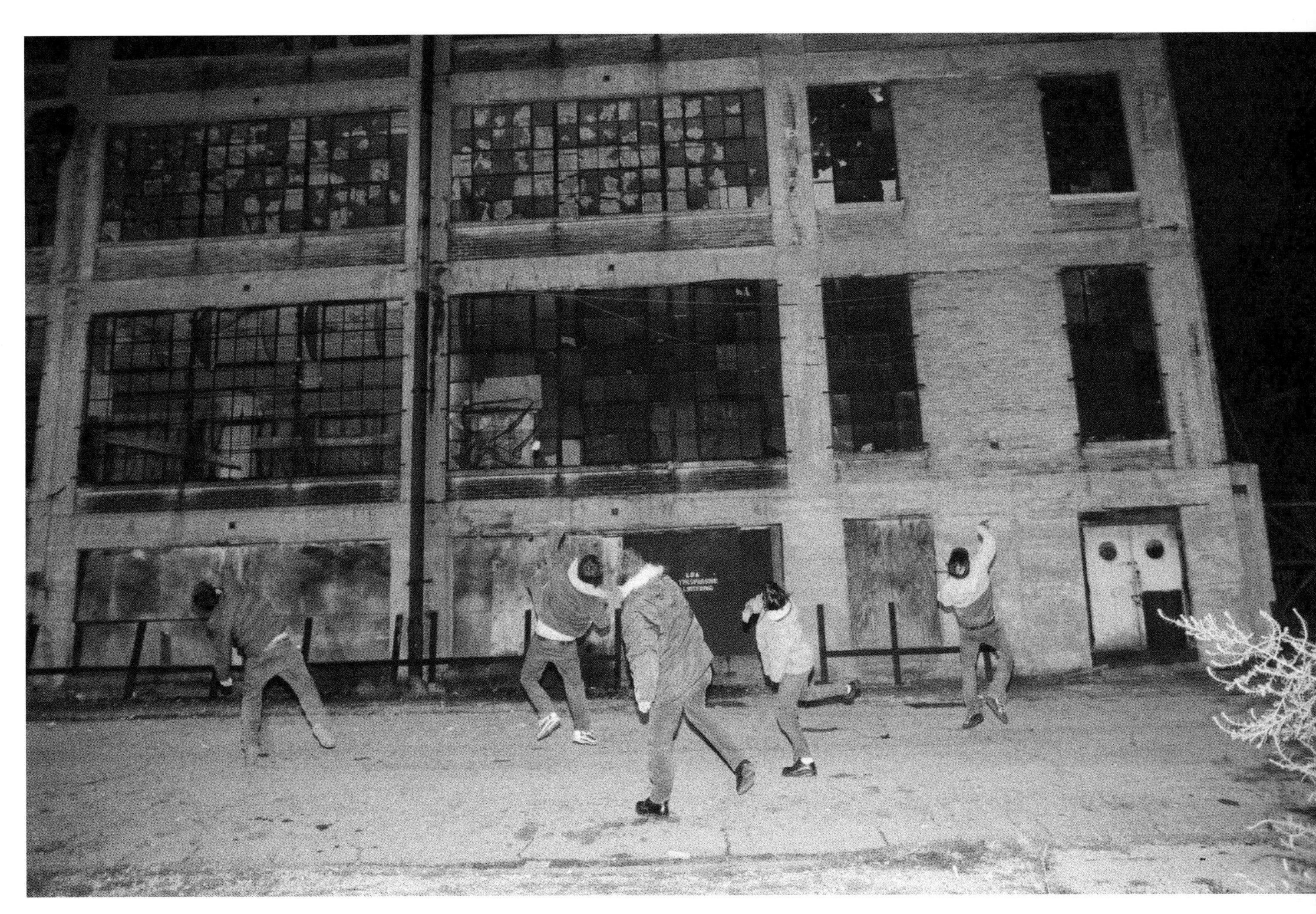

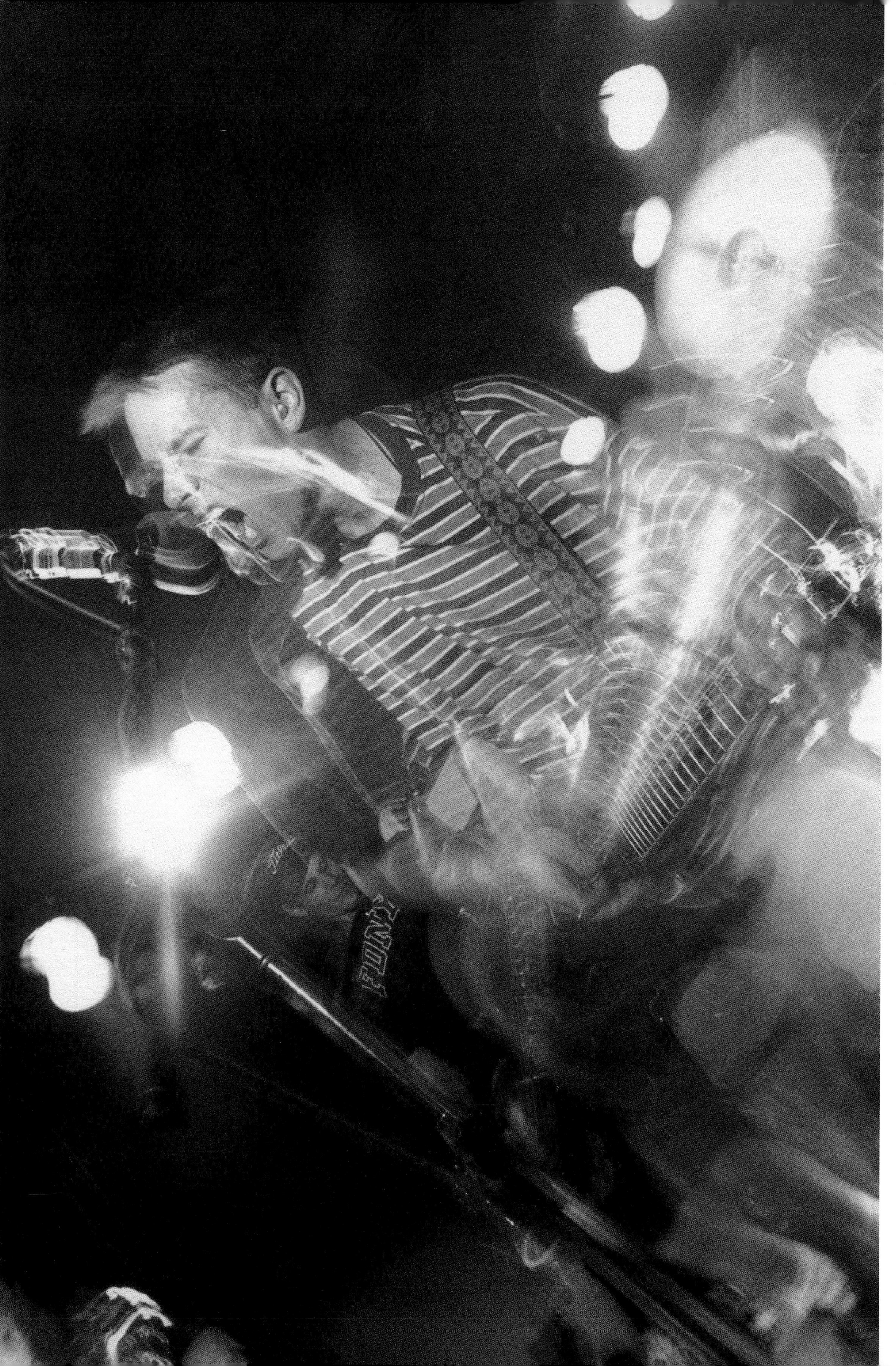

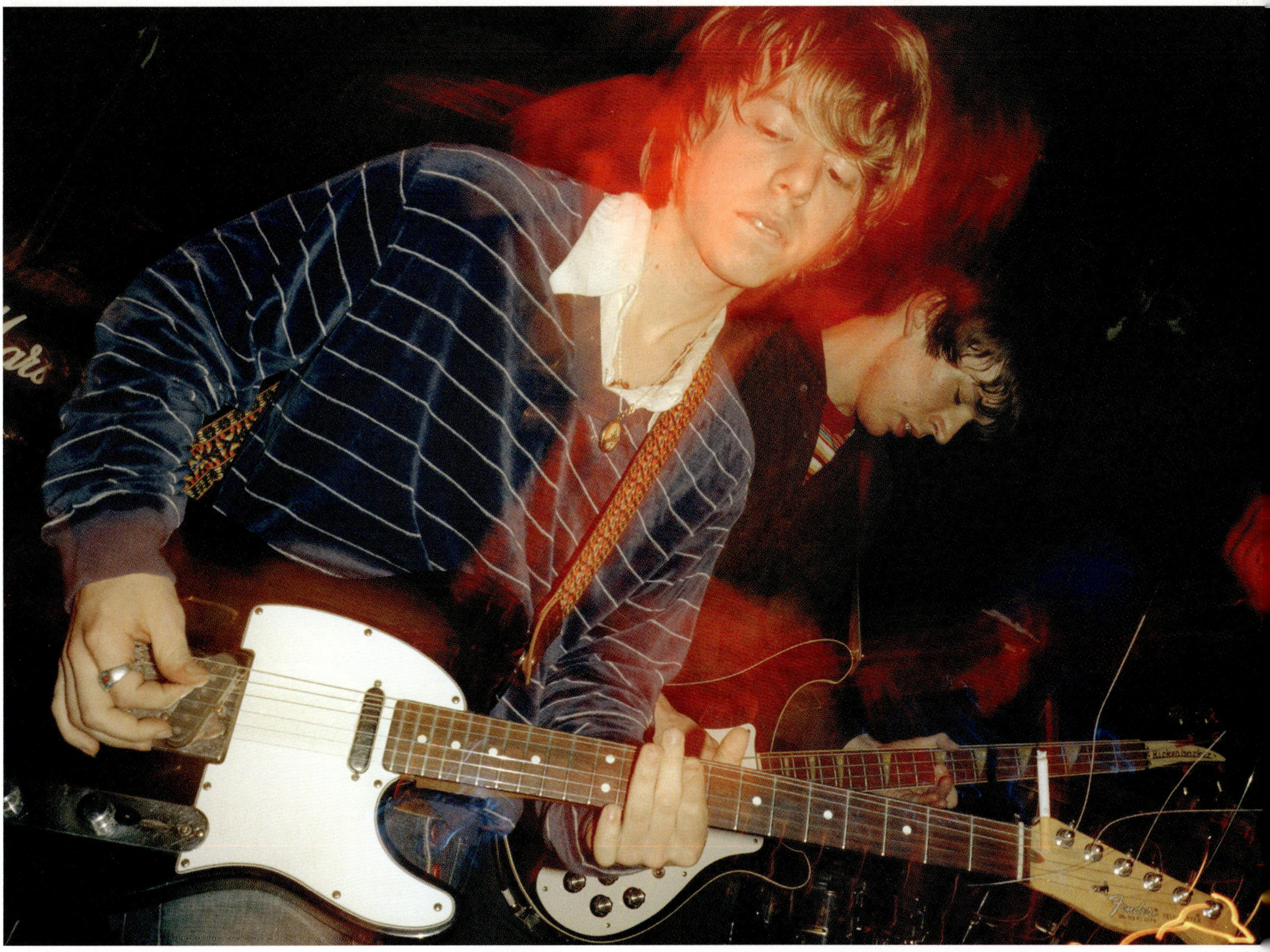

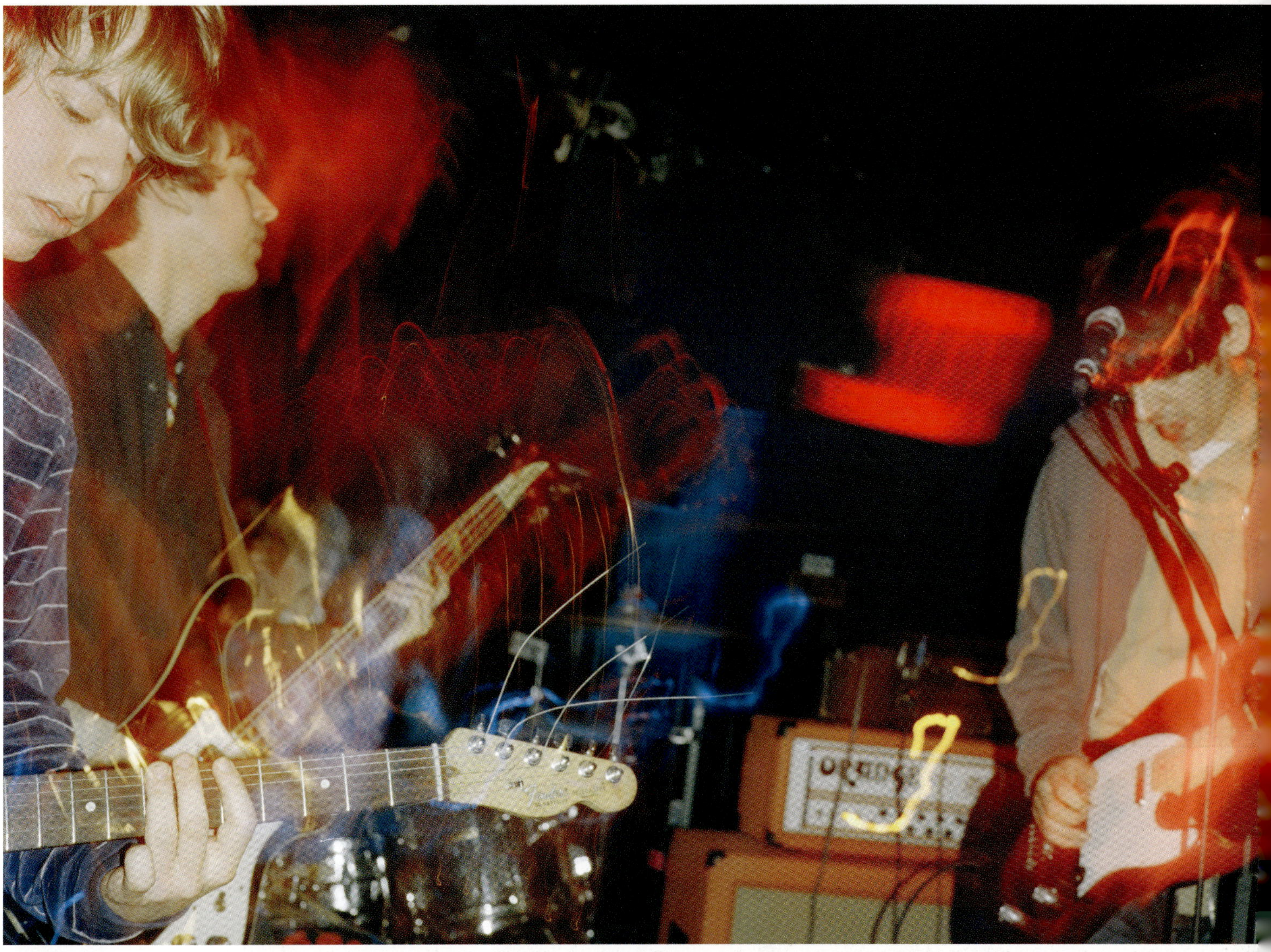

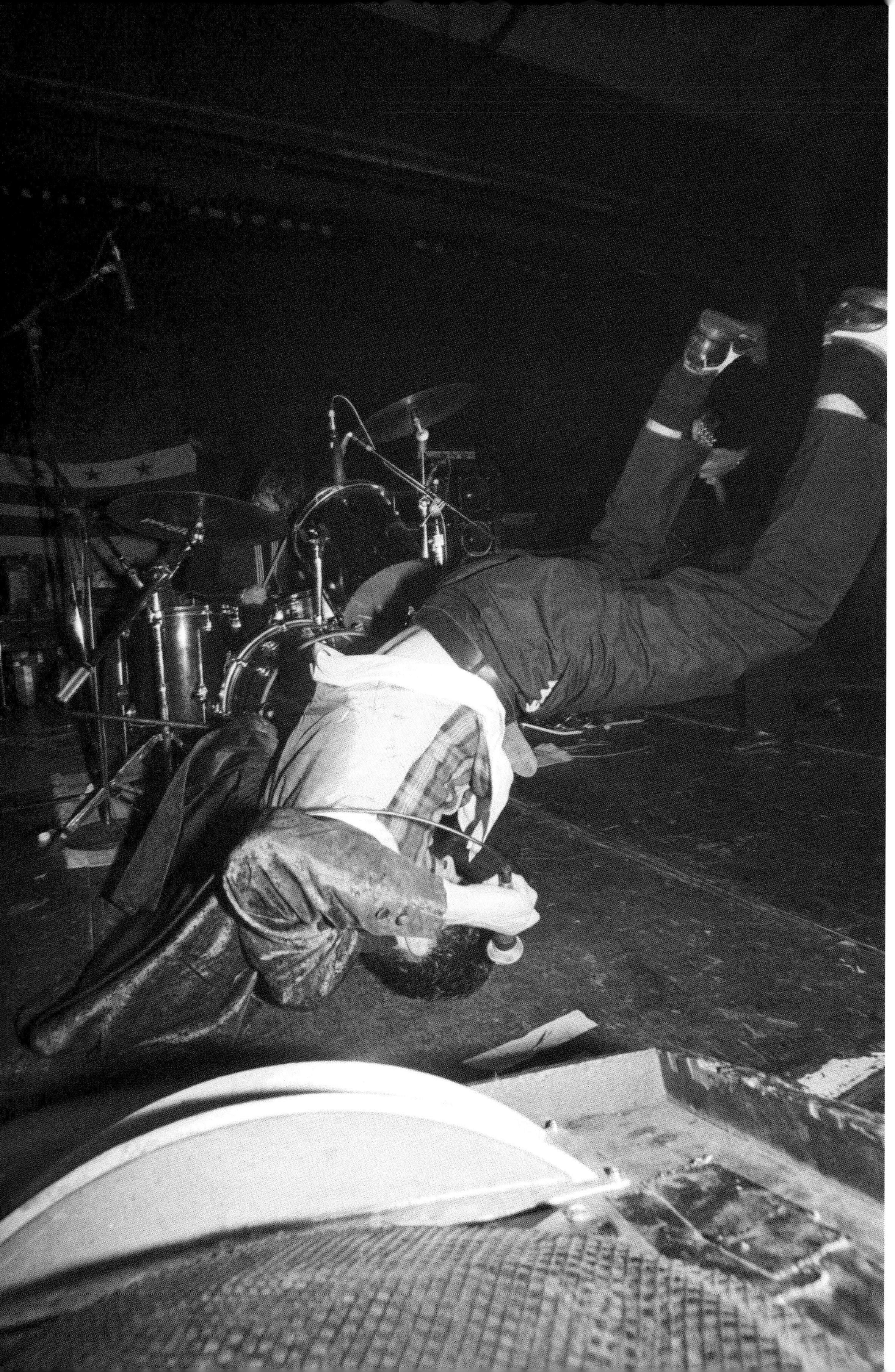

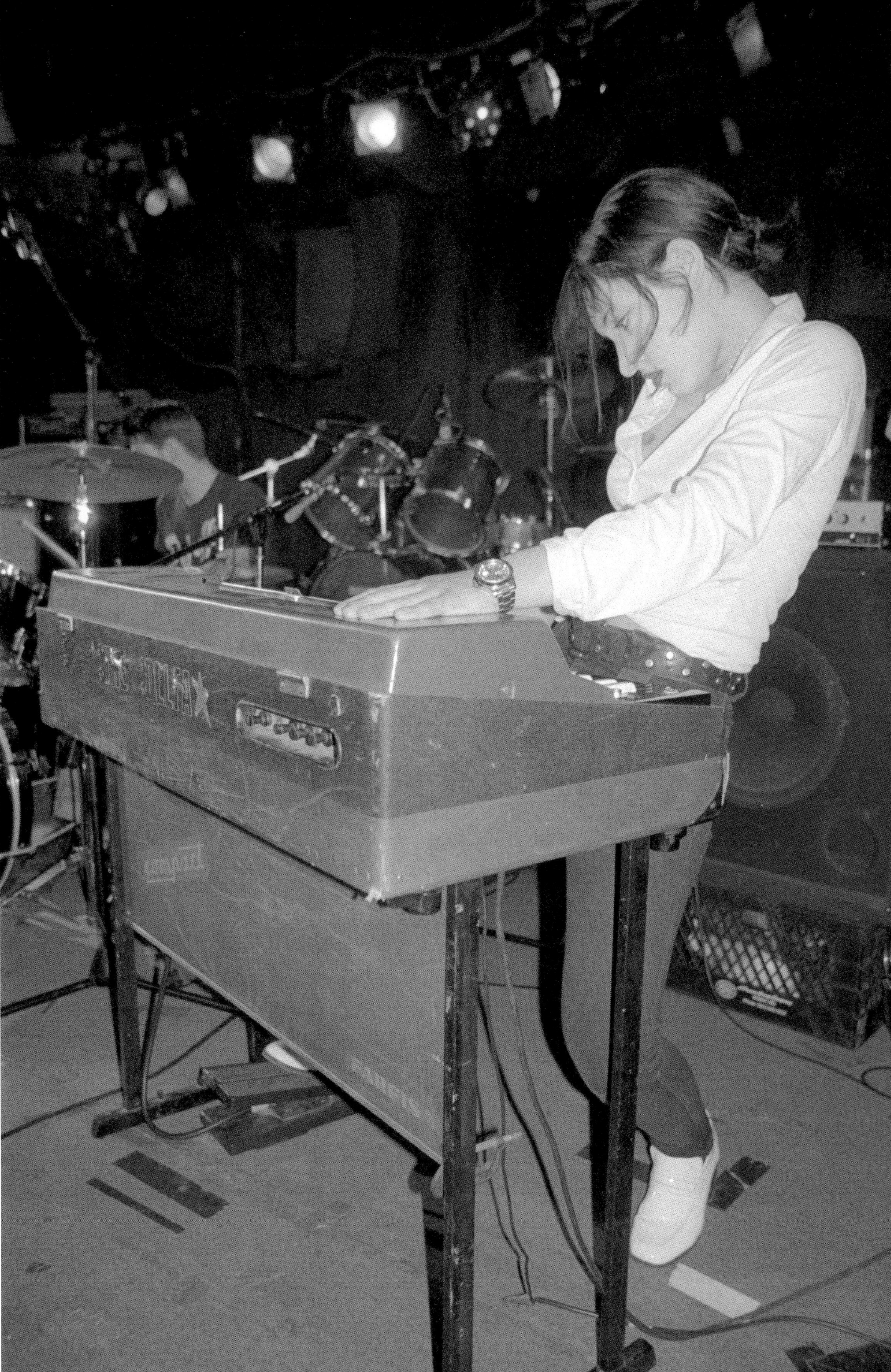

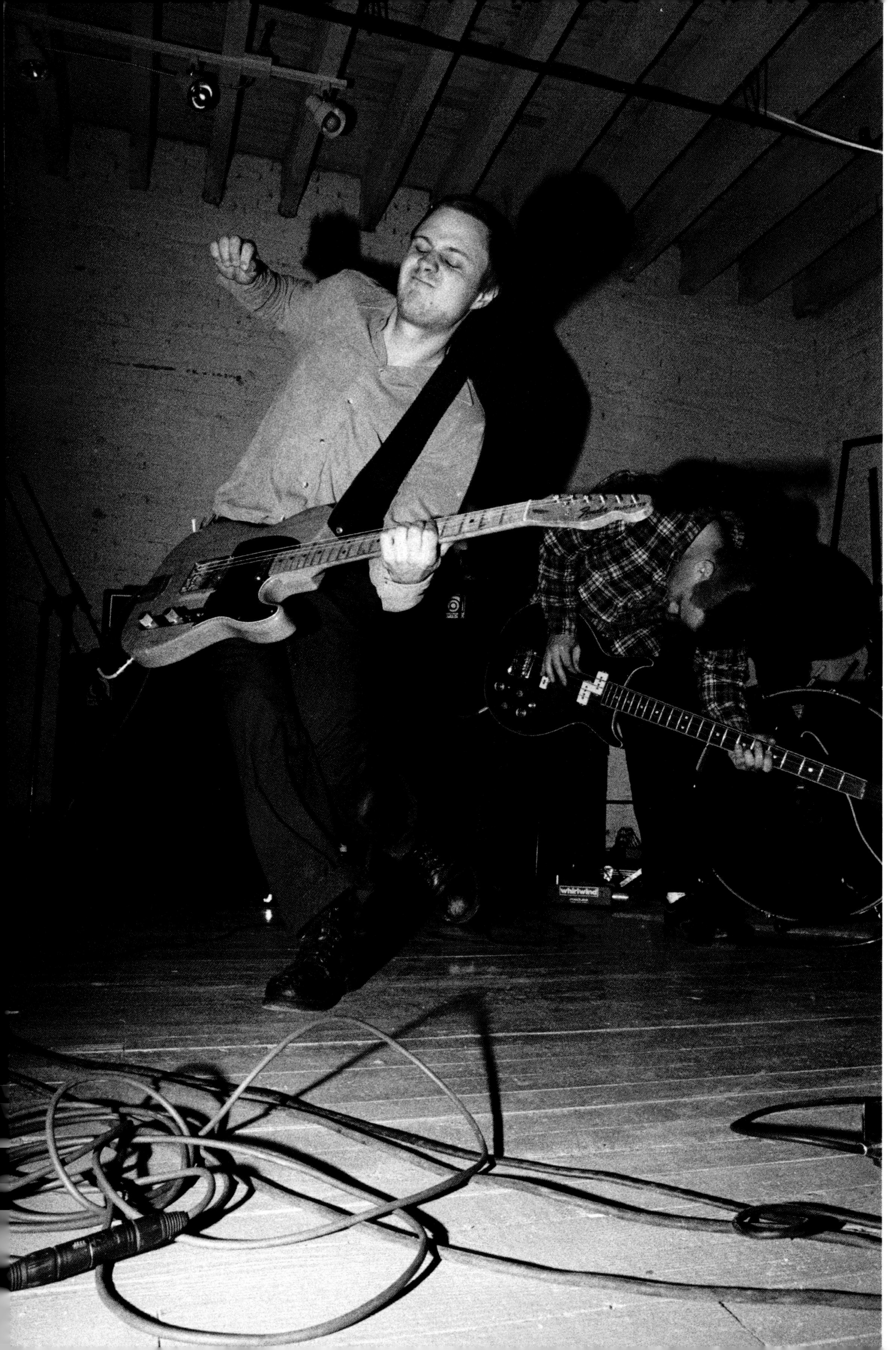
whirlwind

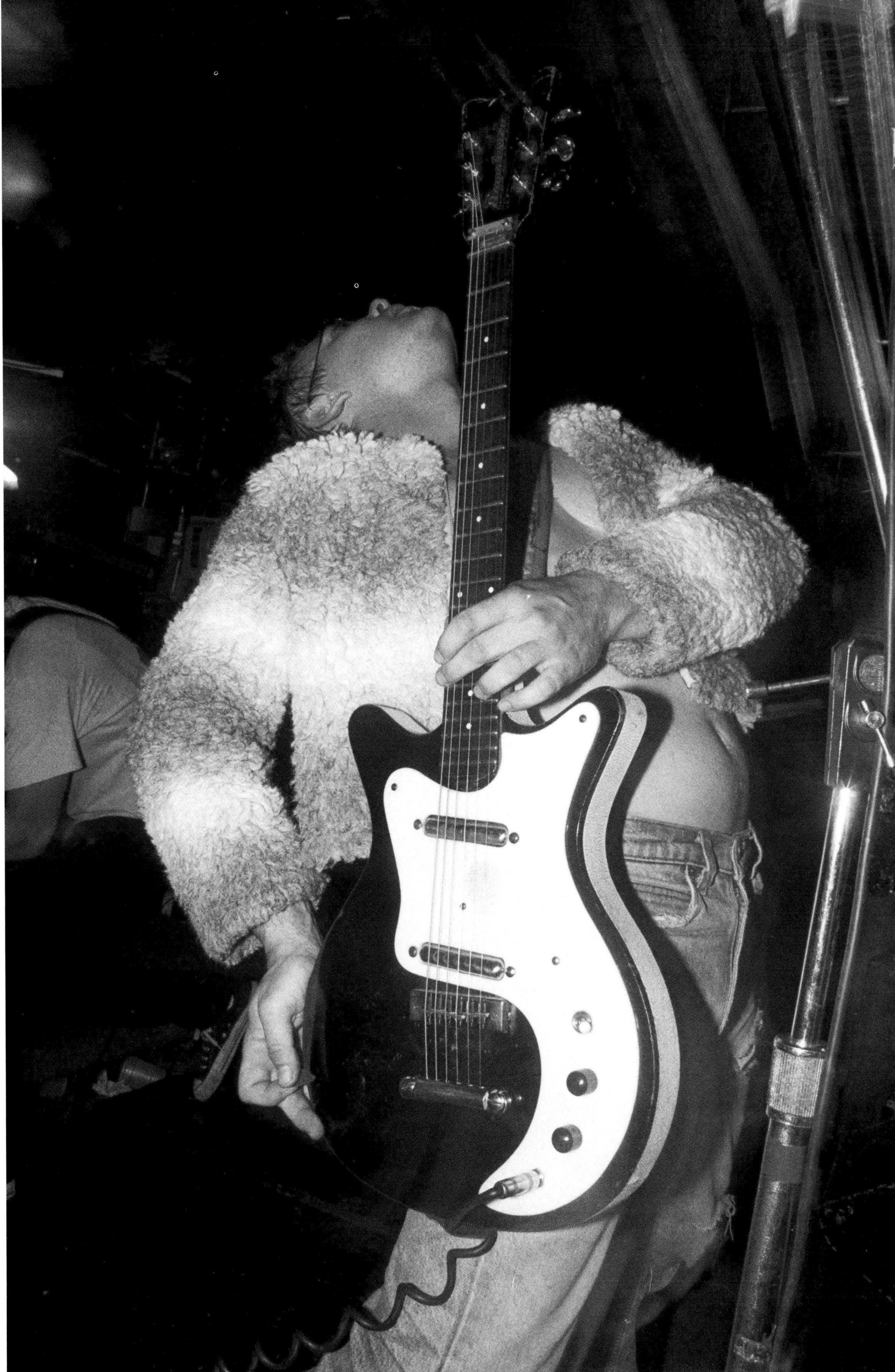

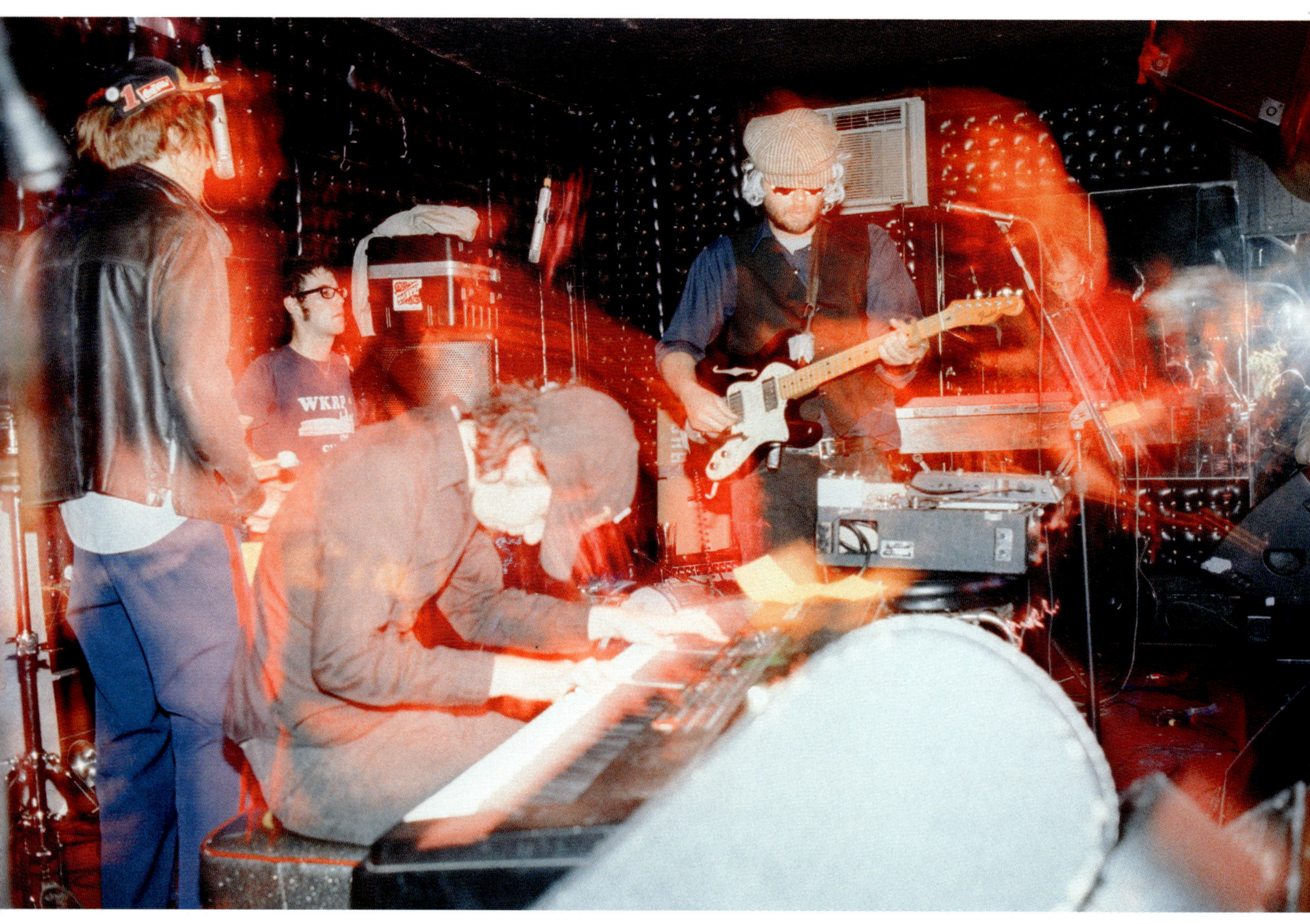
WKRP

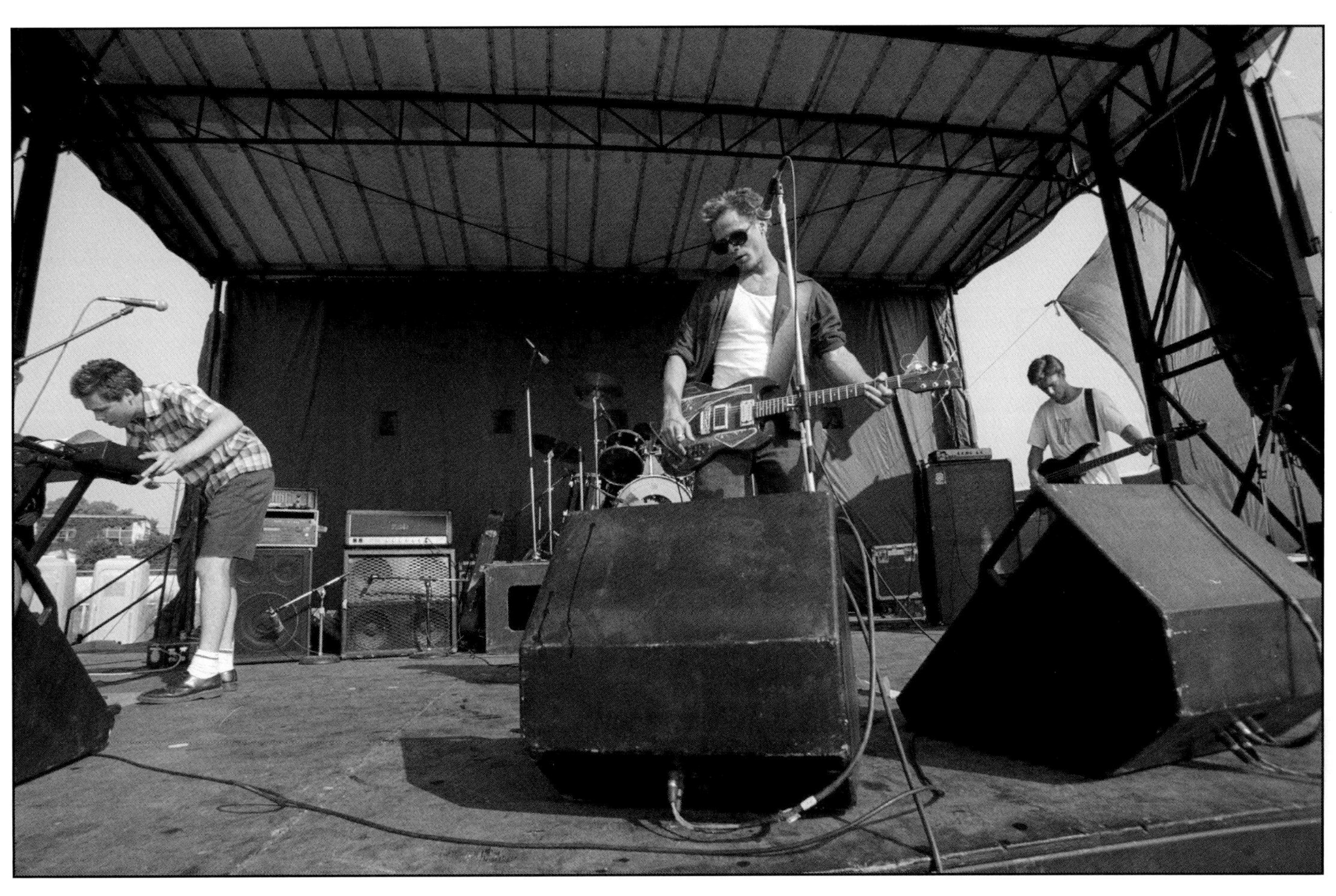

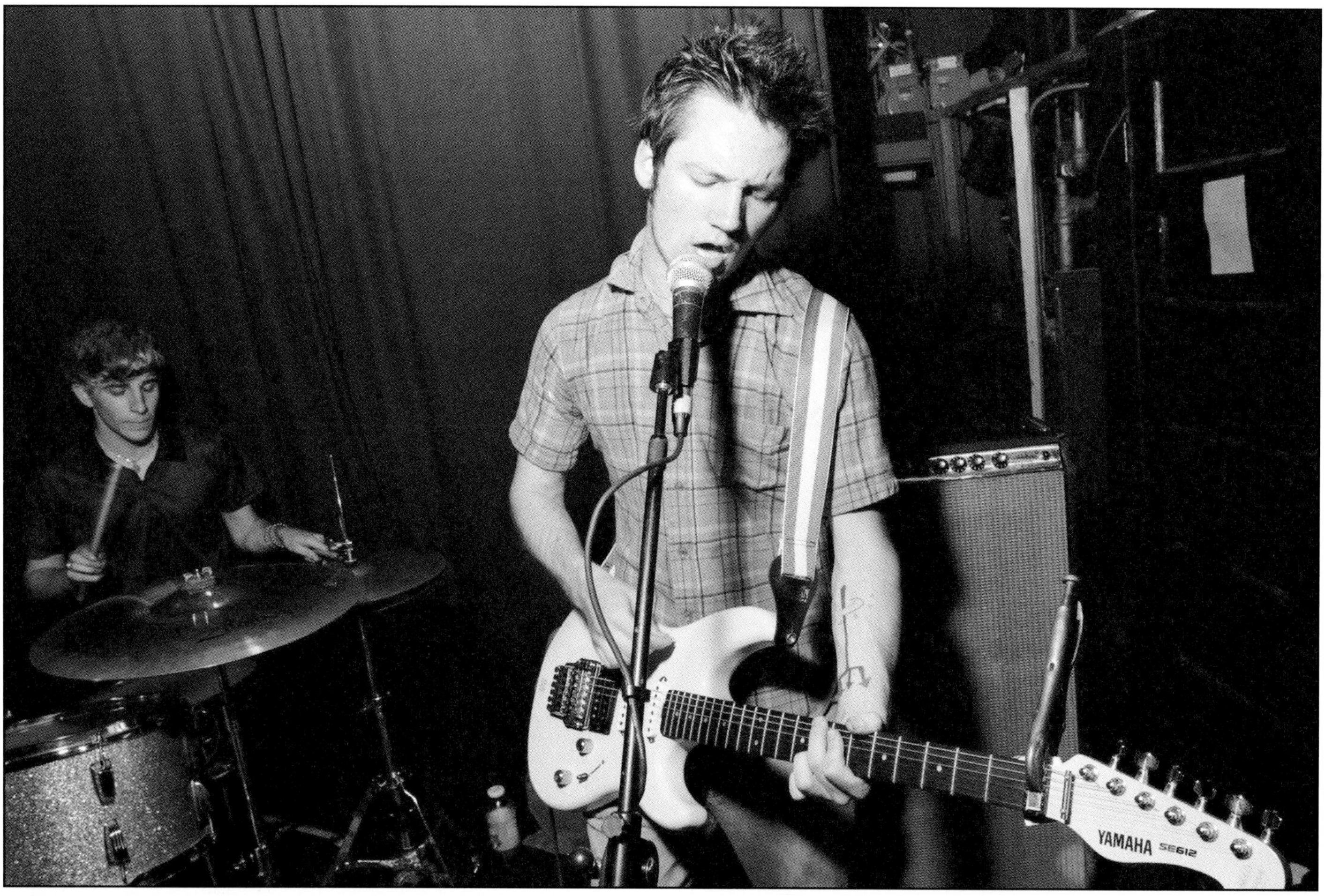

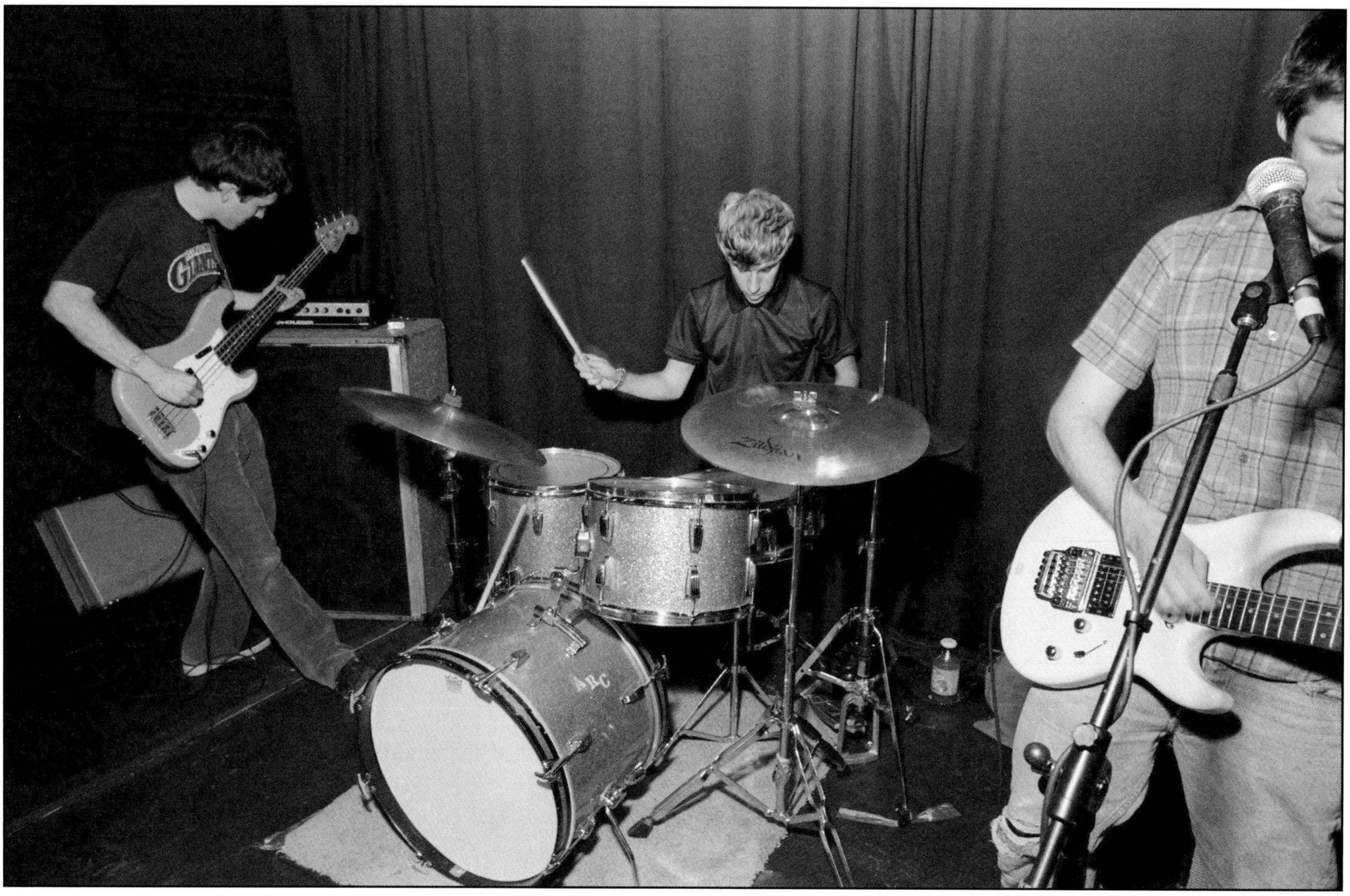

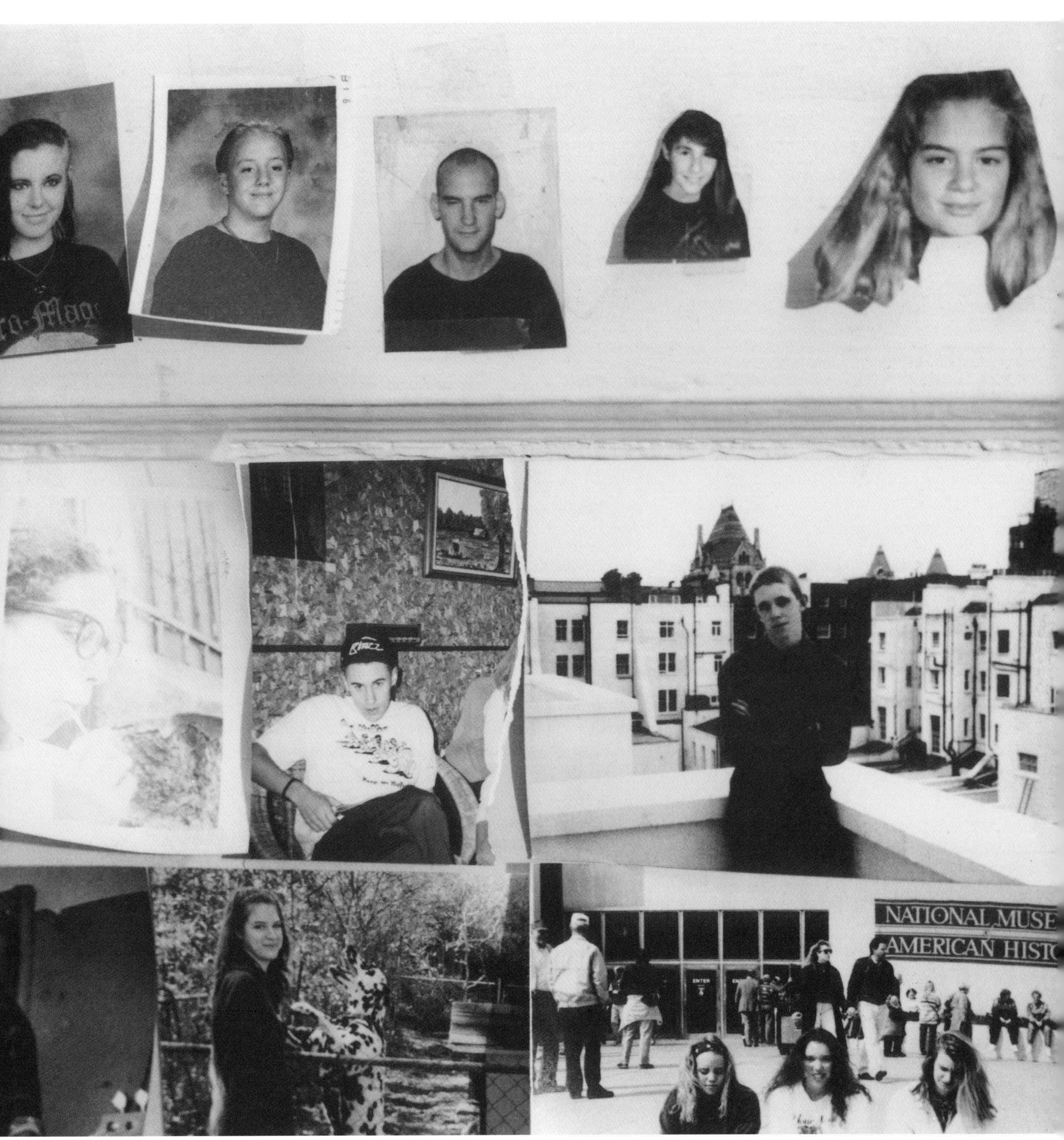
NATIONAL MUSE
AMERICAN HISTO
ENTER

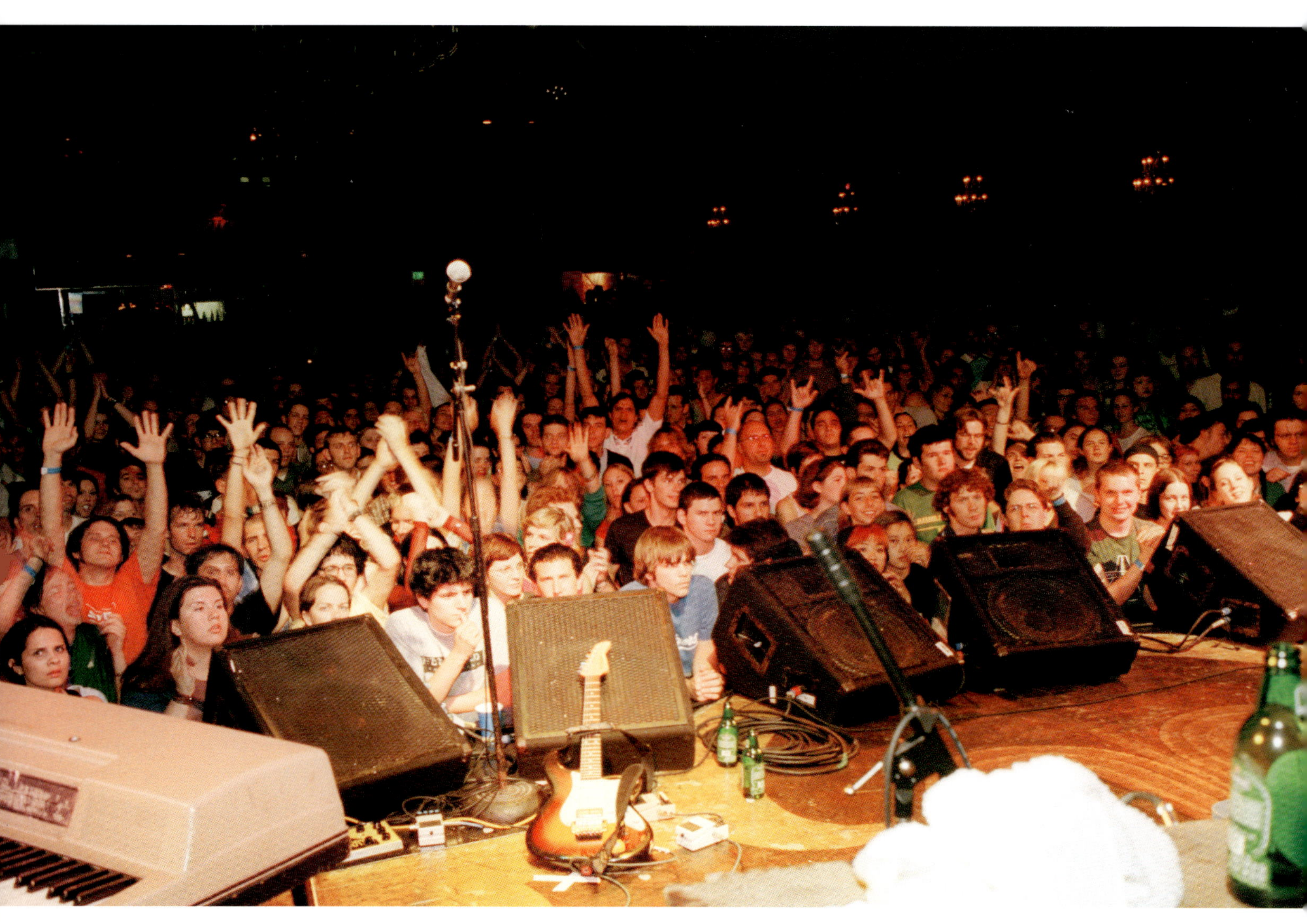

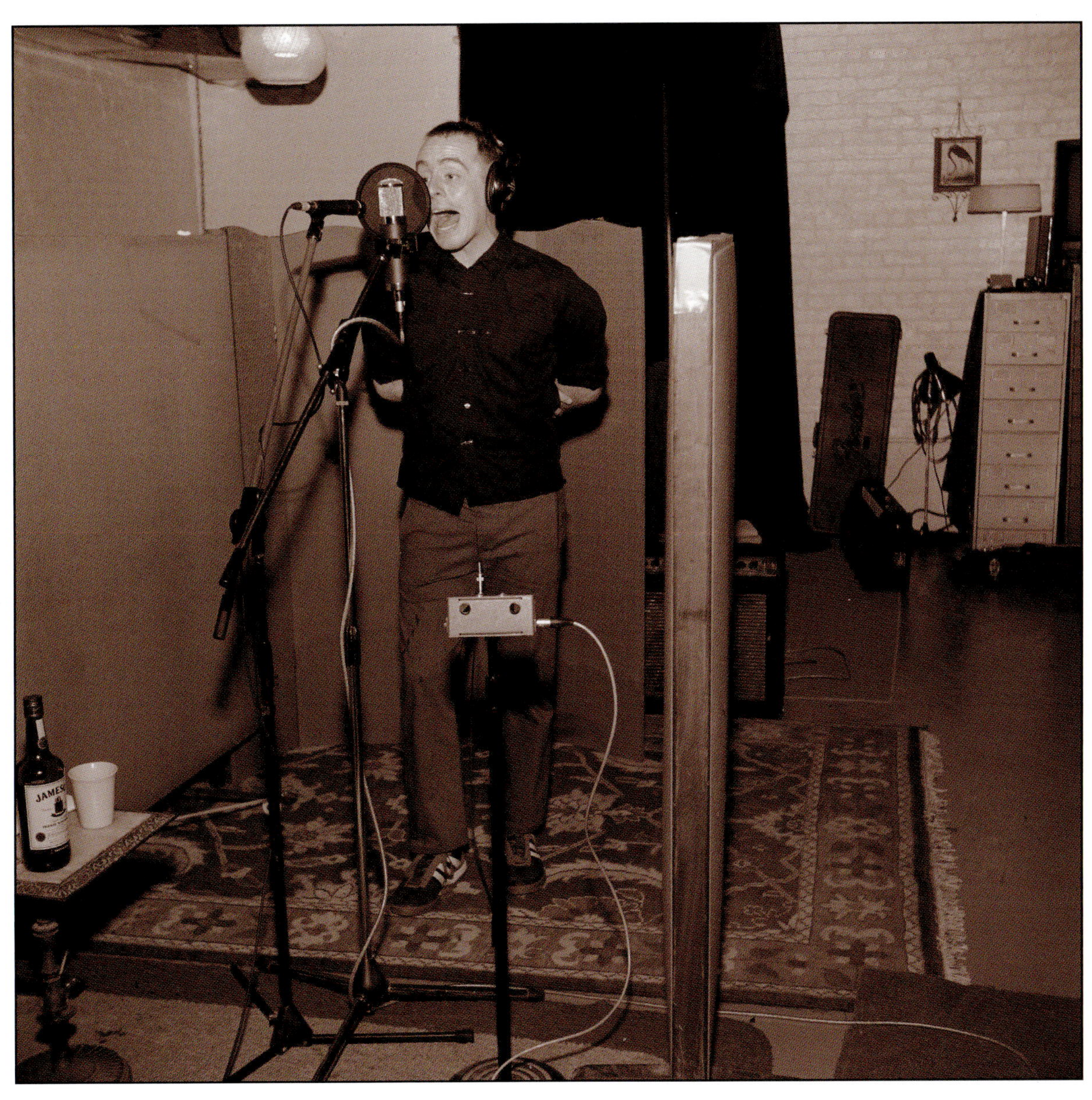

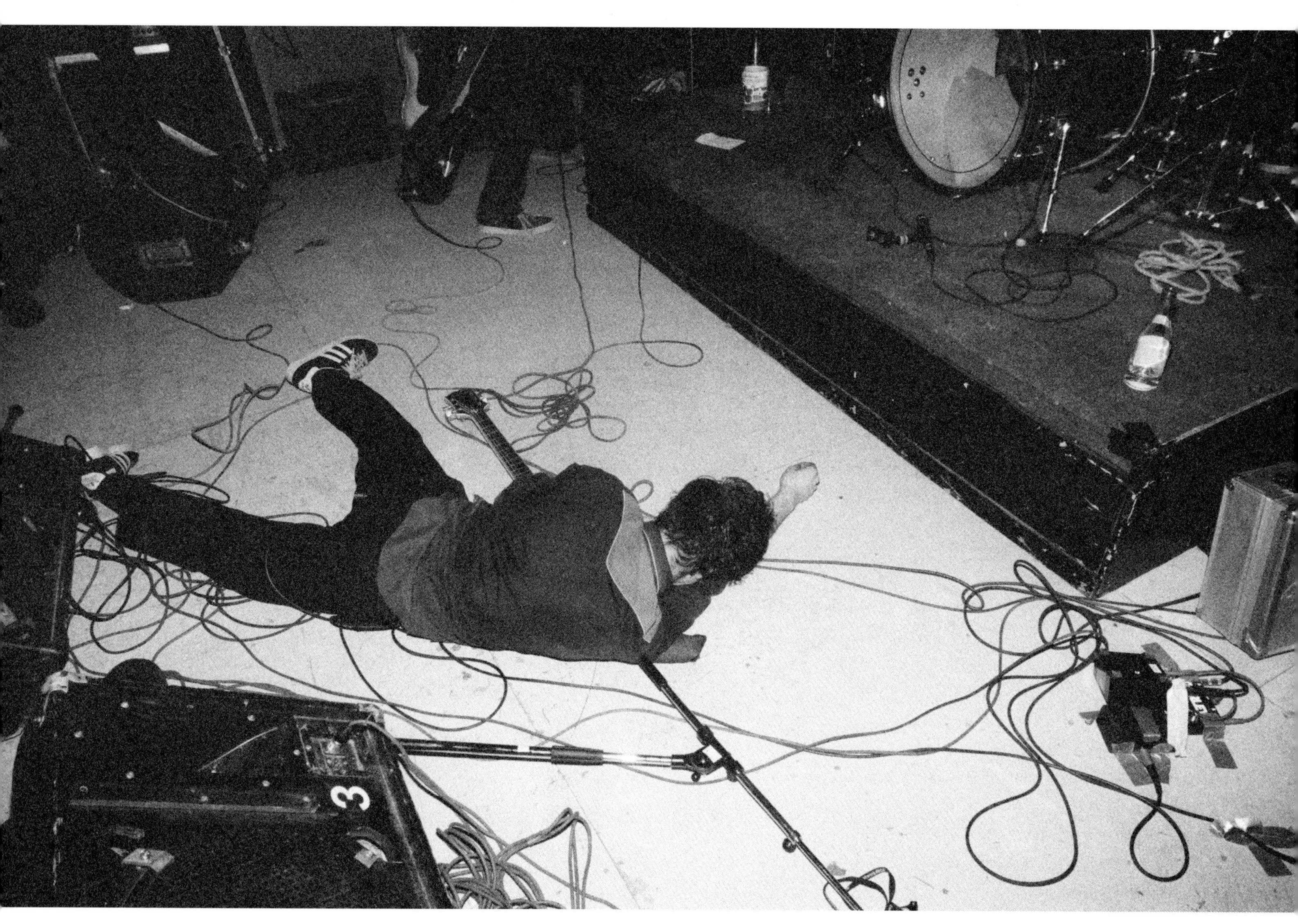
3

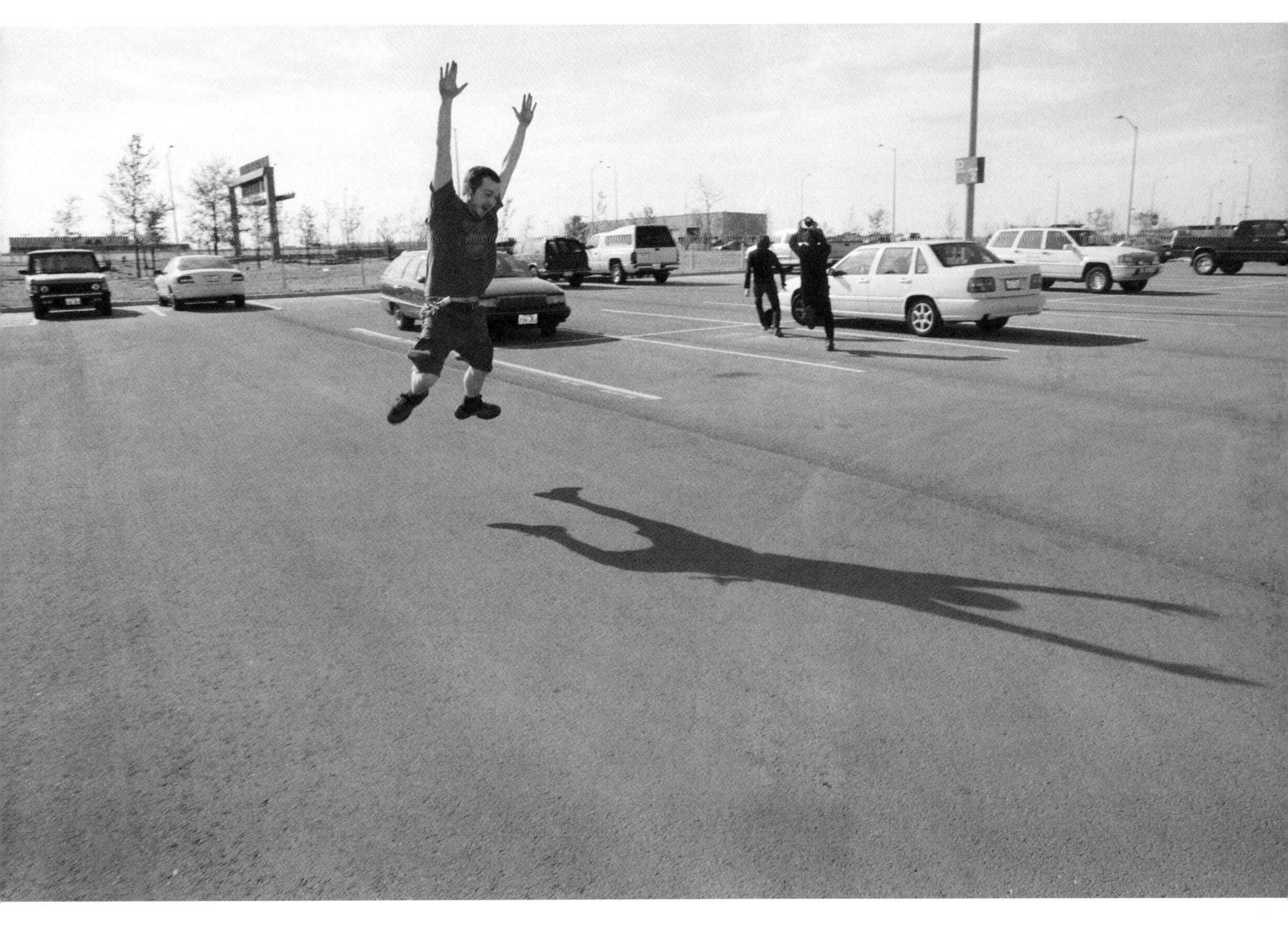

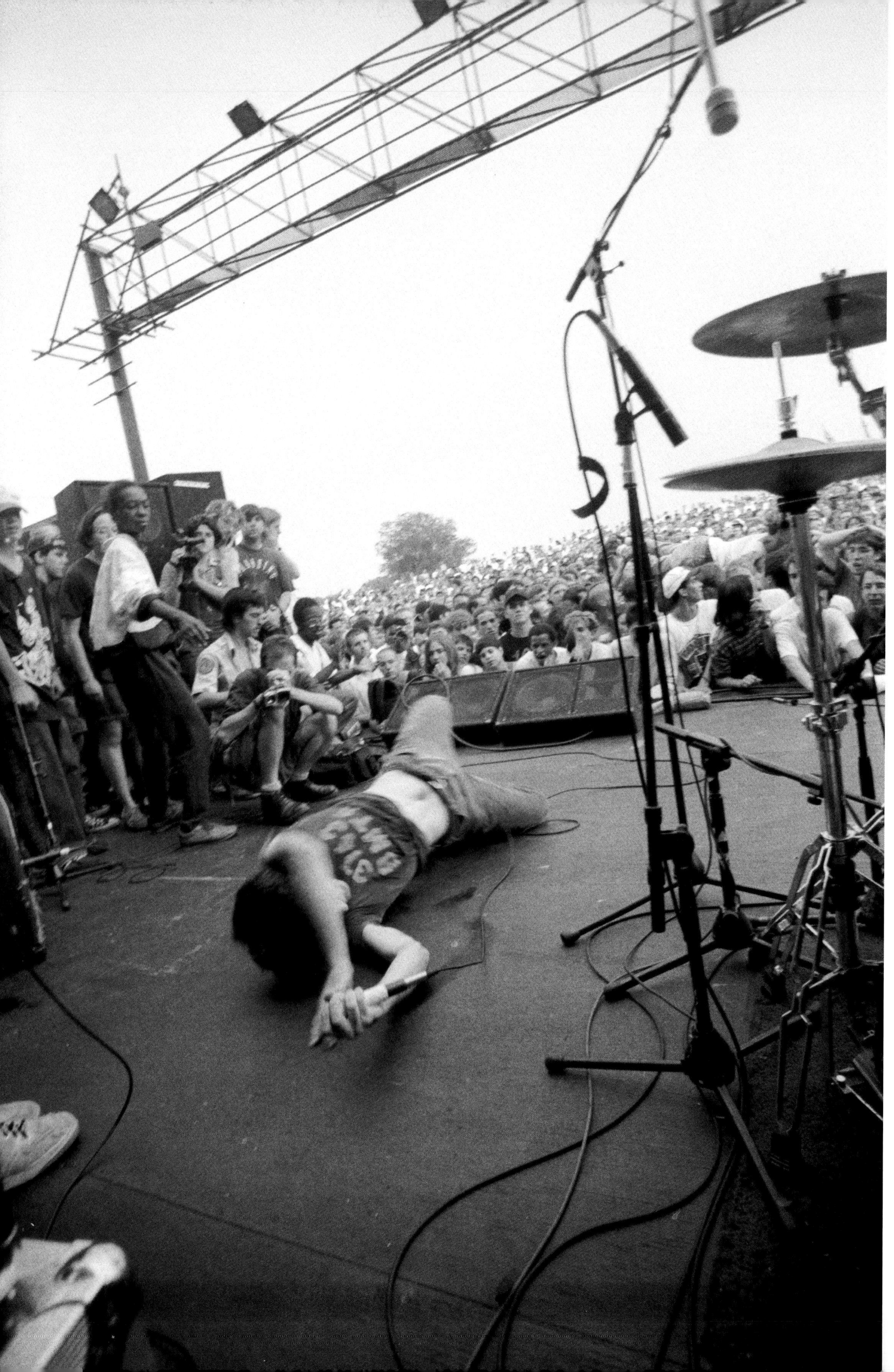

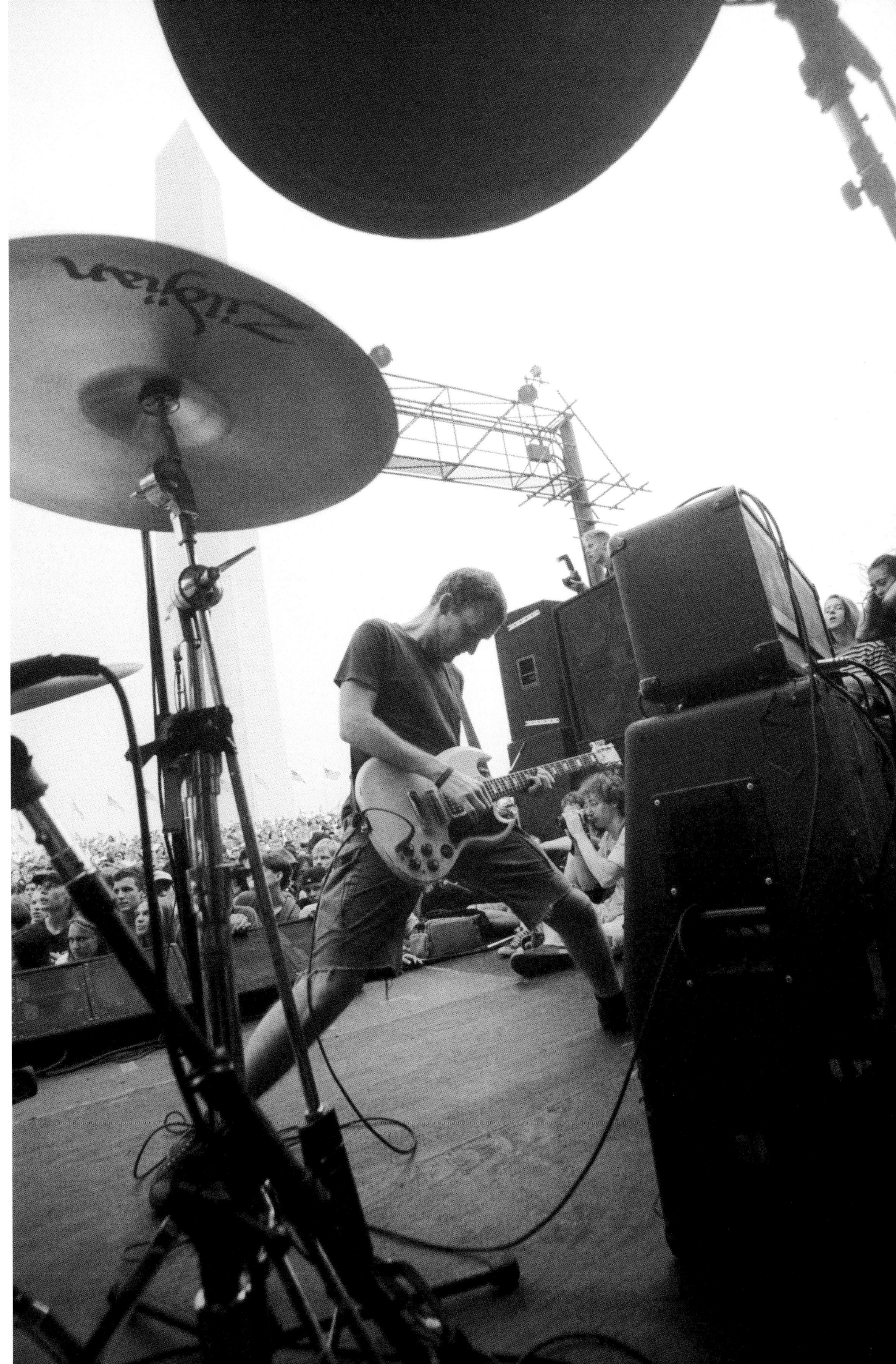
Zildjian

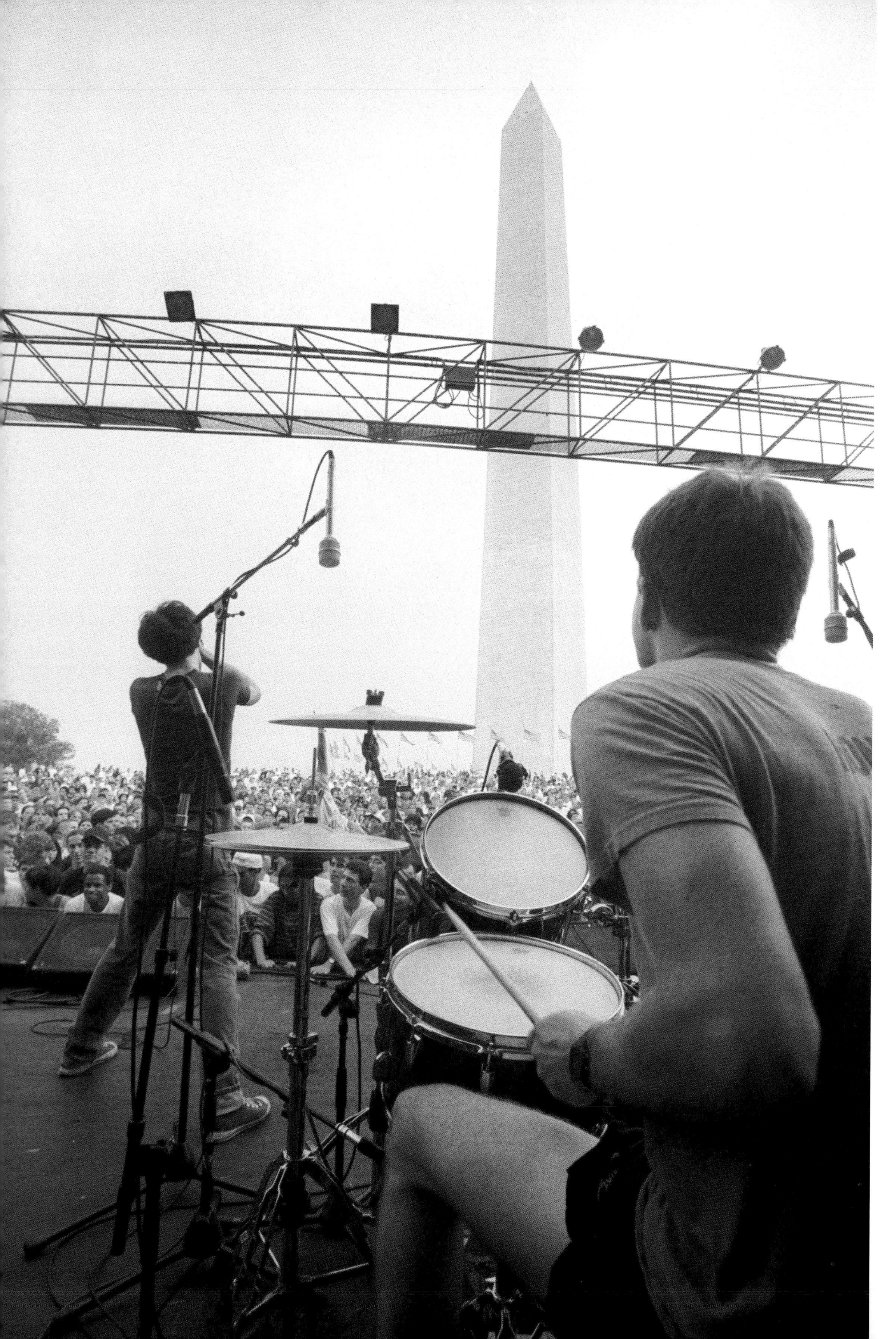

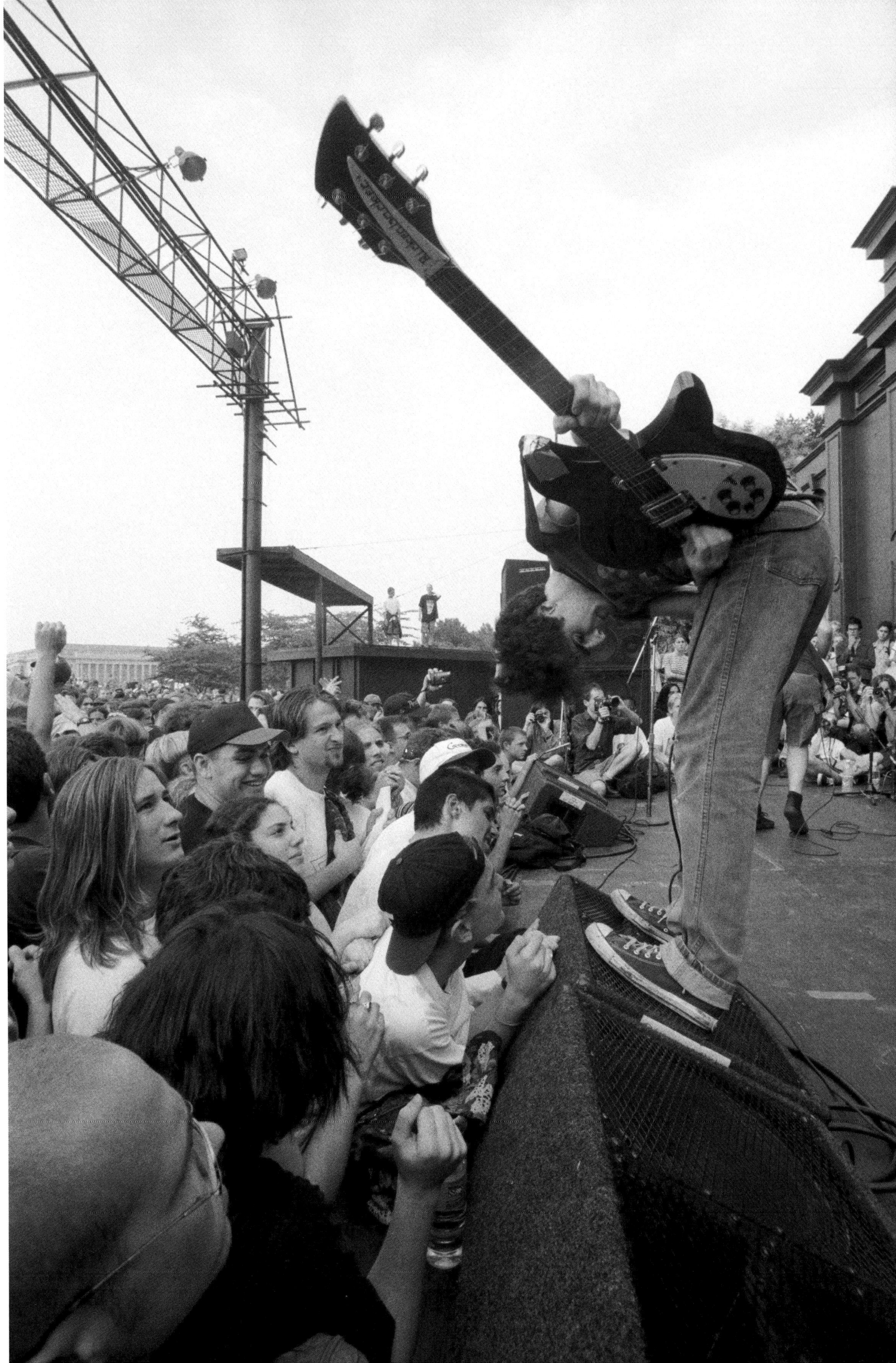

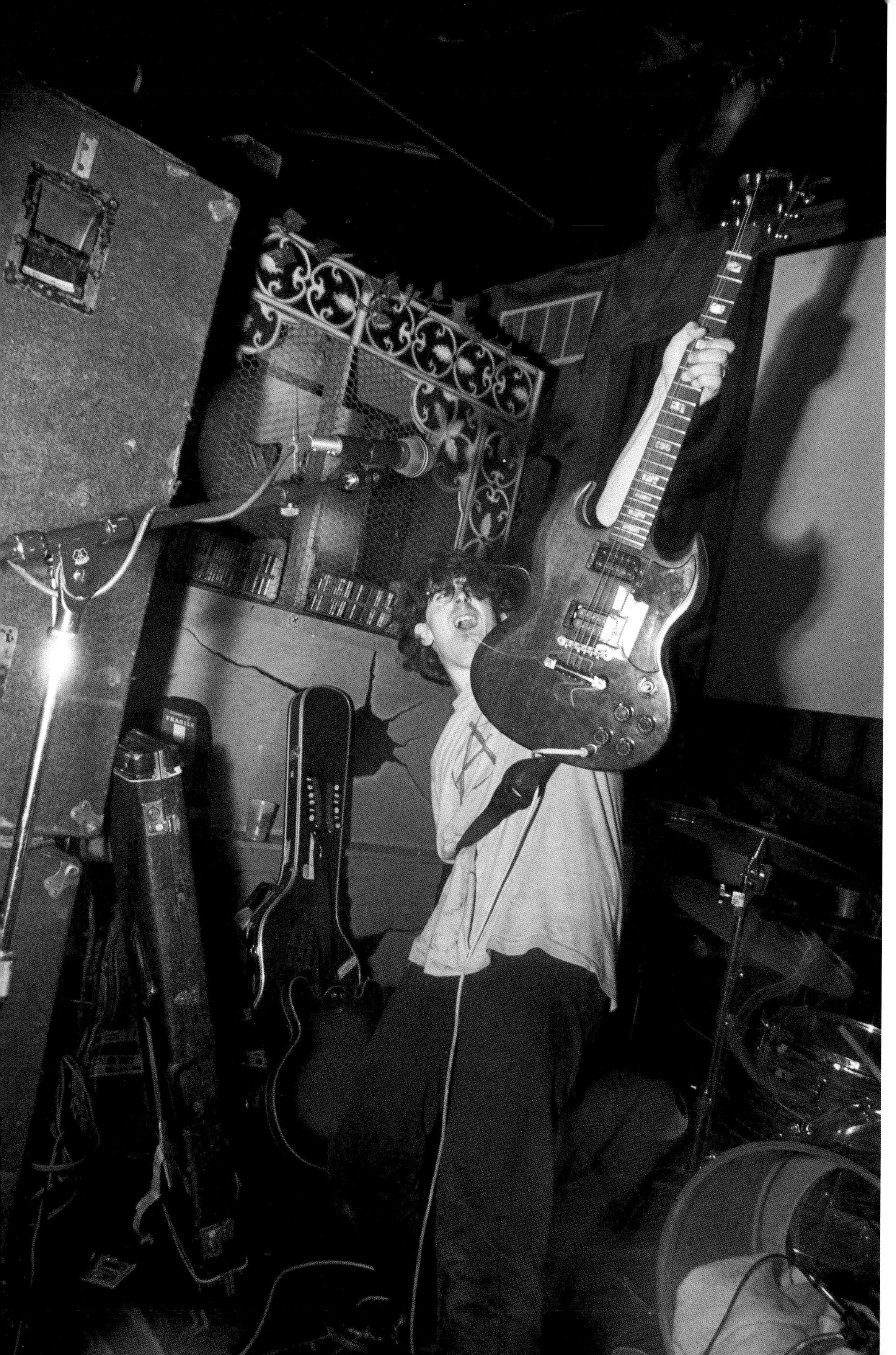
FRAGILE

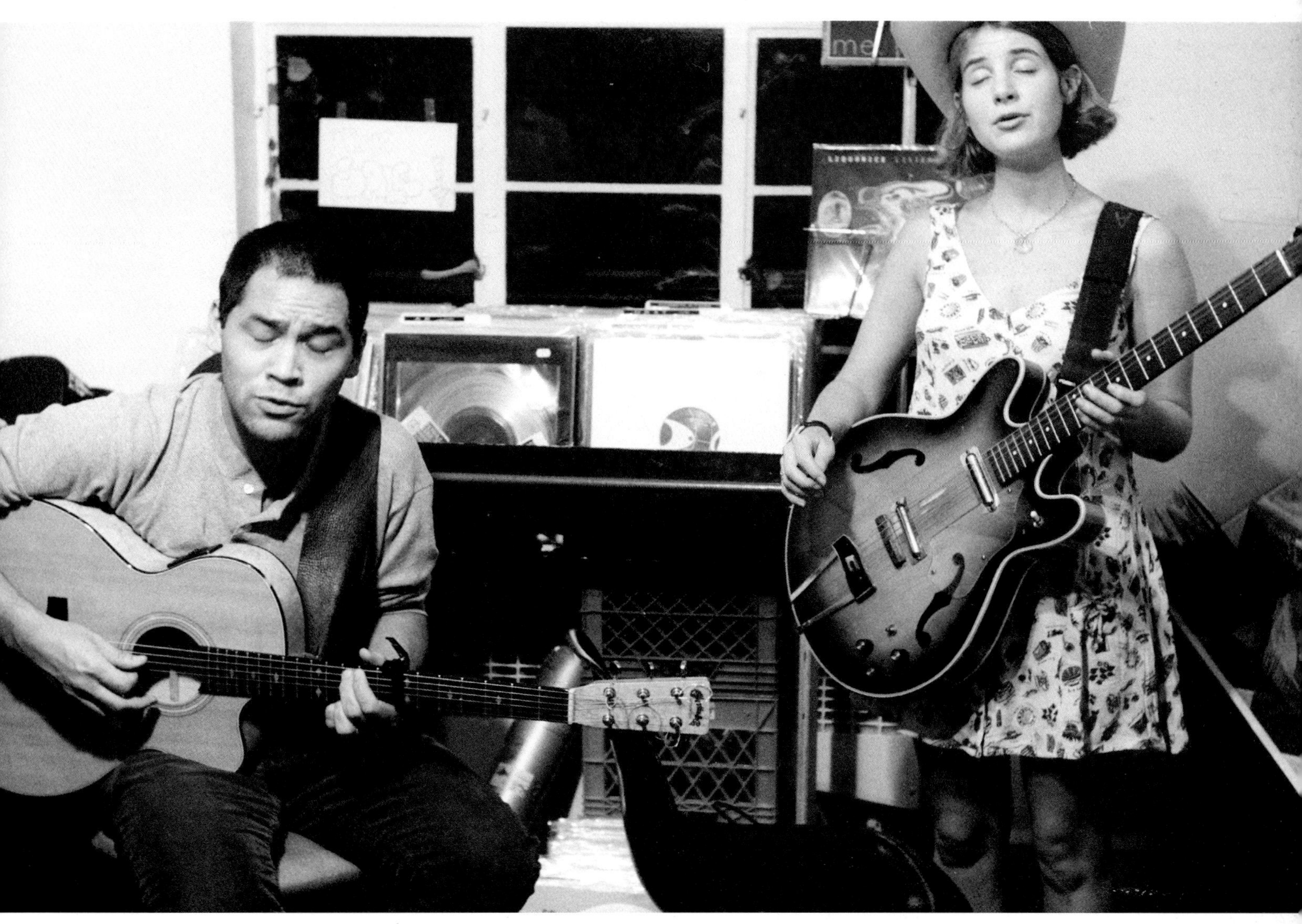

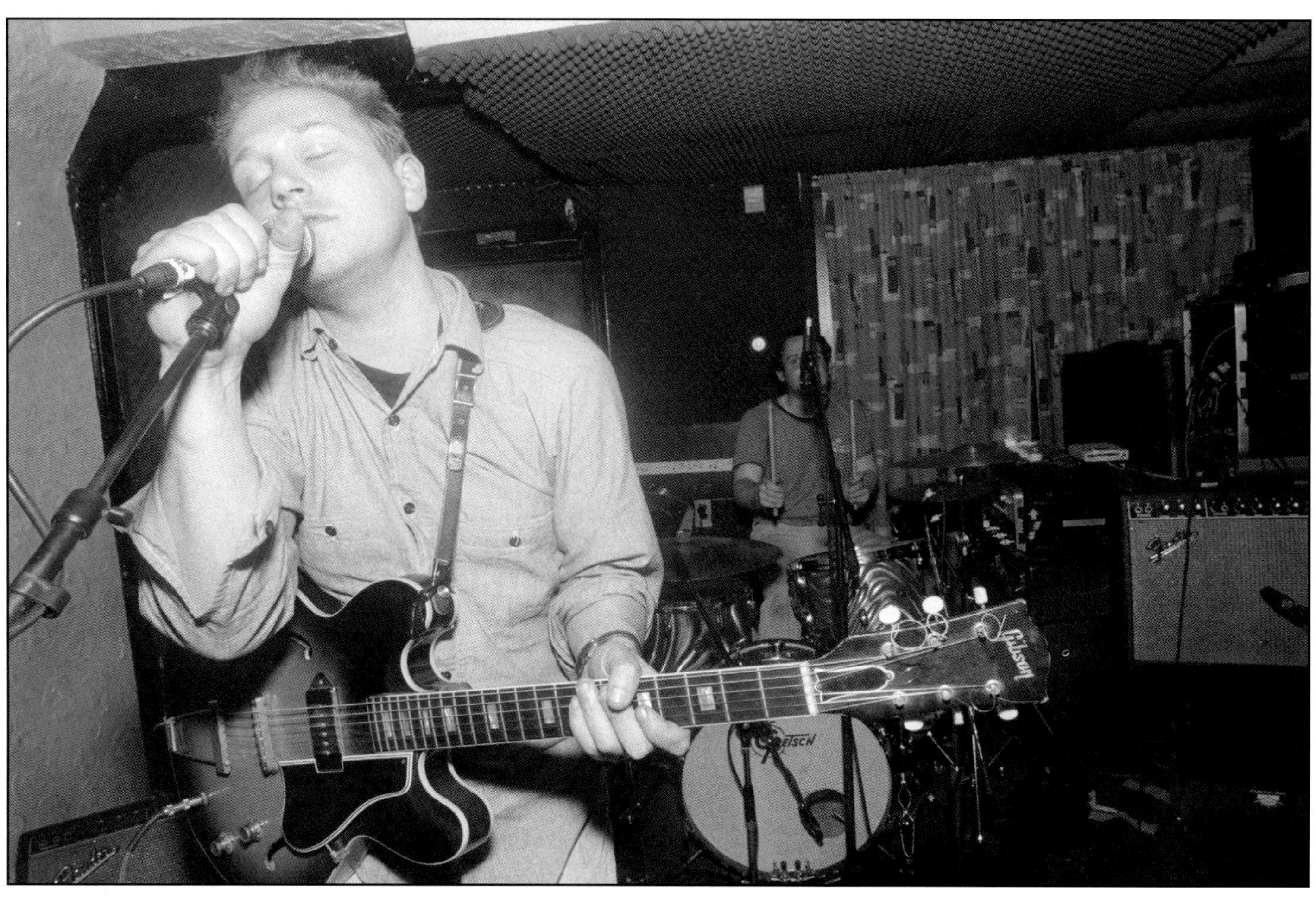
Gibson

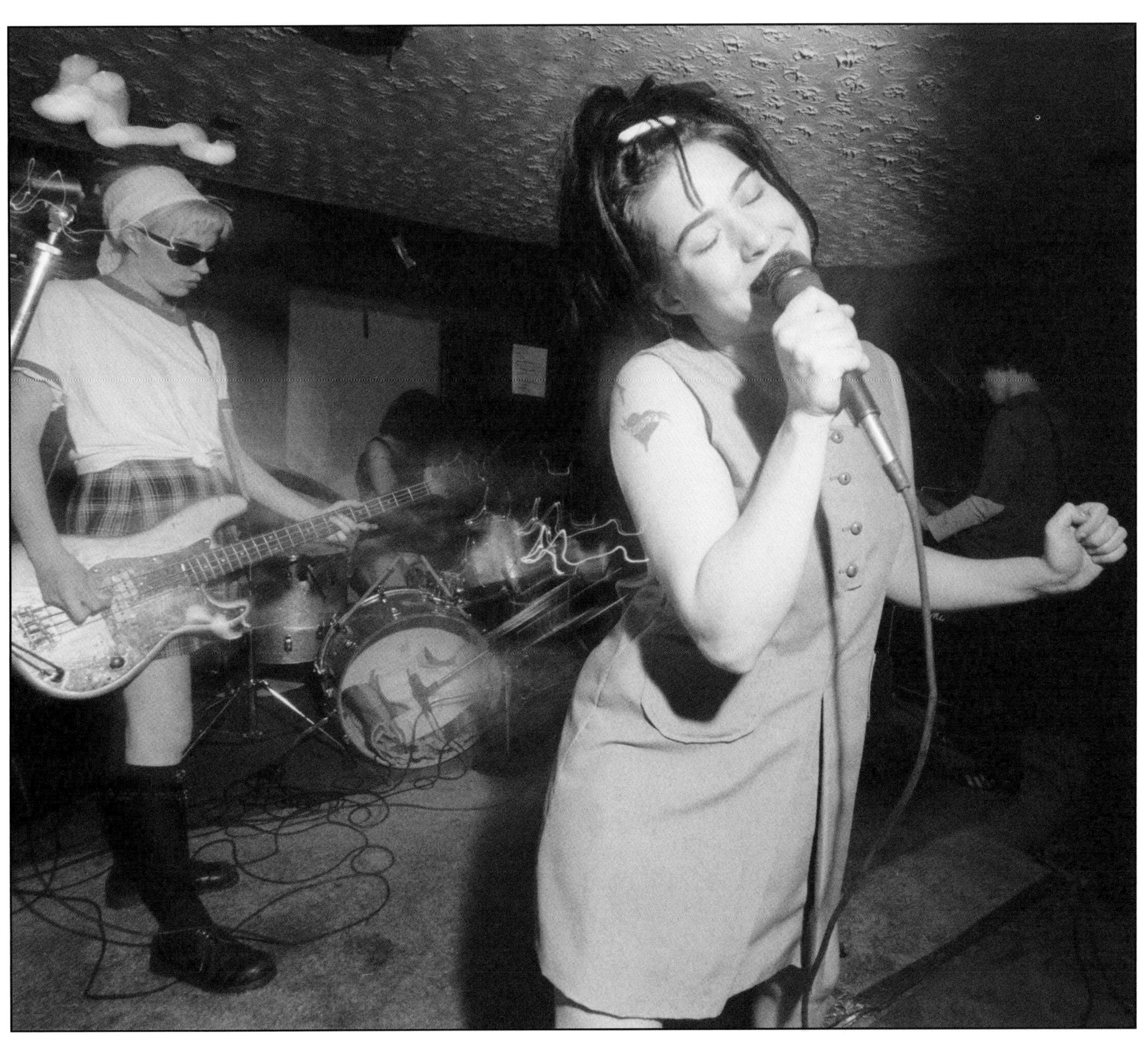

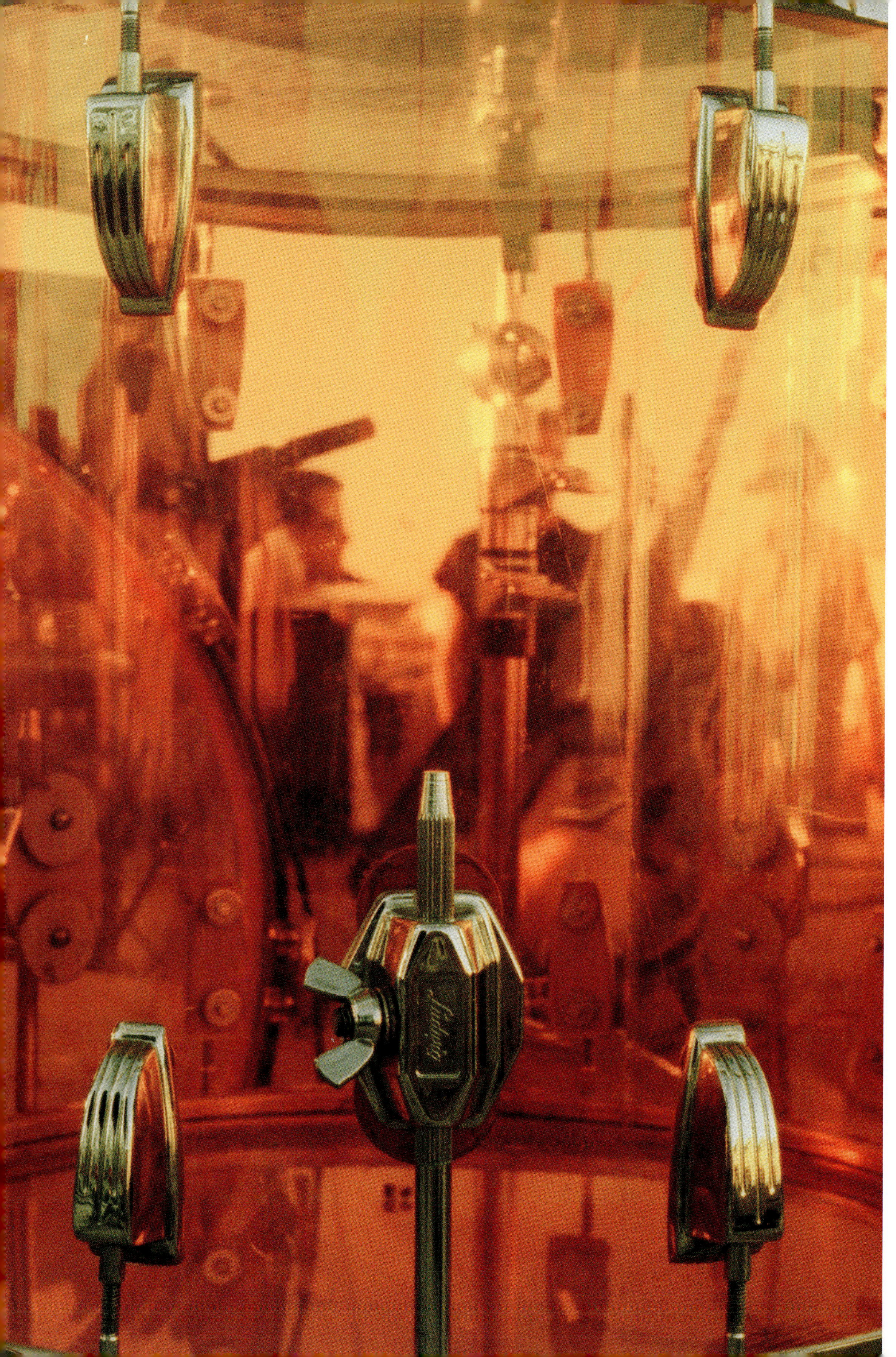
Ludwig

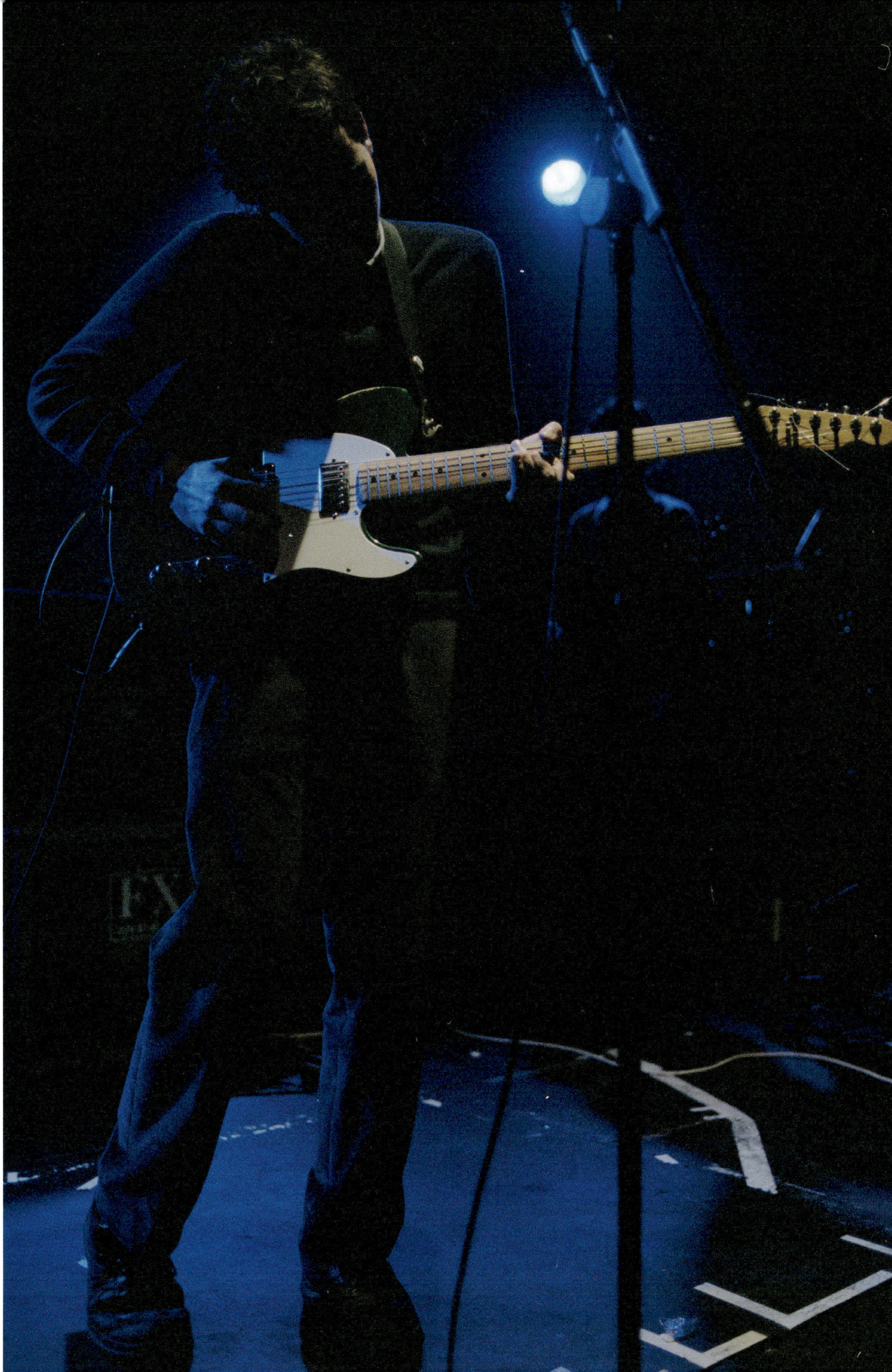

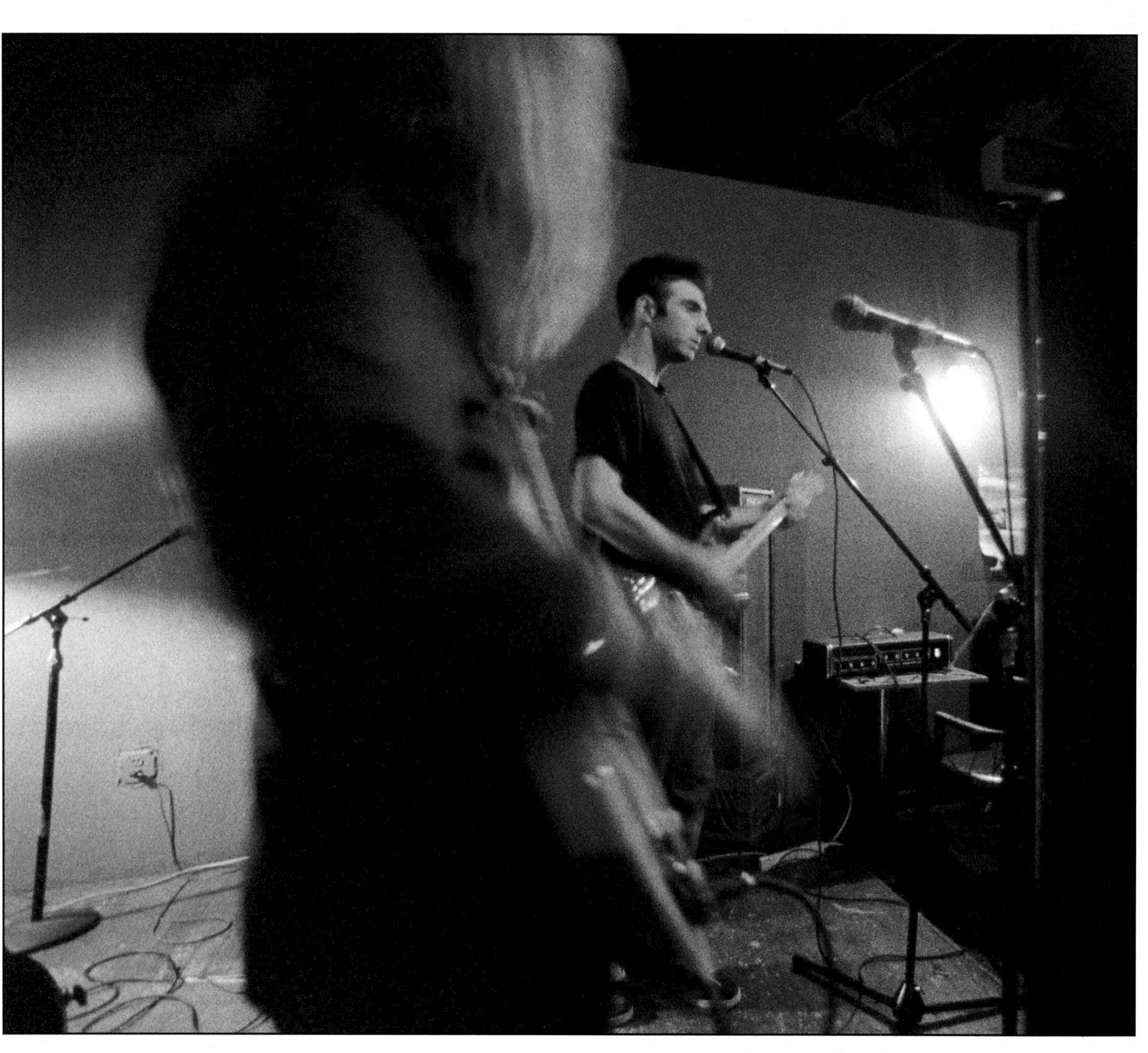

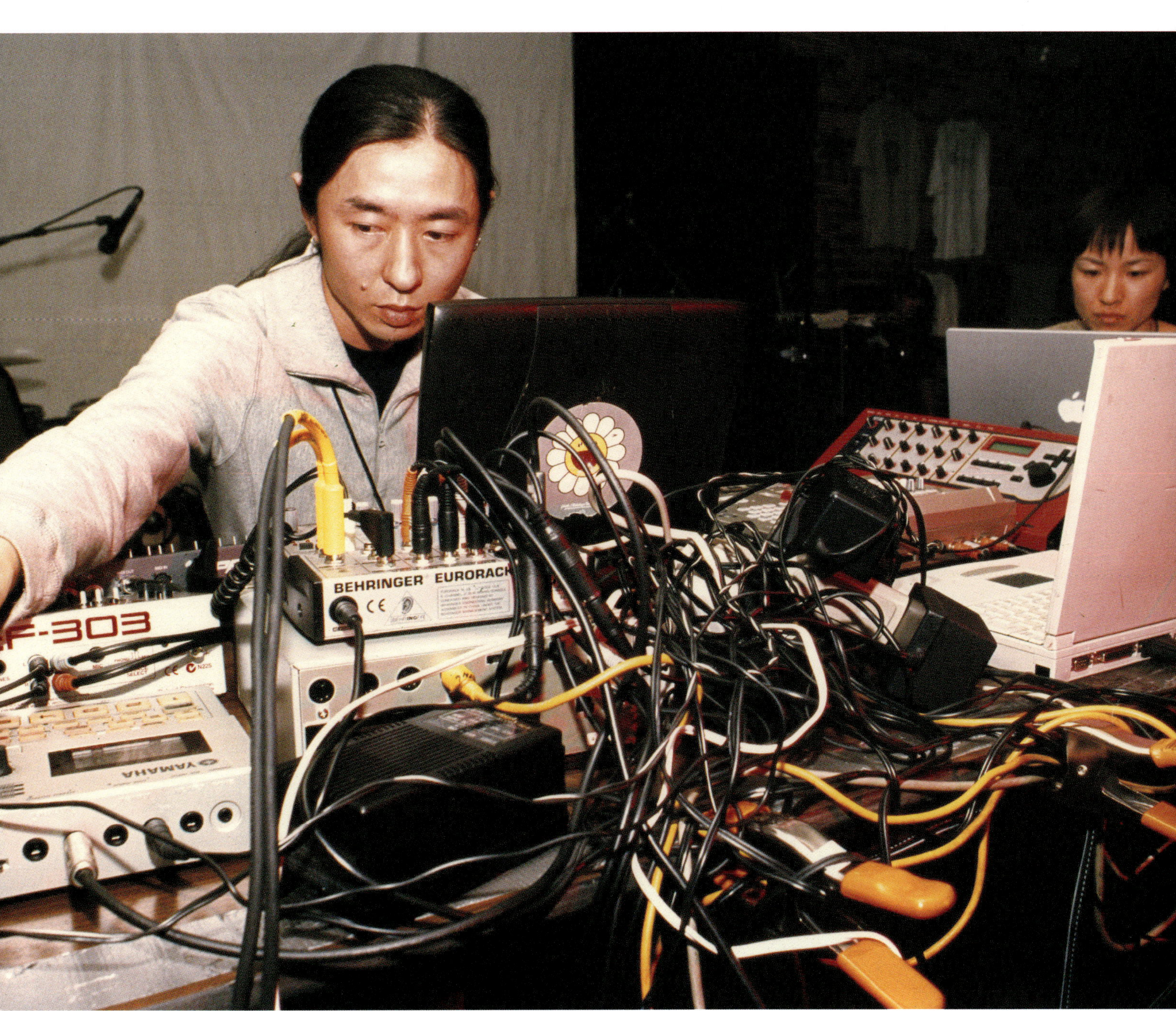
BEHRINGER EURORACK
F-303

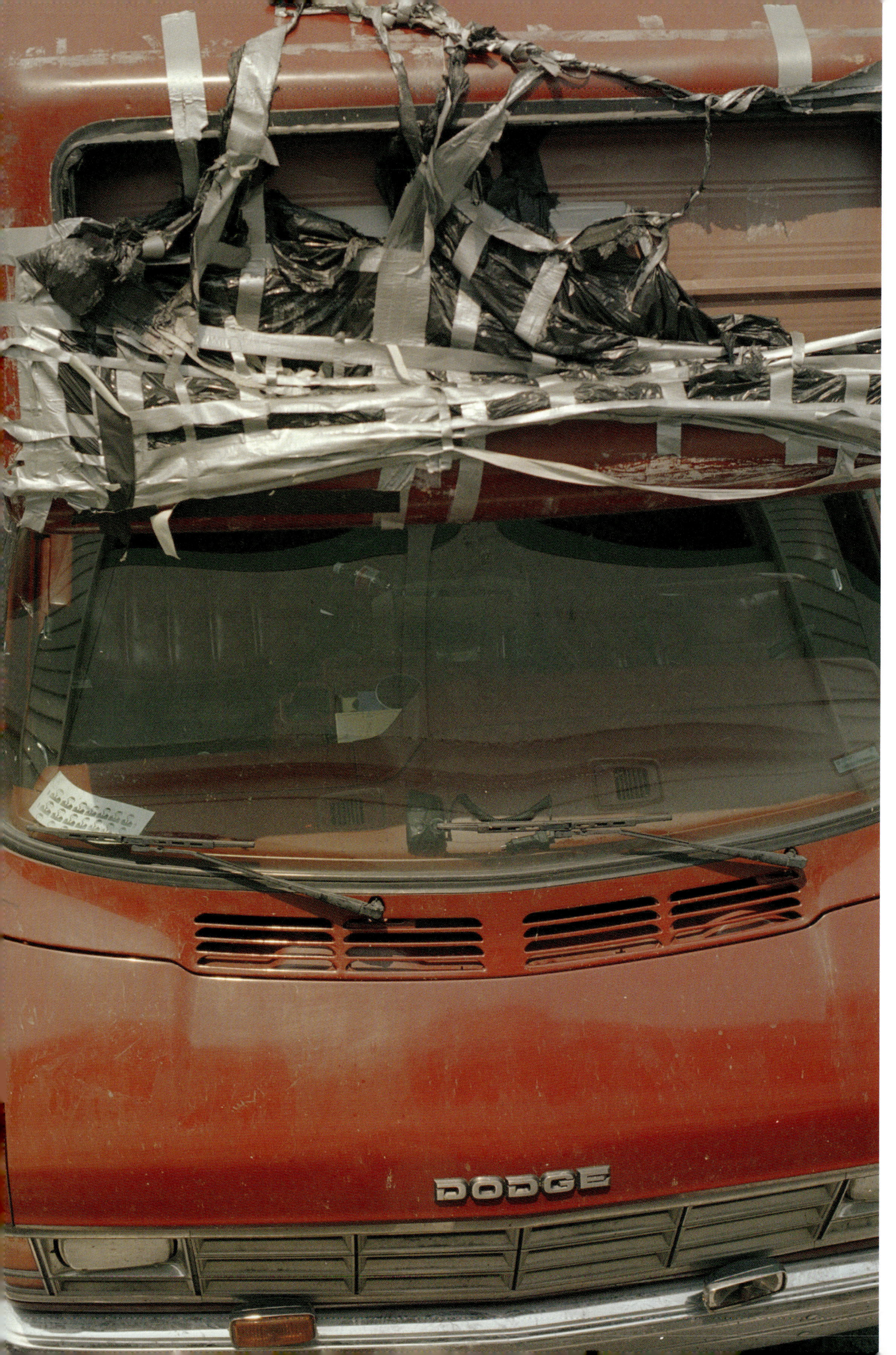
DODGE

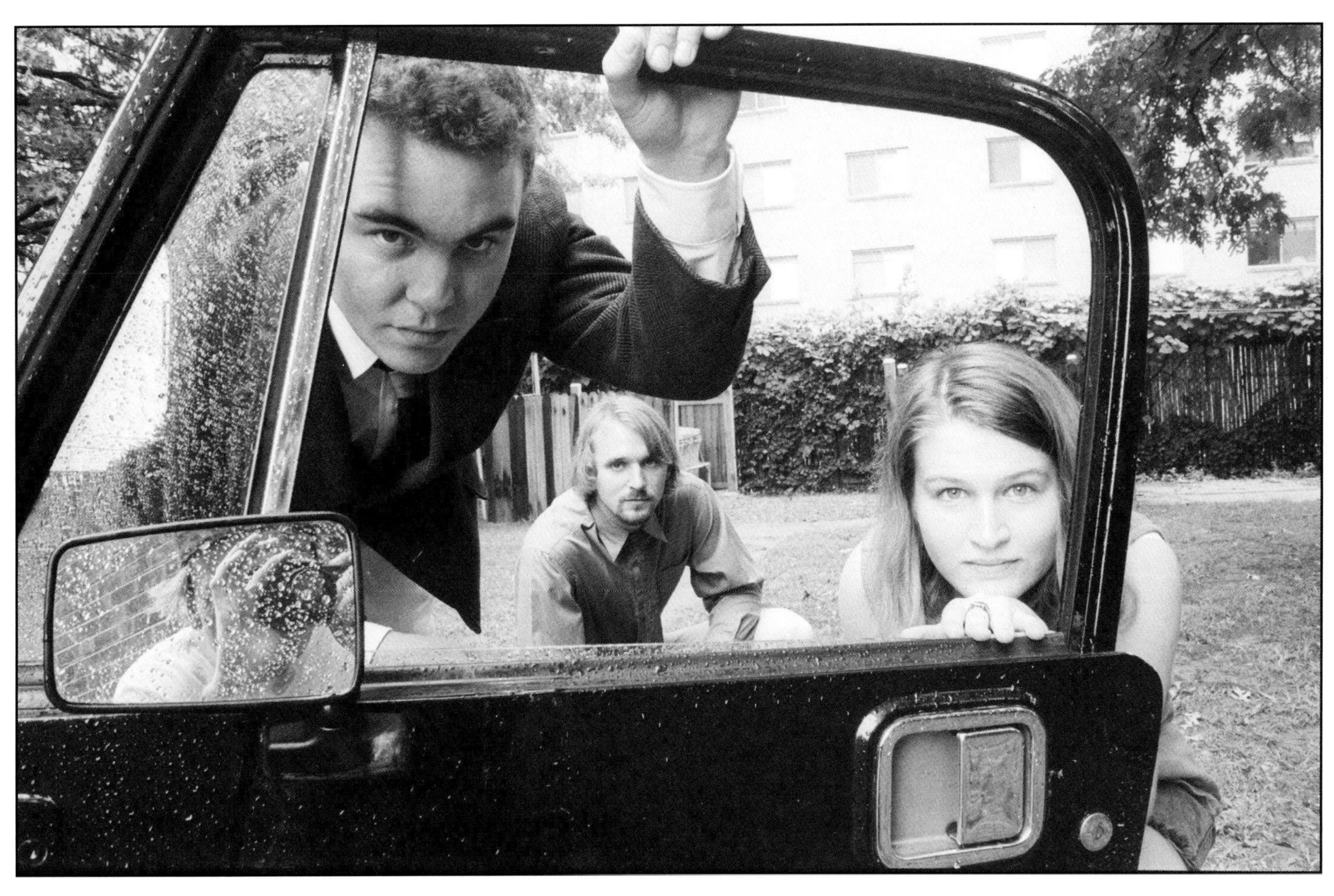

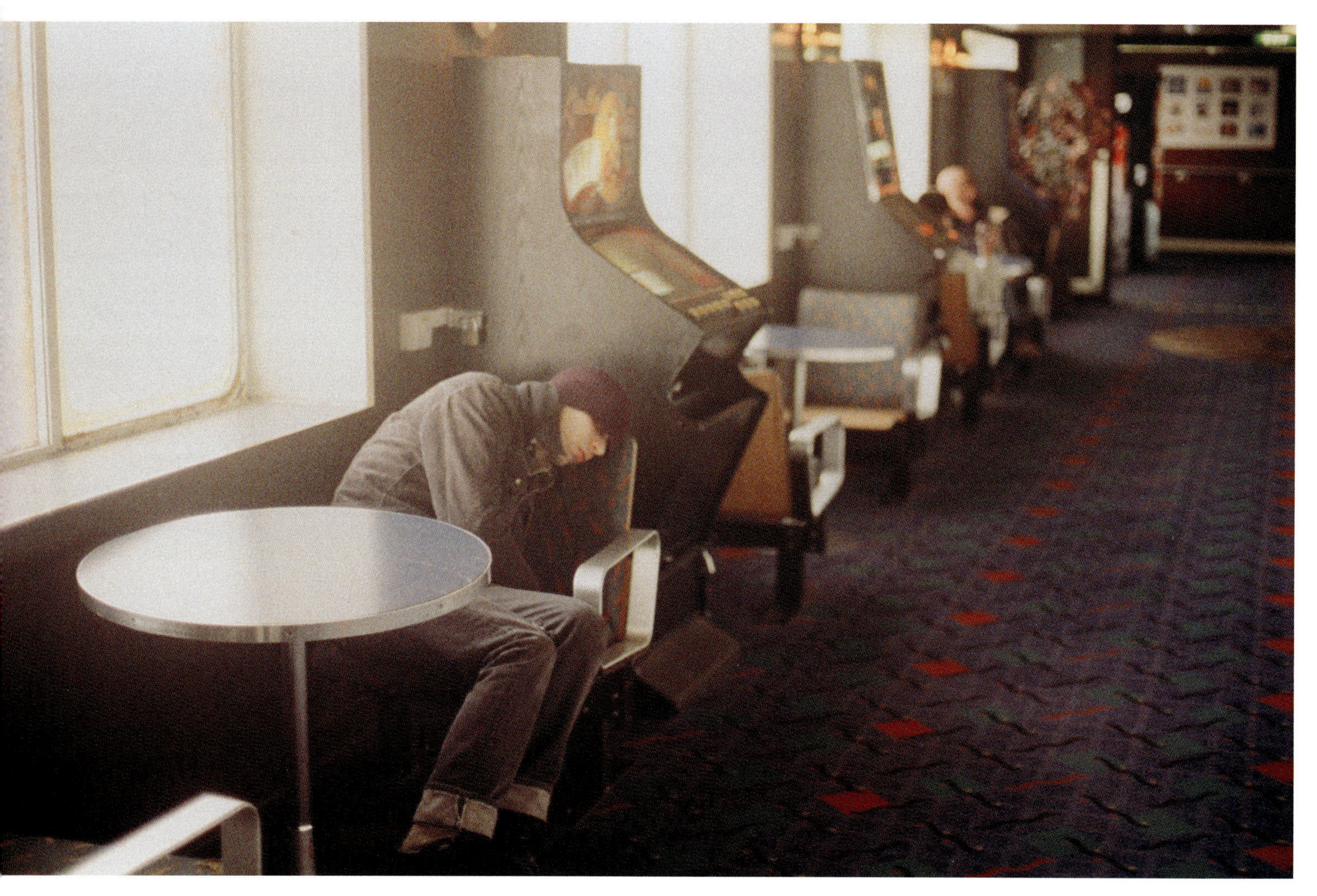

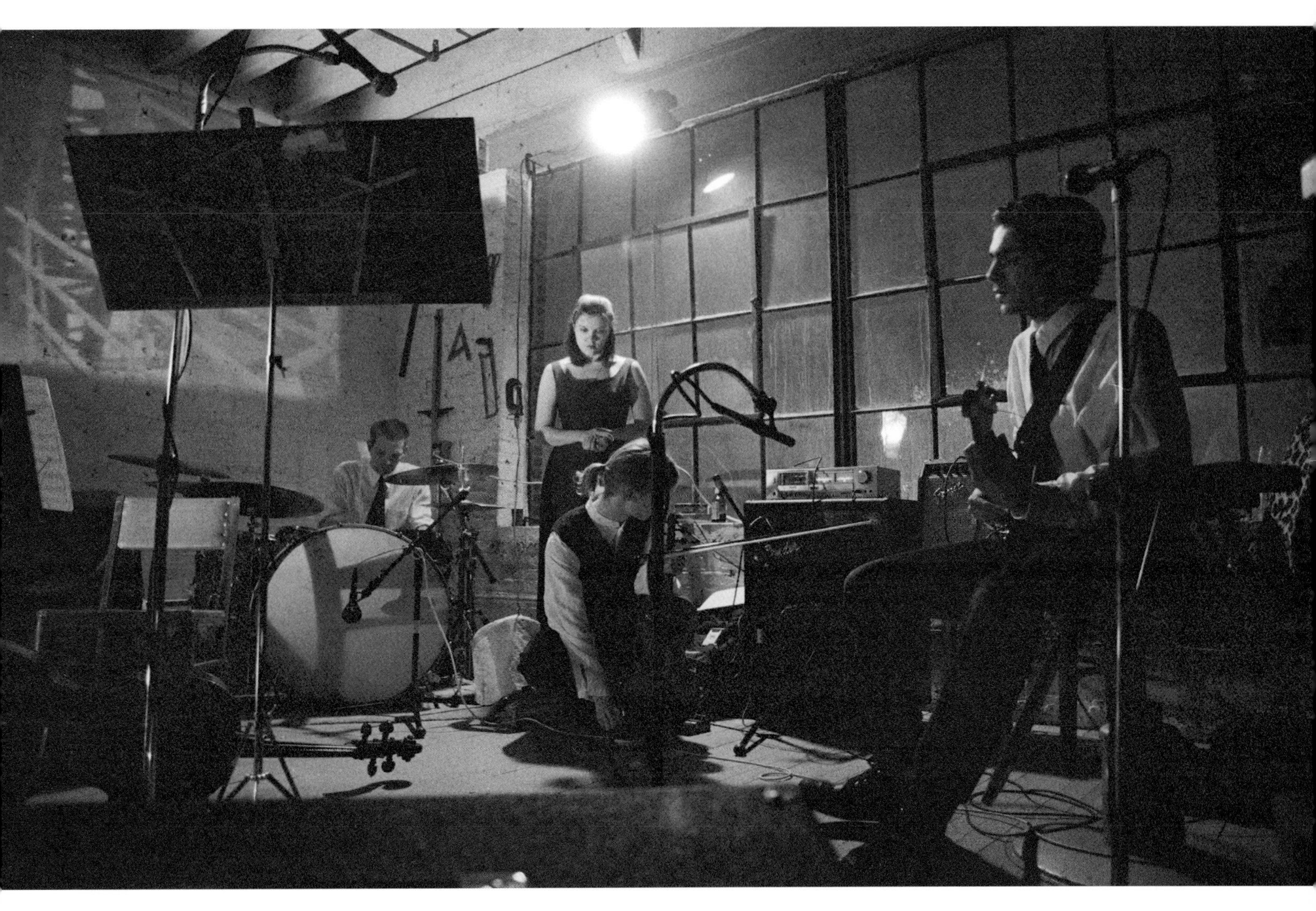

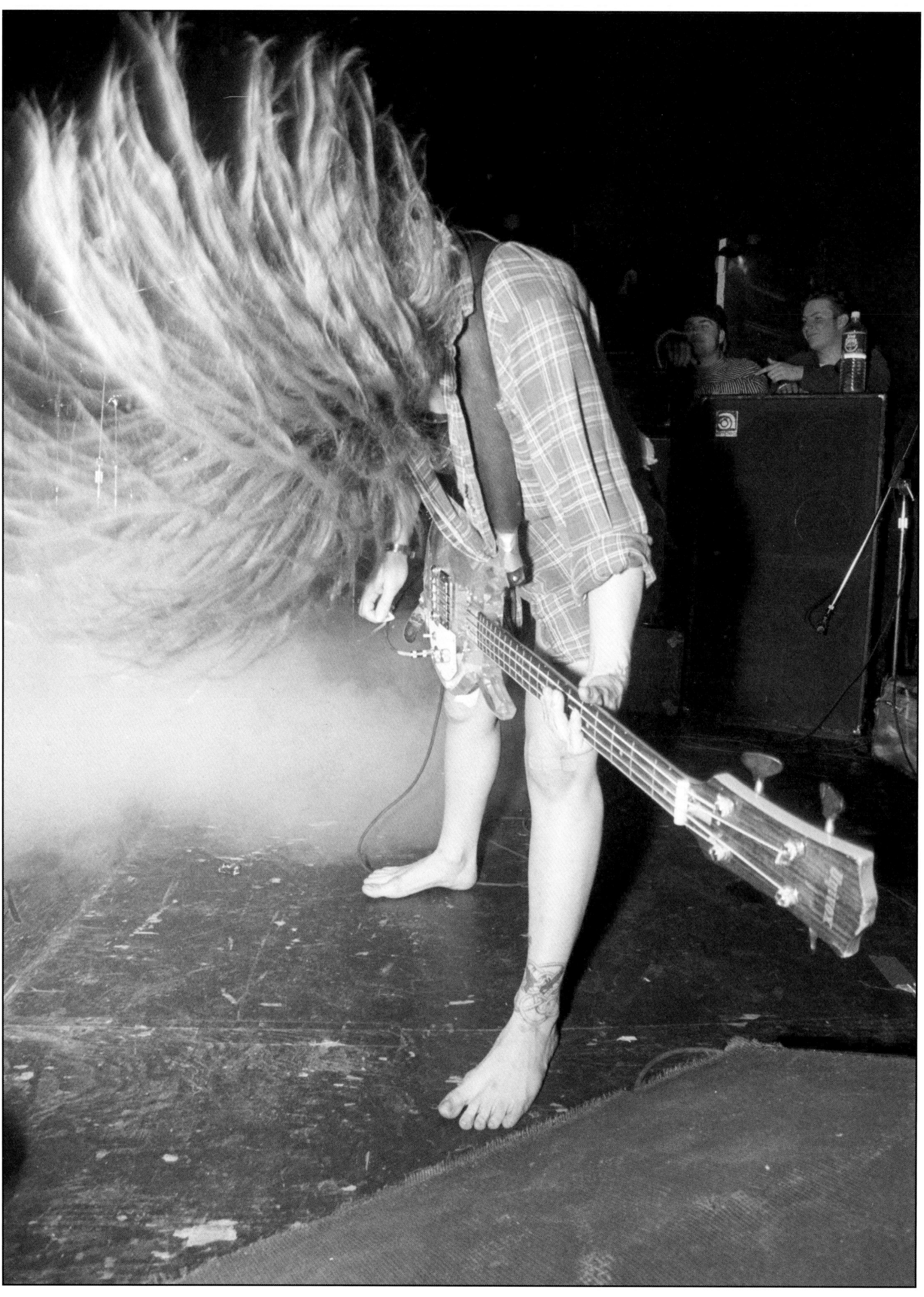

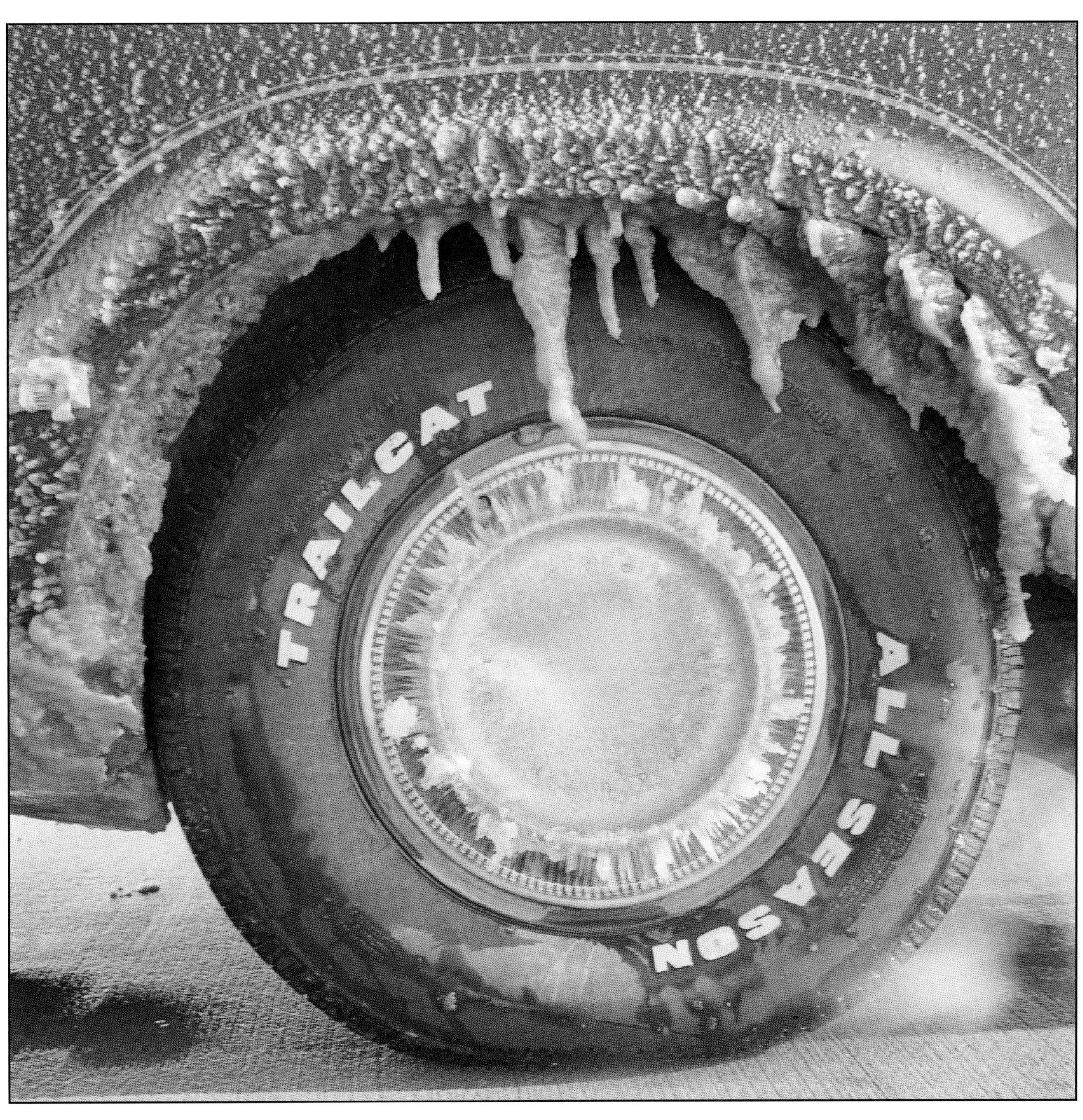
TRAILCAT
ALL SEASON

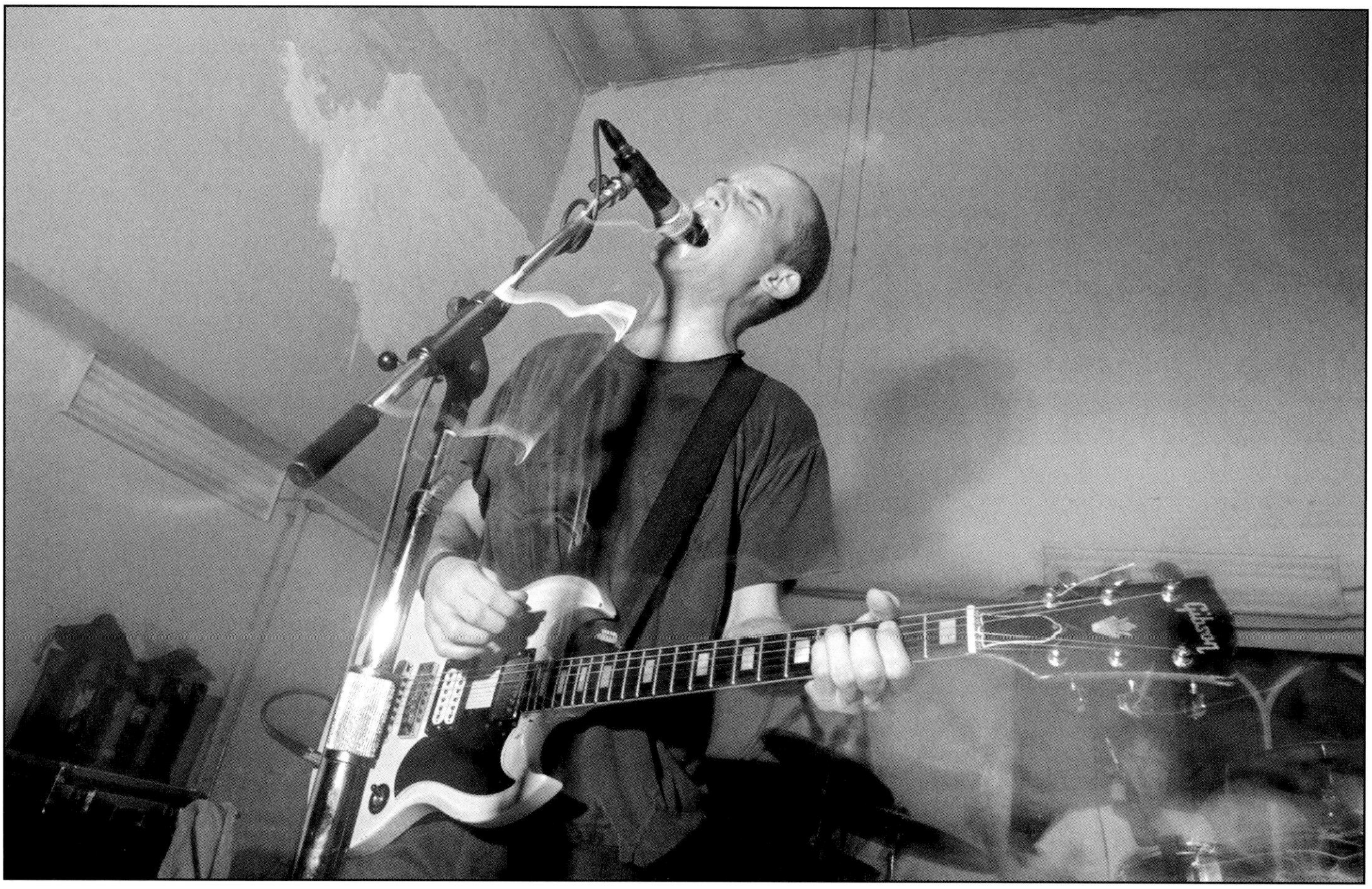

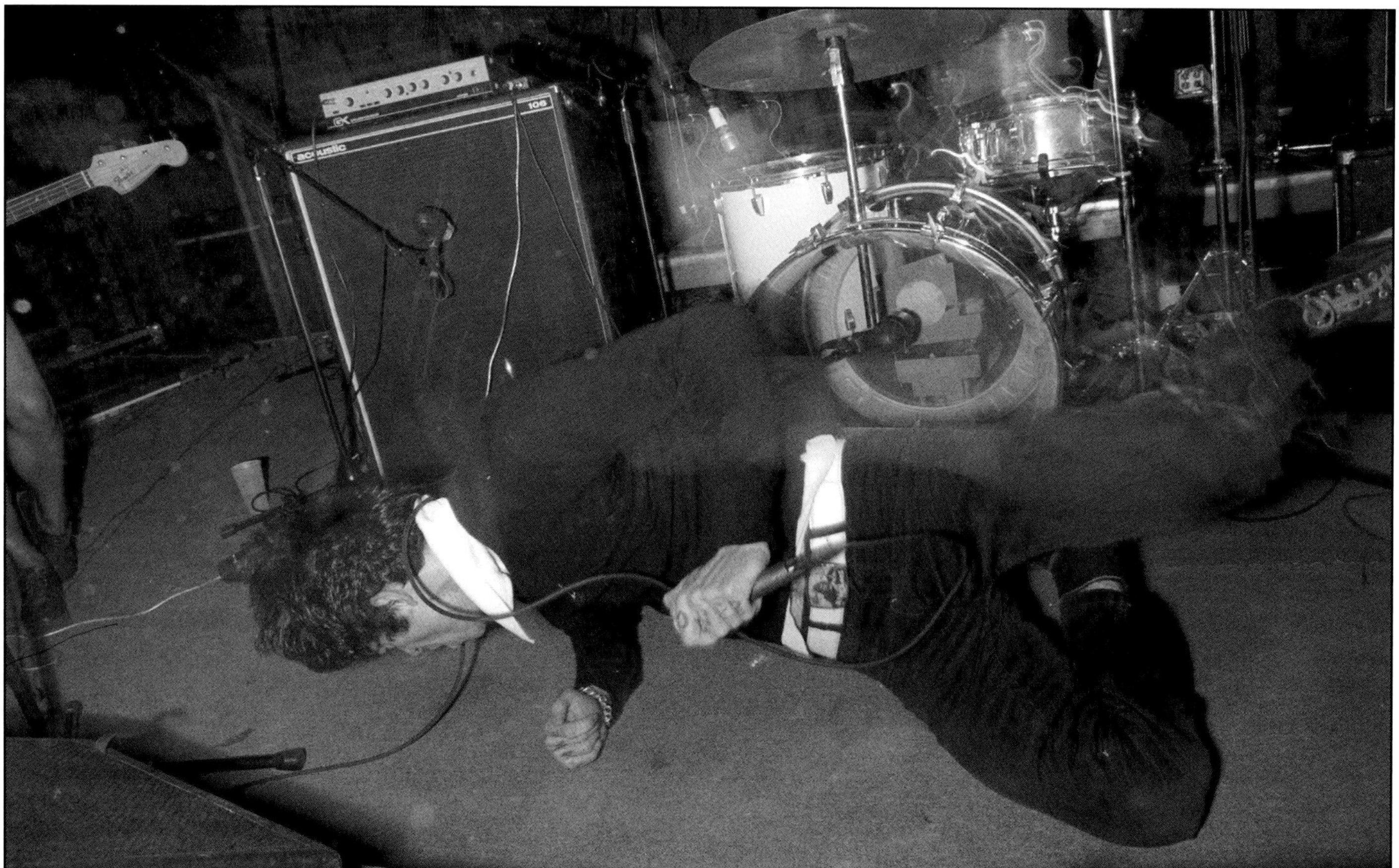

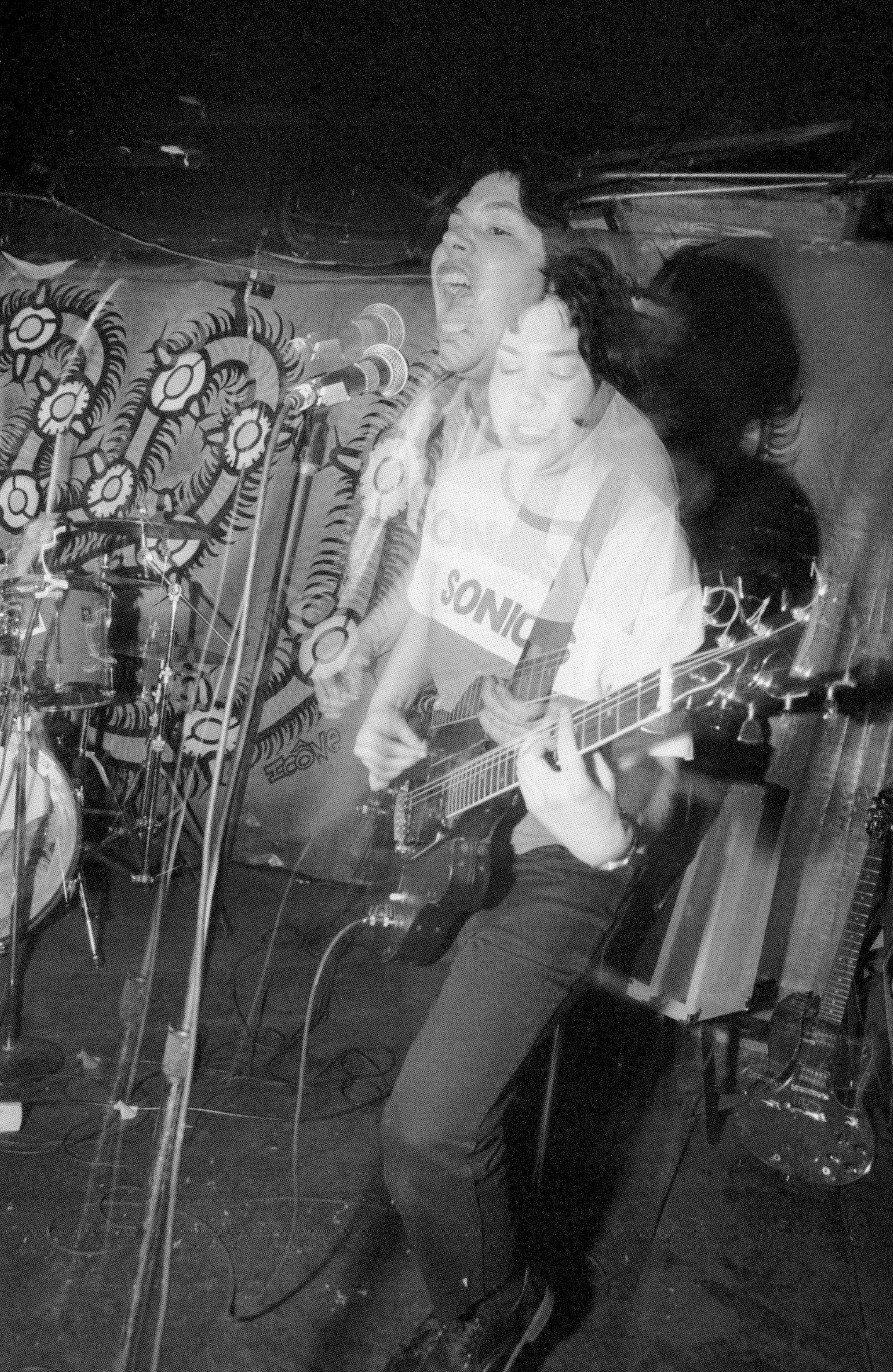
SONIC

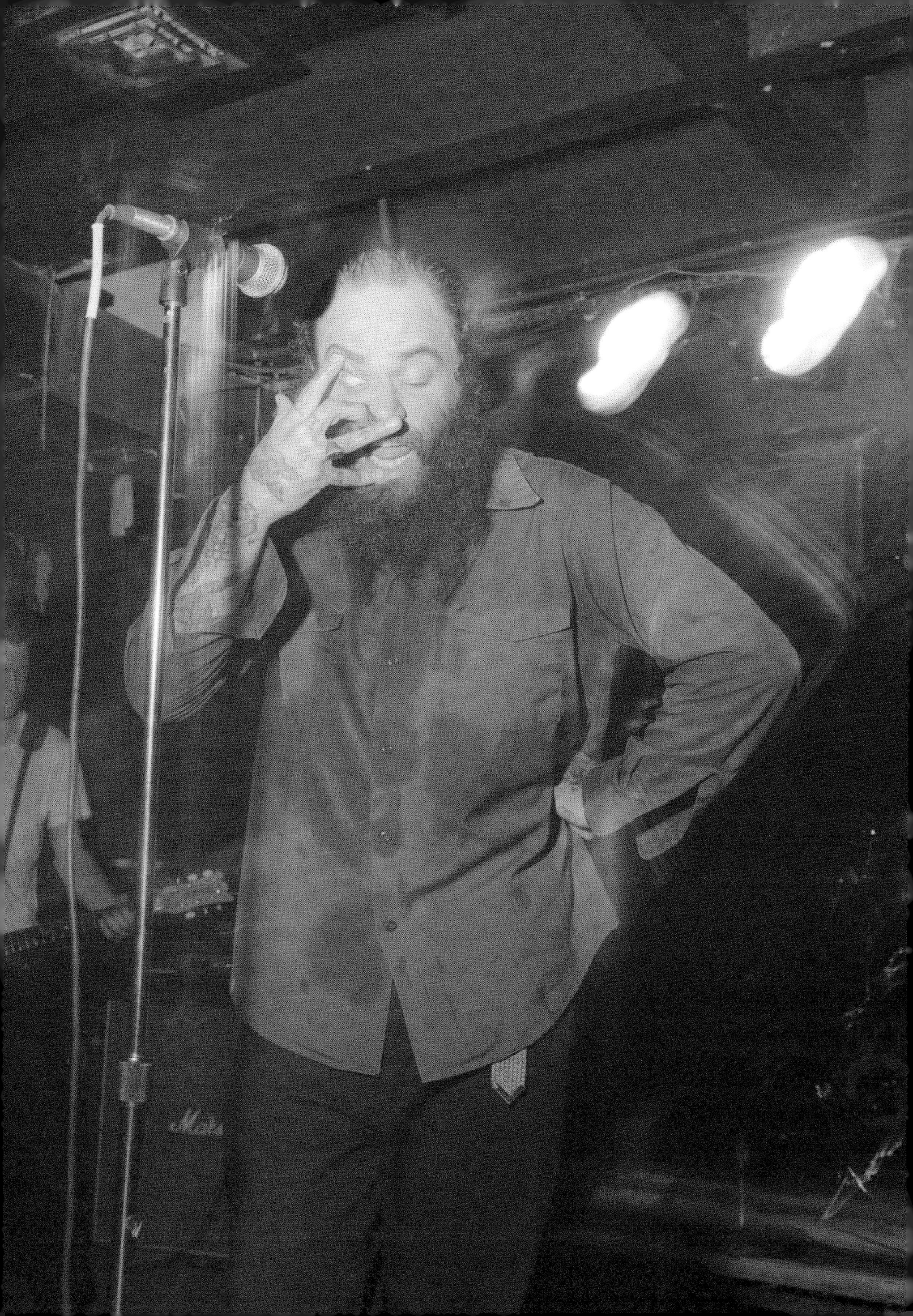

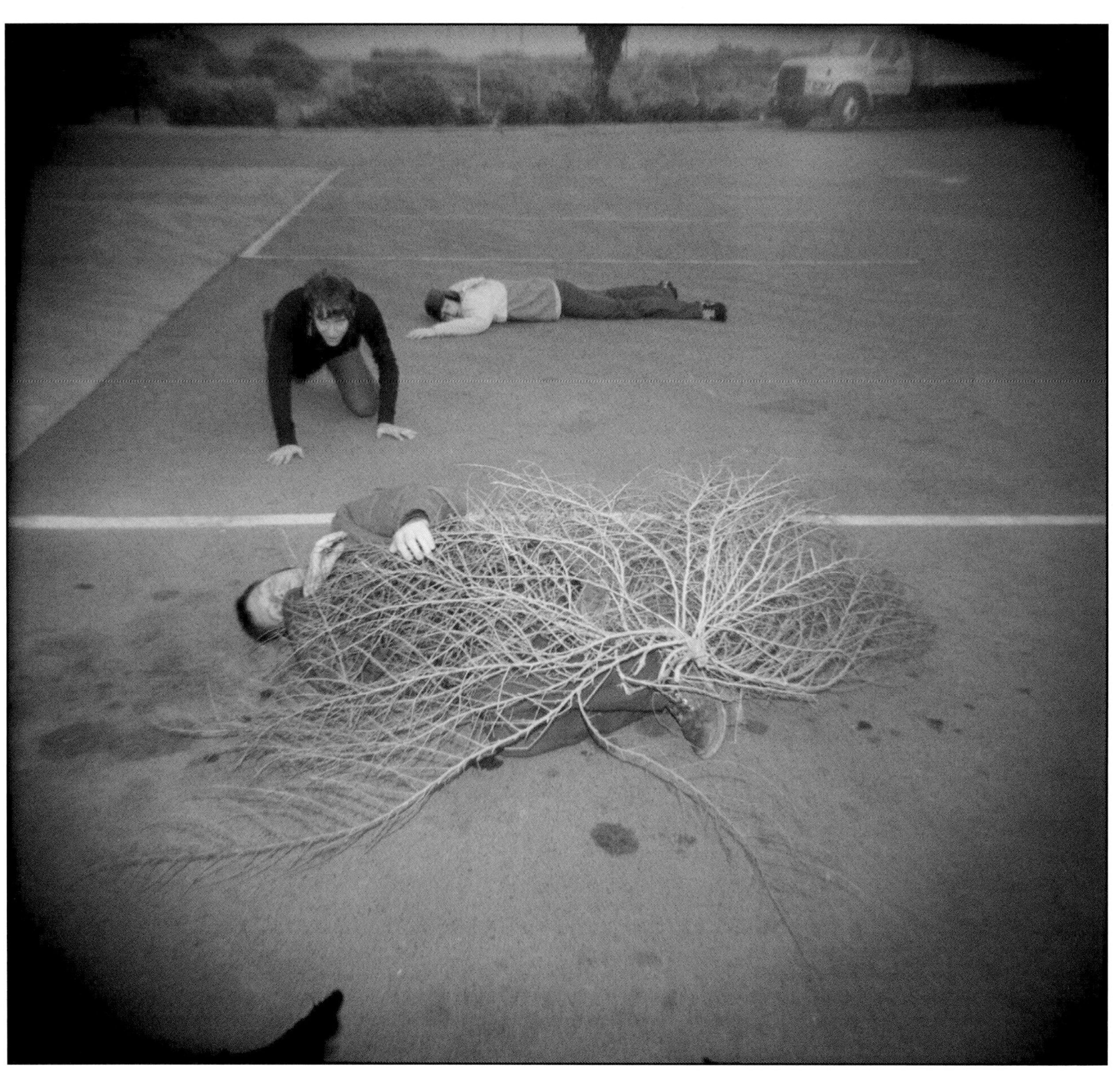

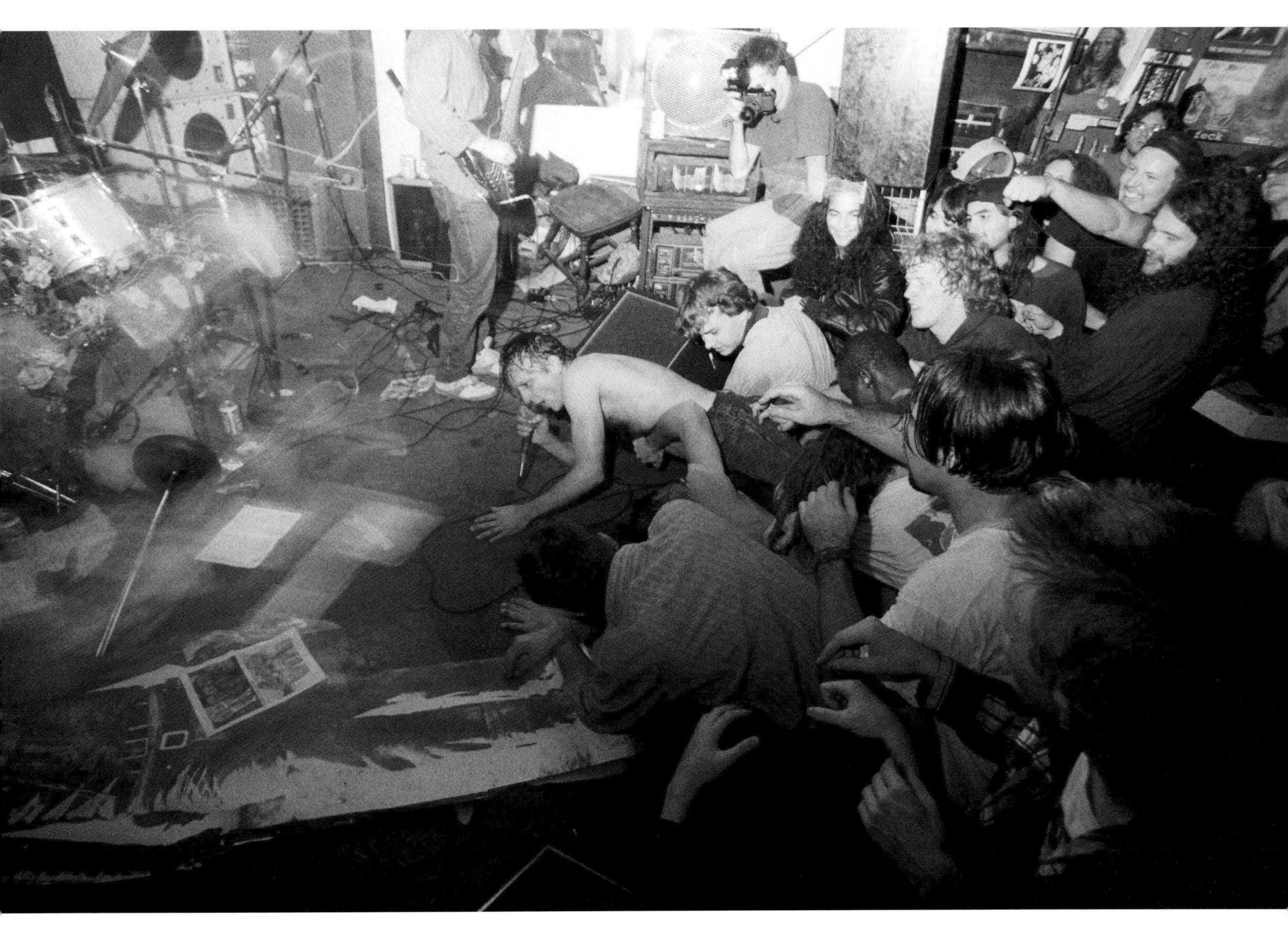

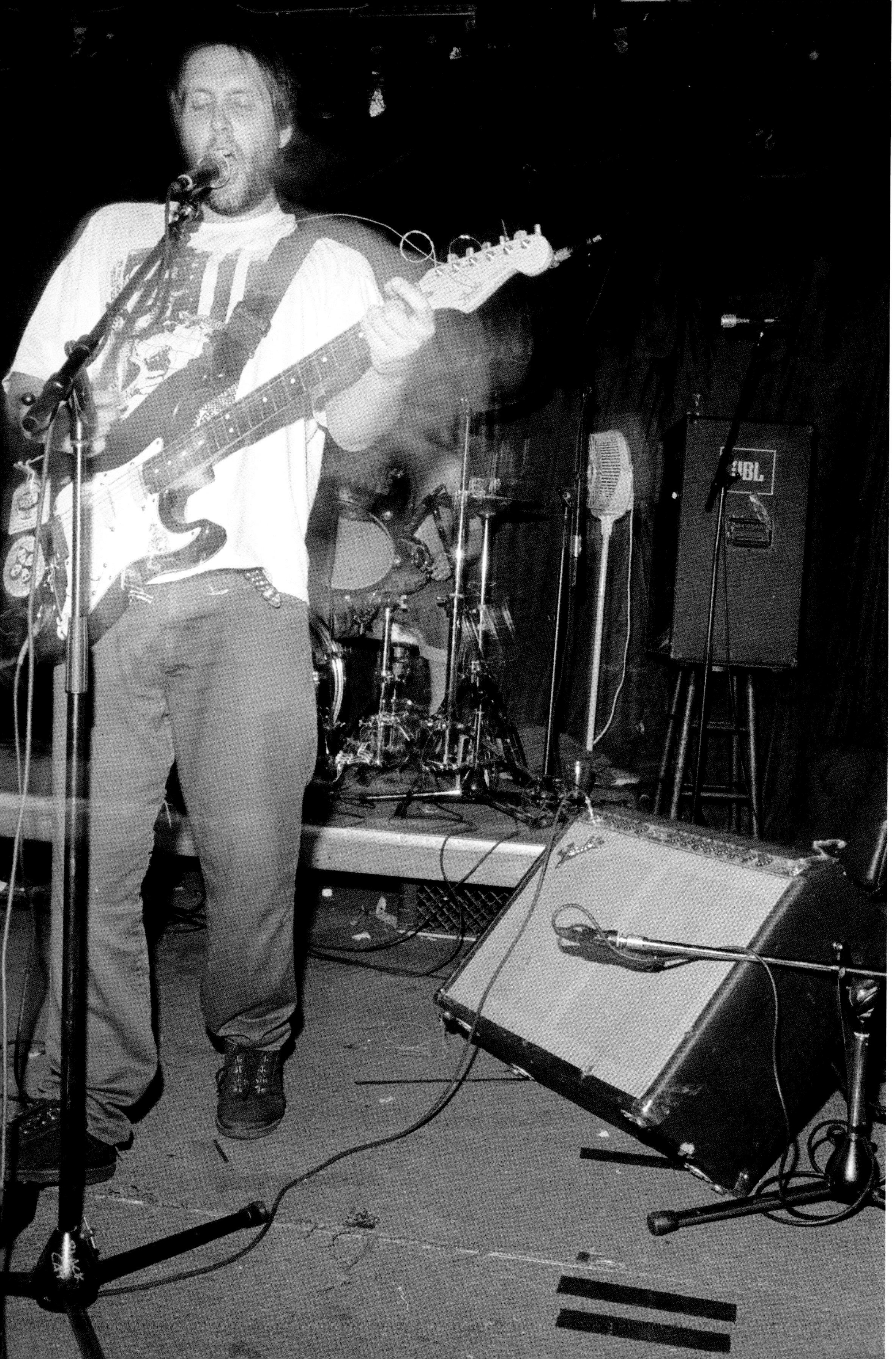
JBL

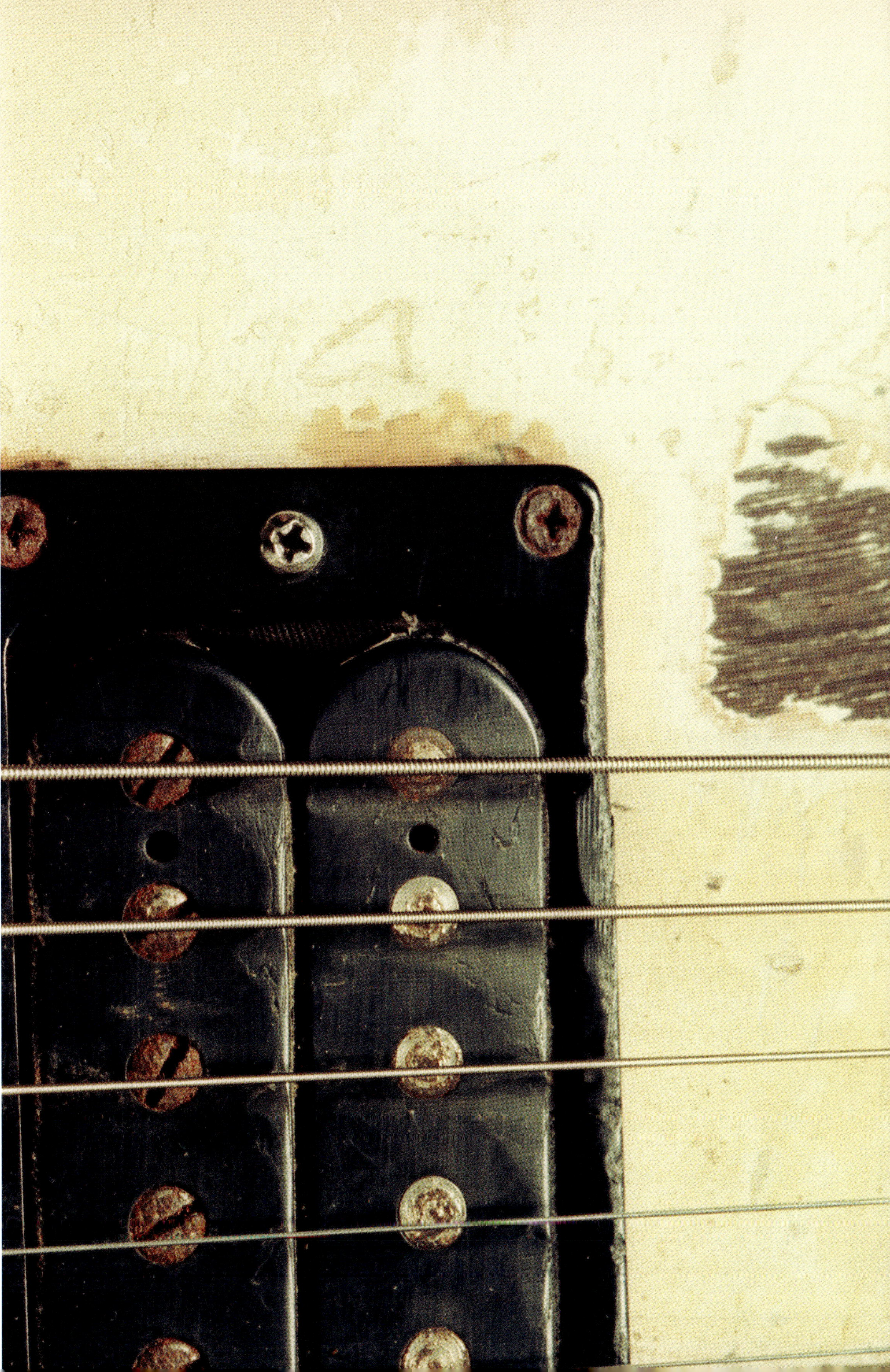

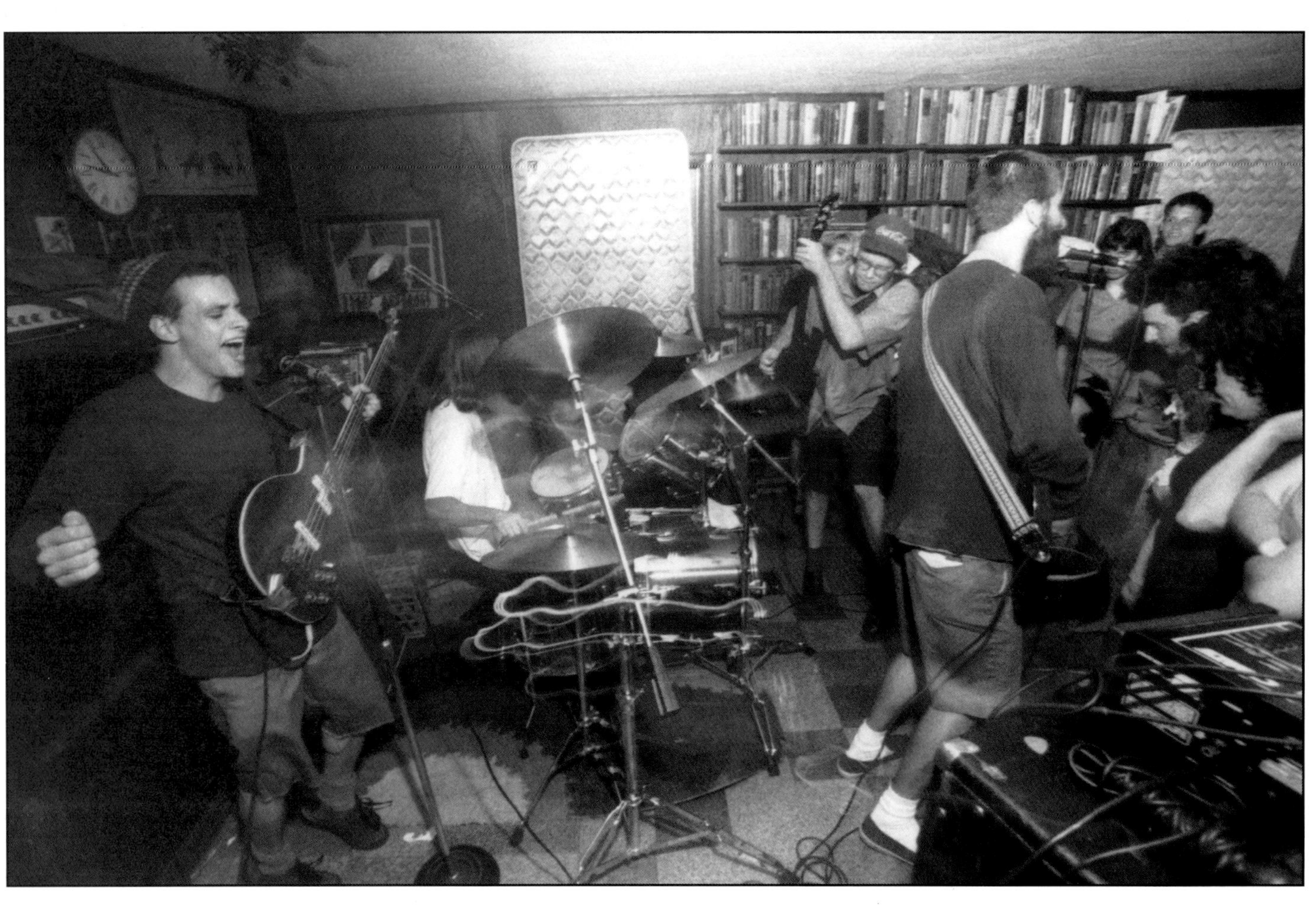

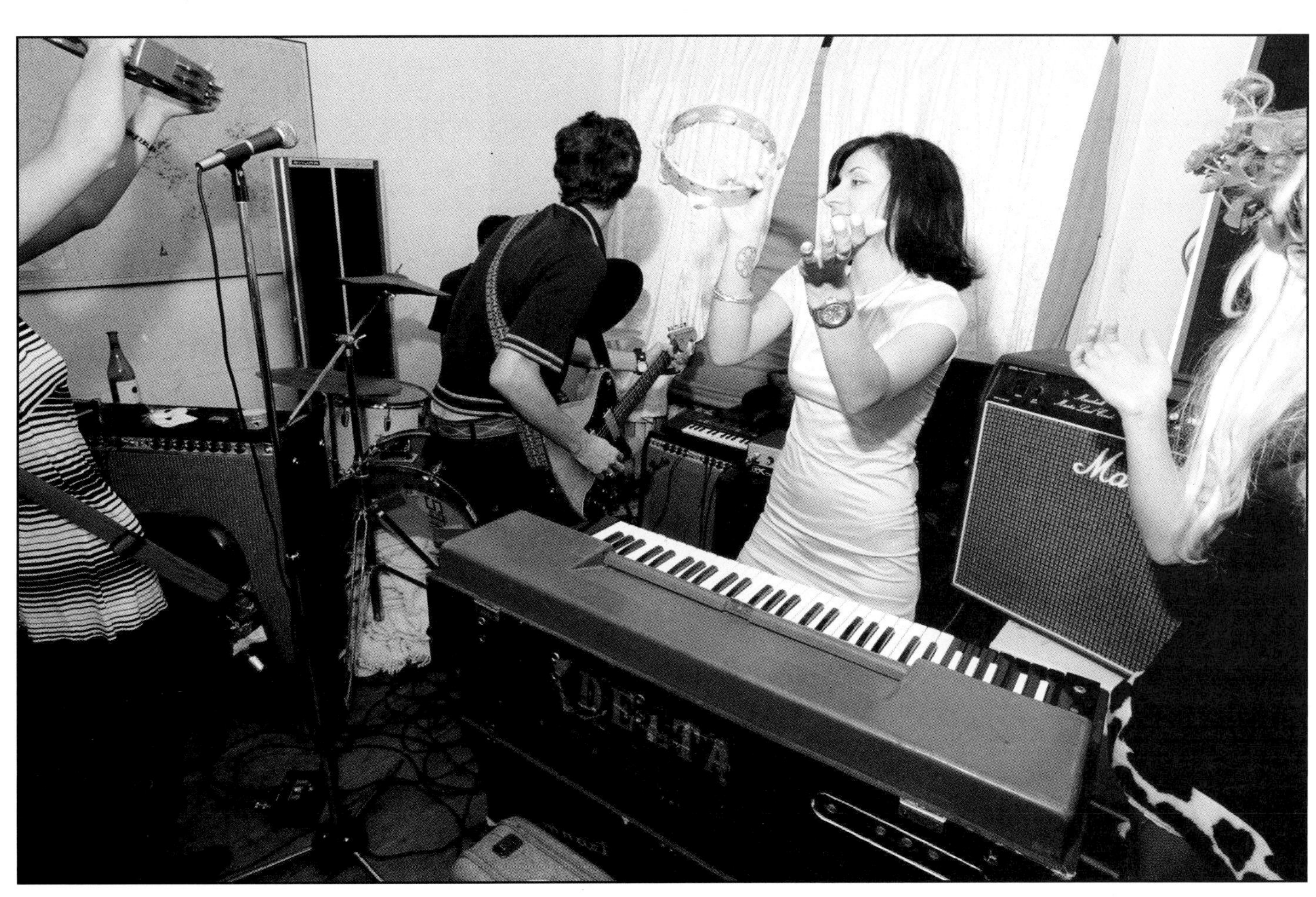
DELTA

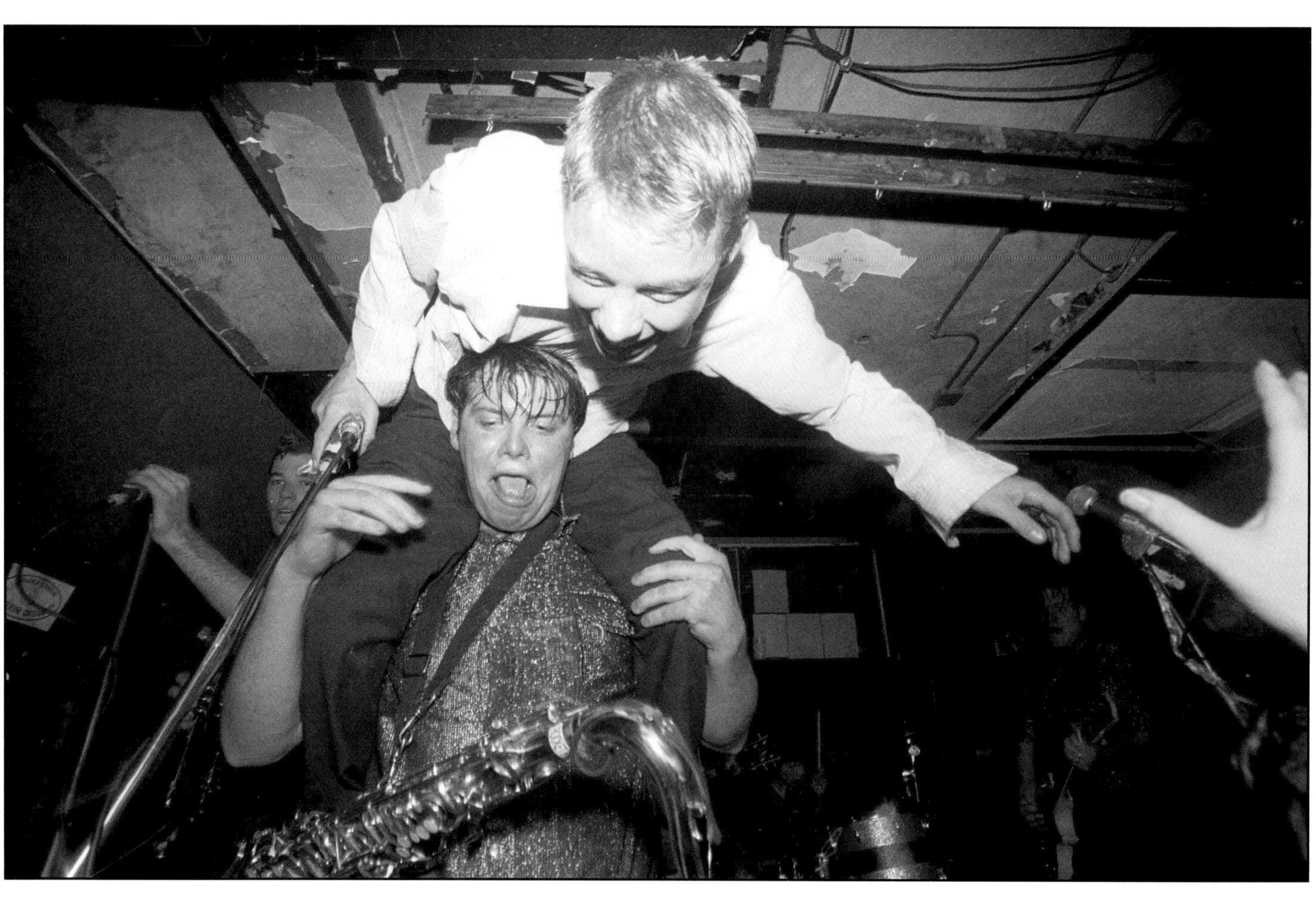

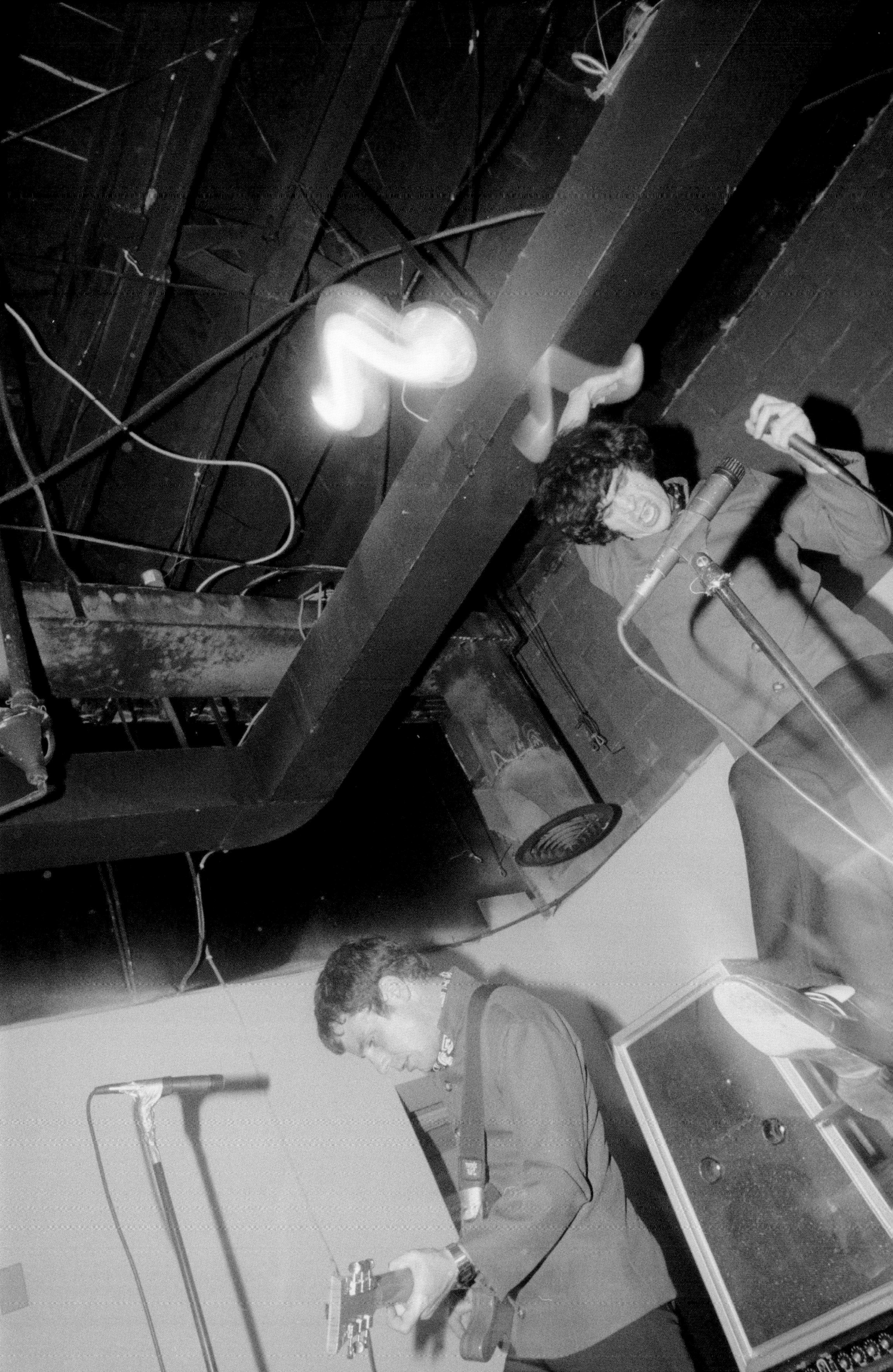

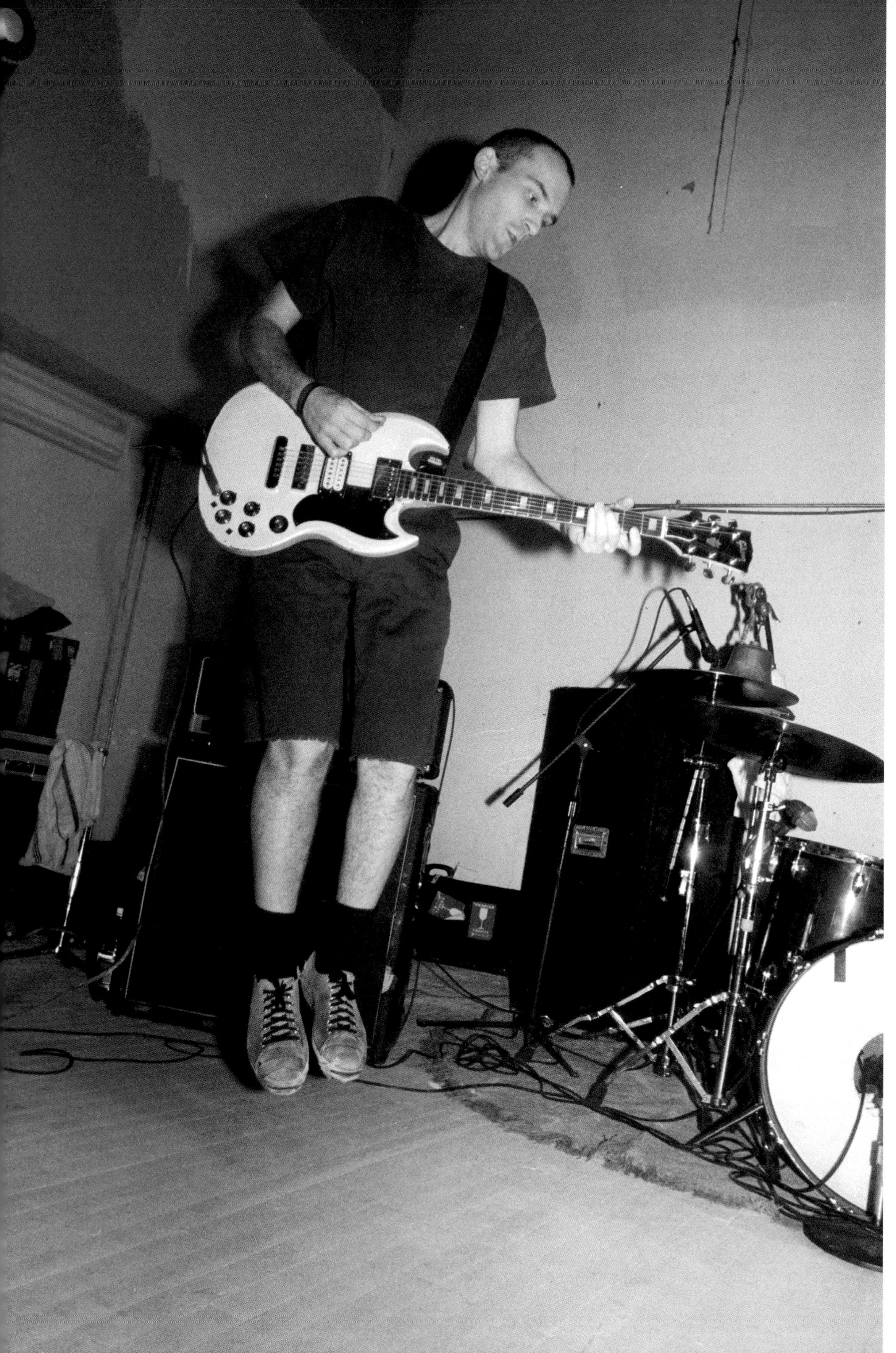

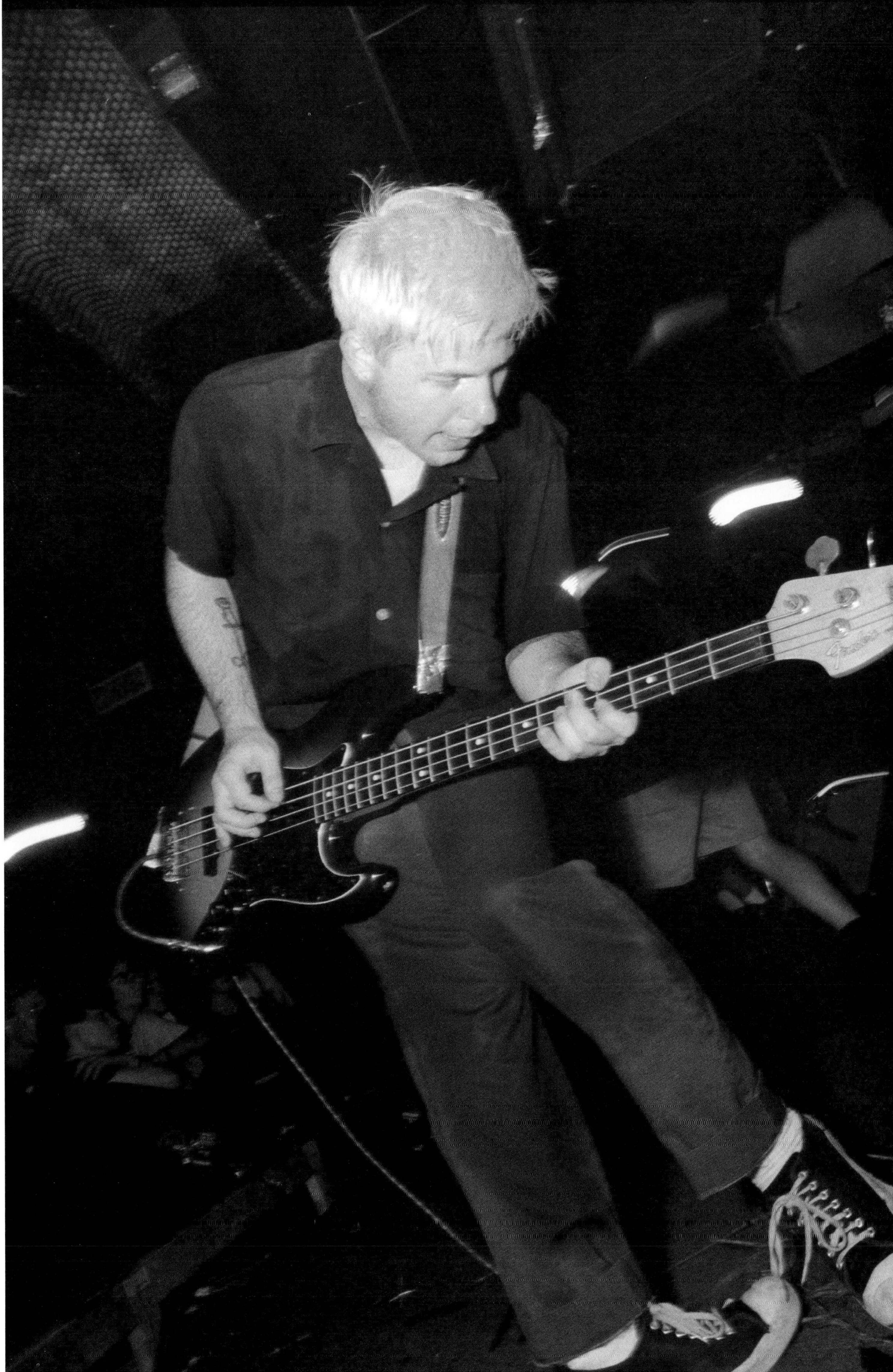

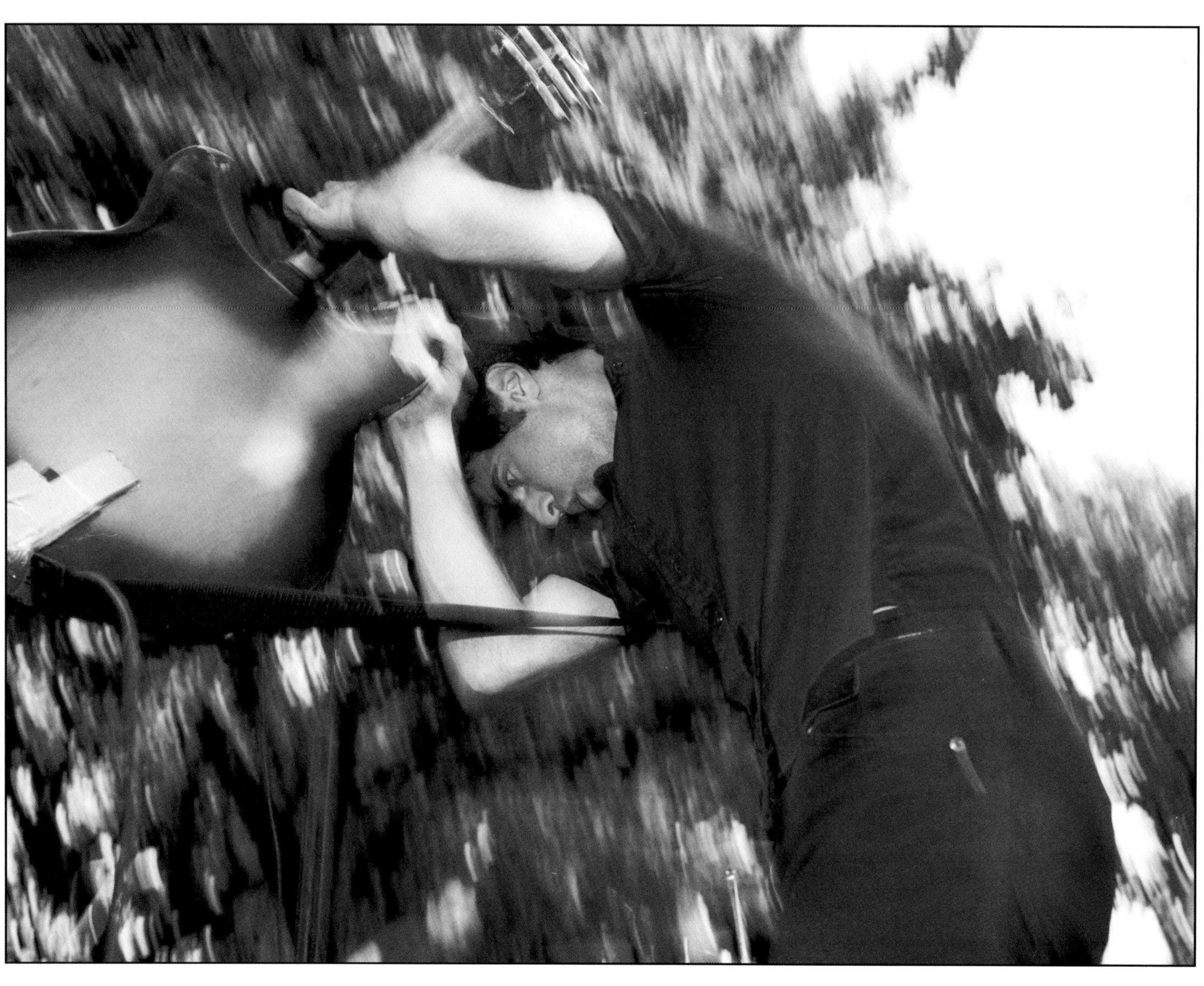

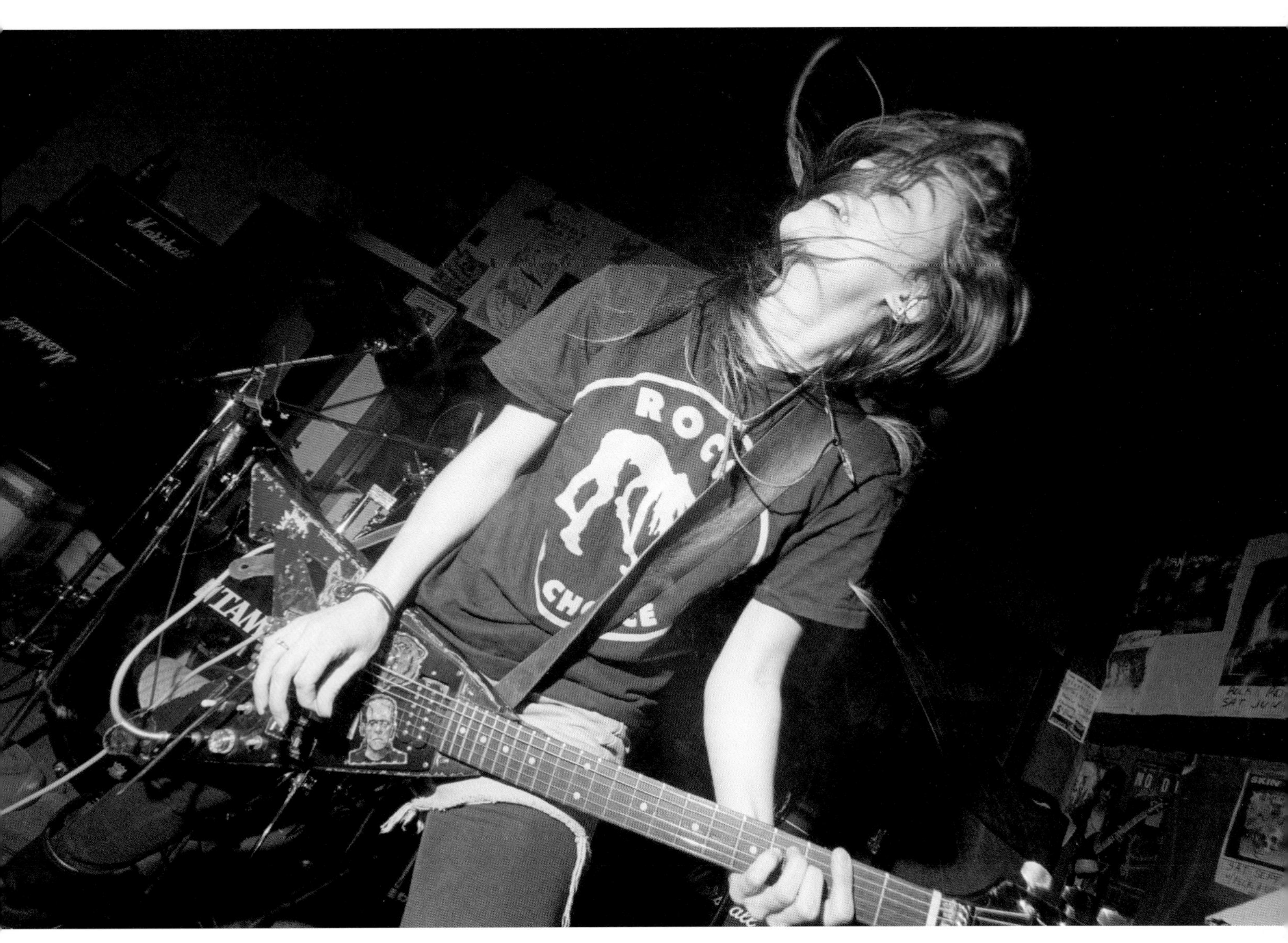

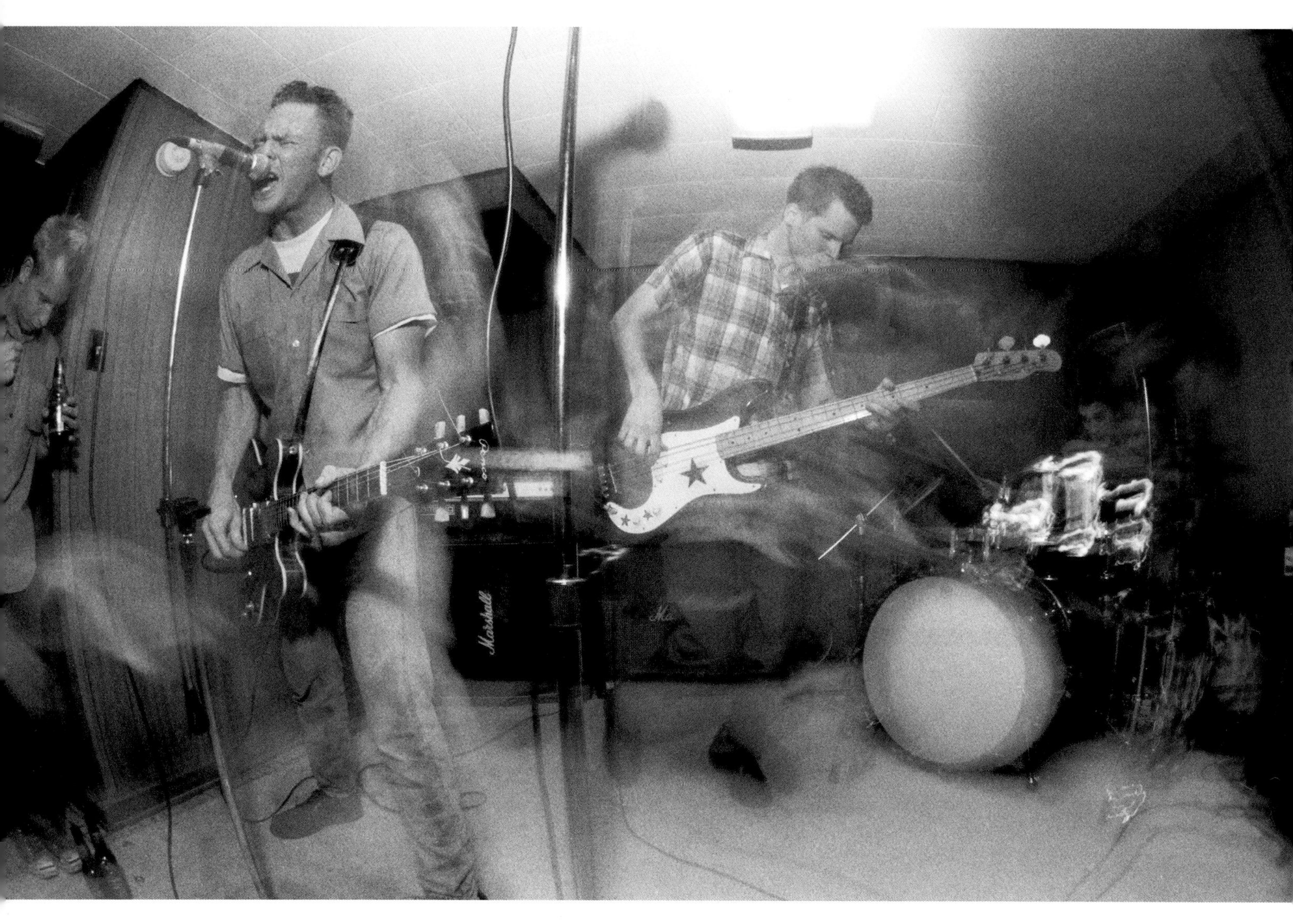
Marshall

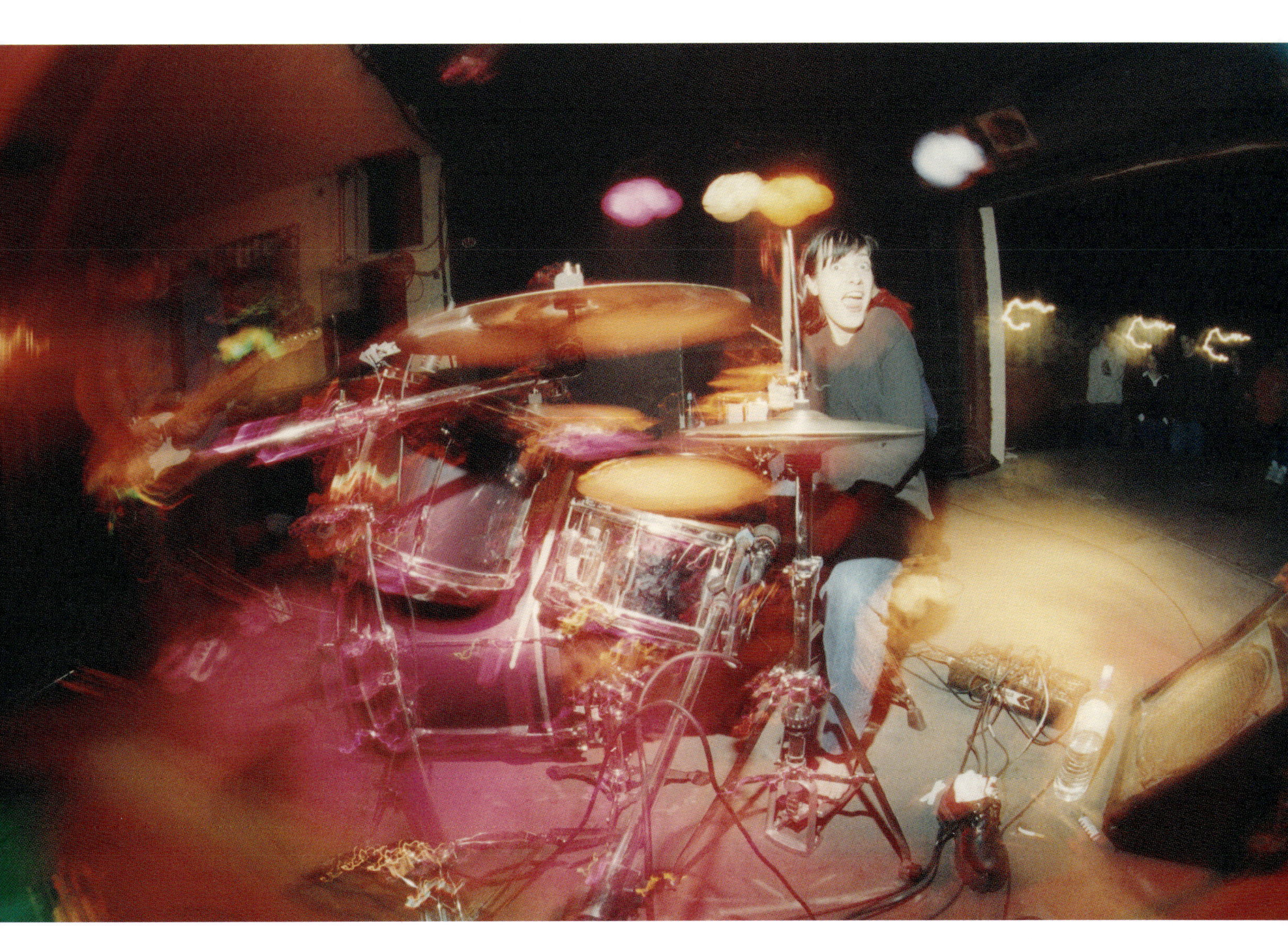

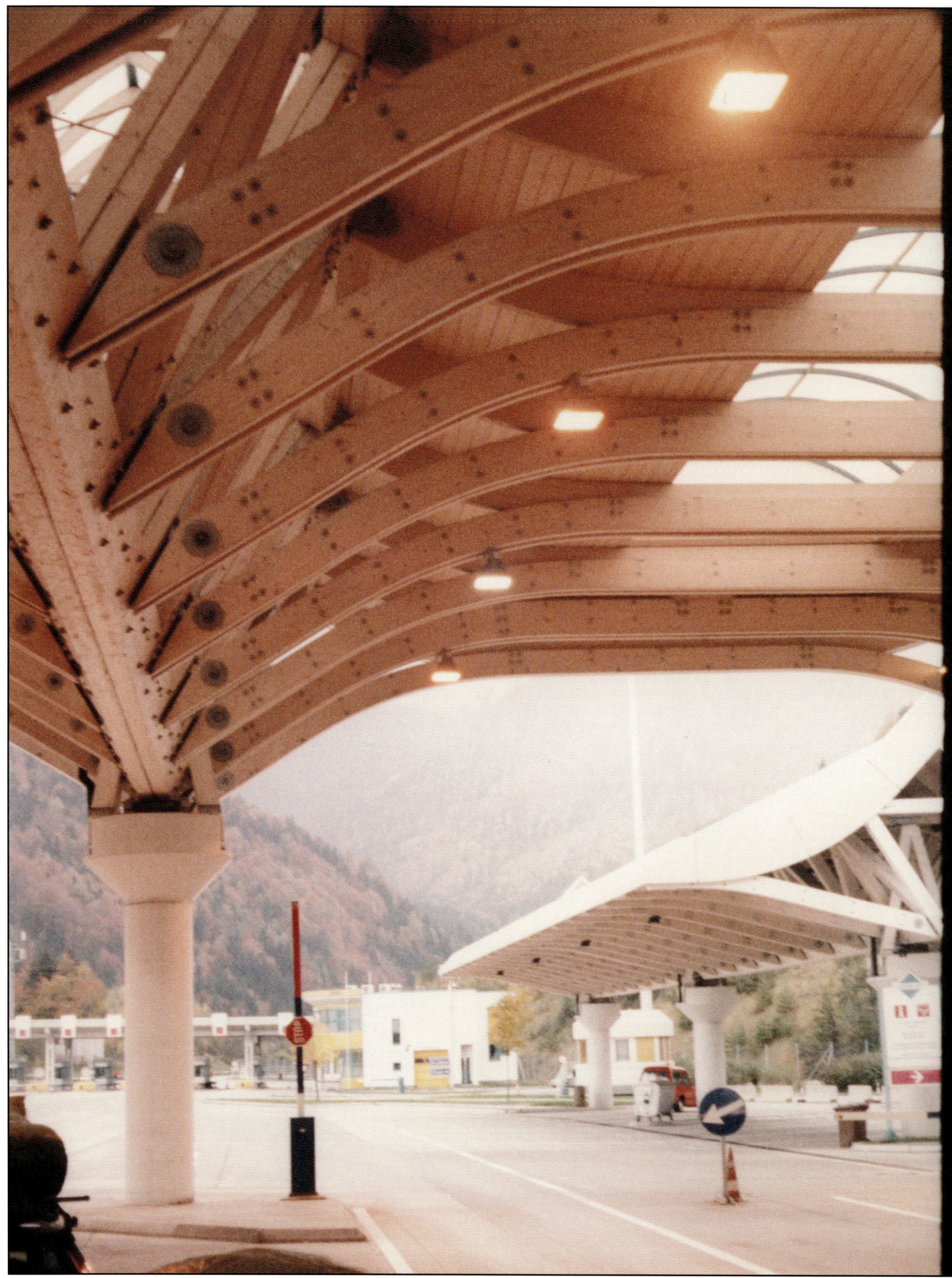

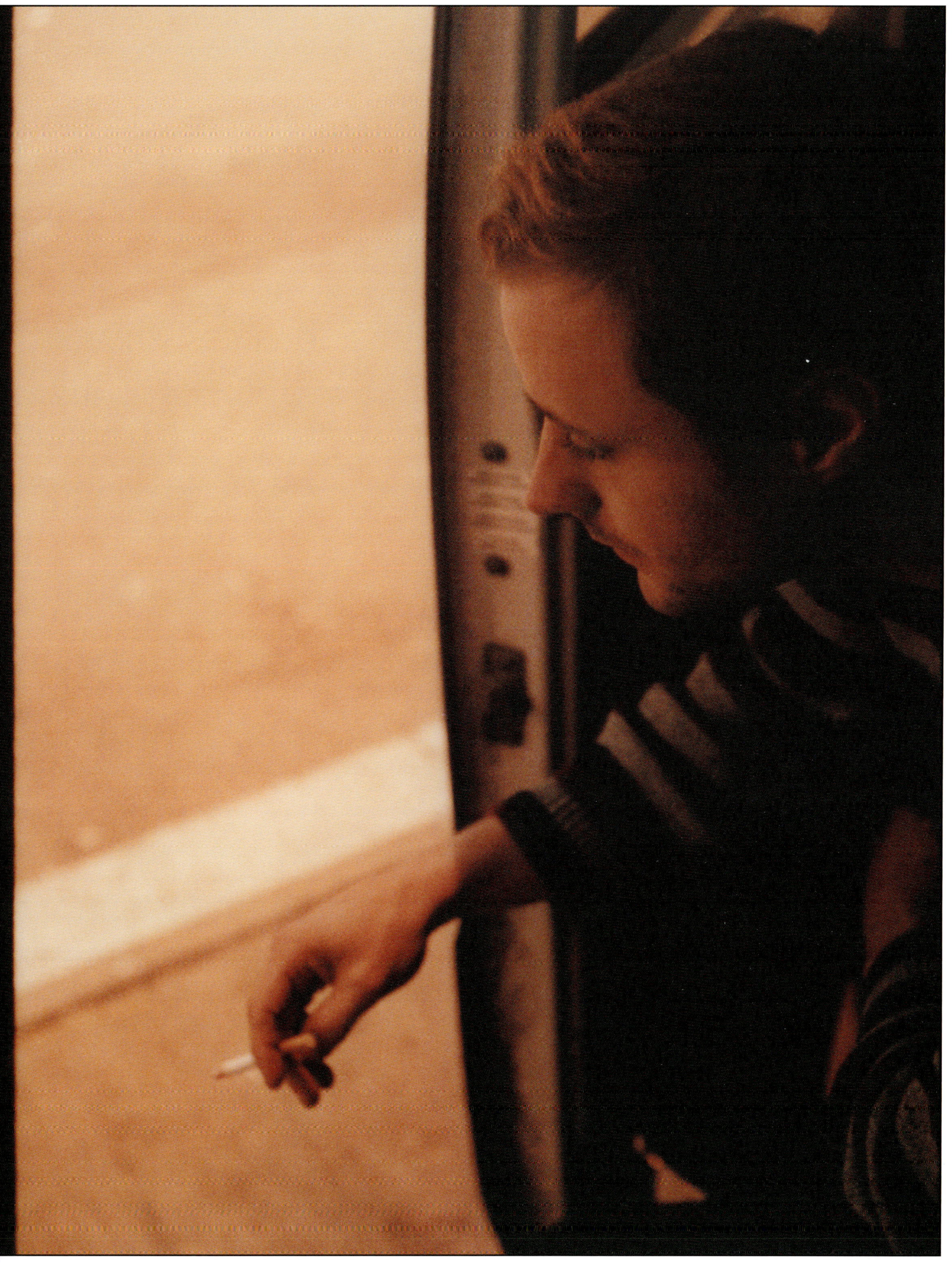

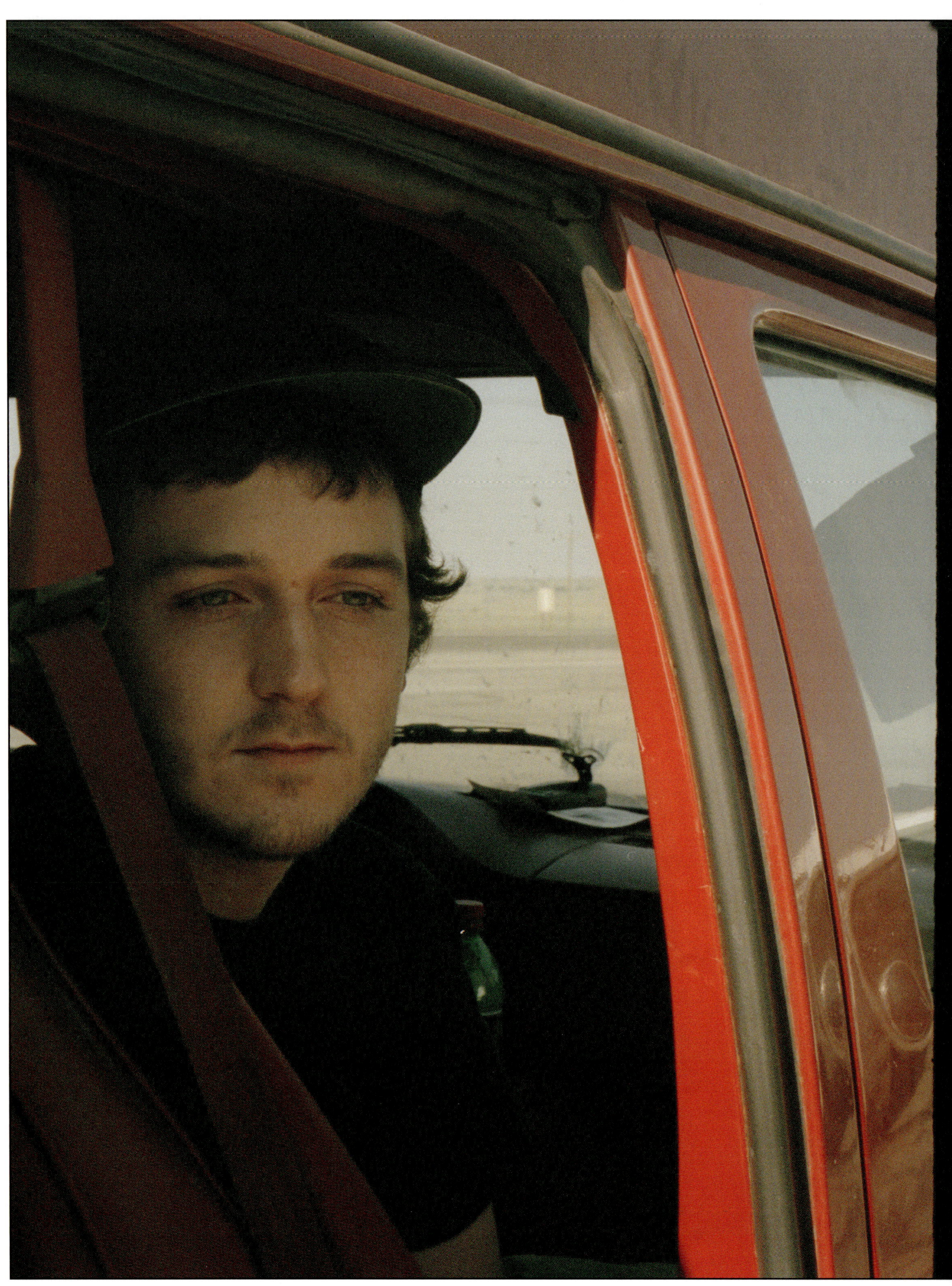

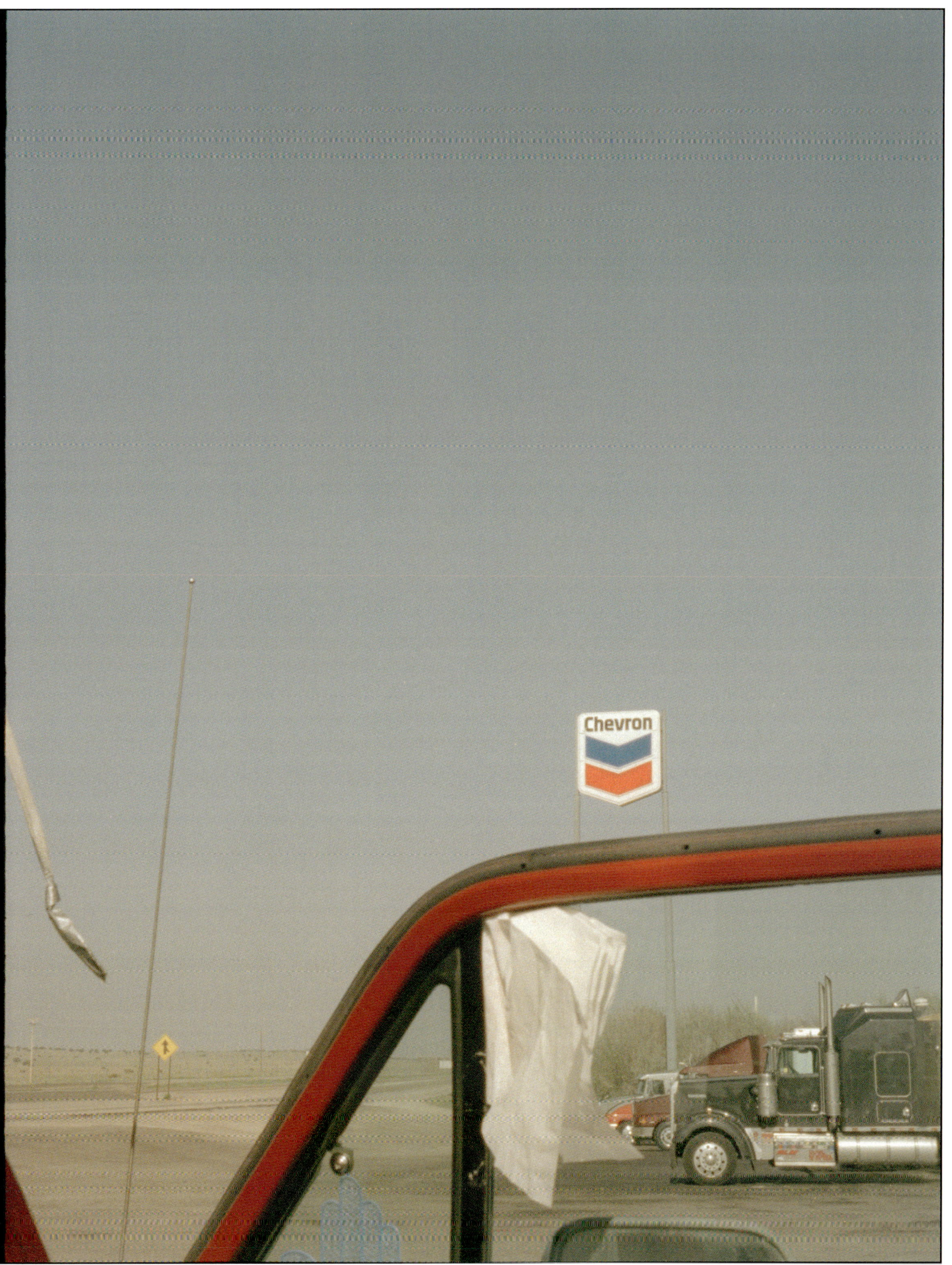
Chevron

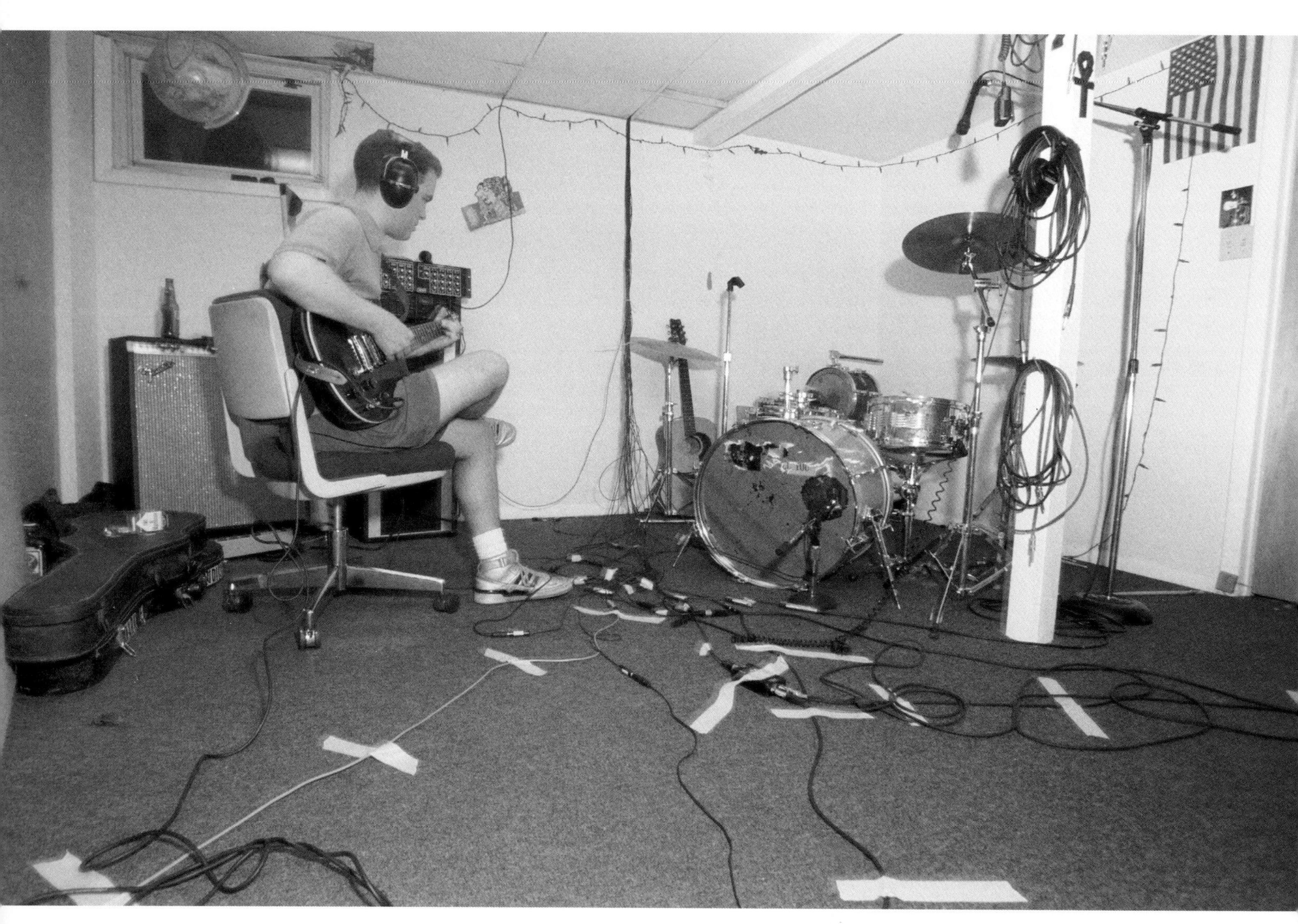

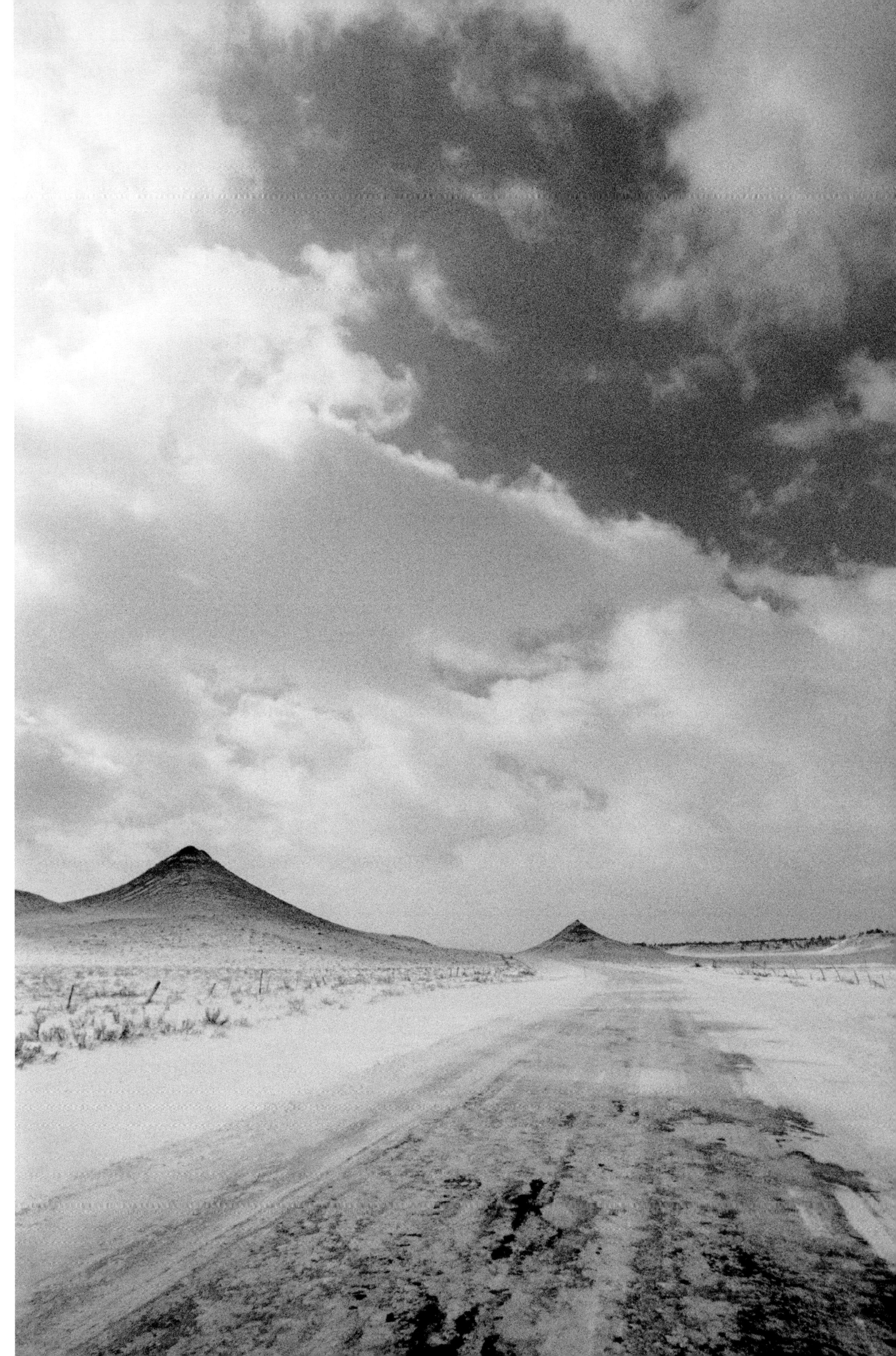

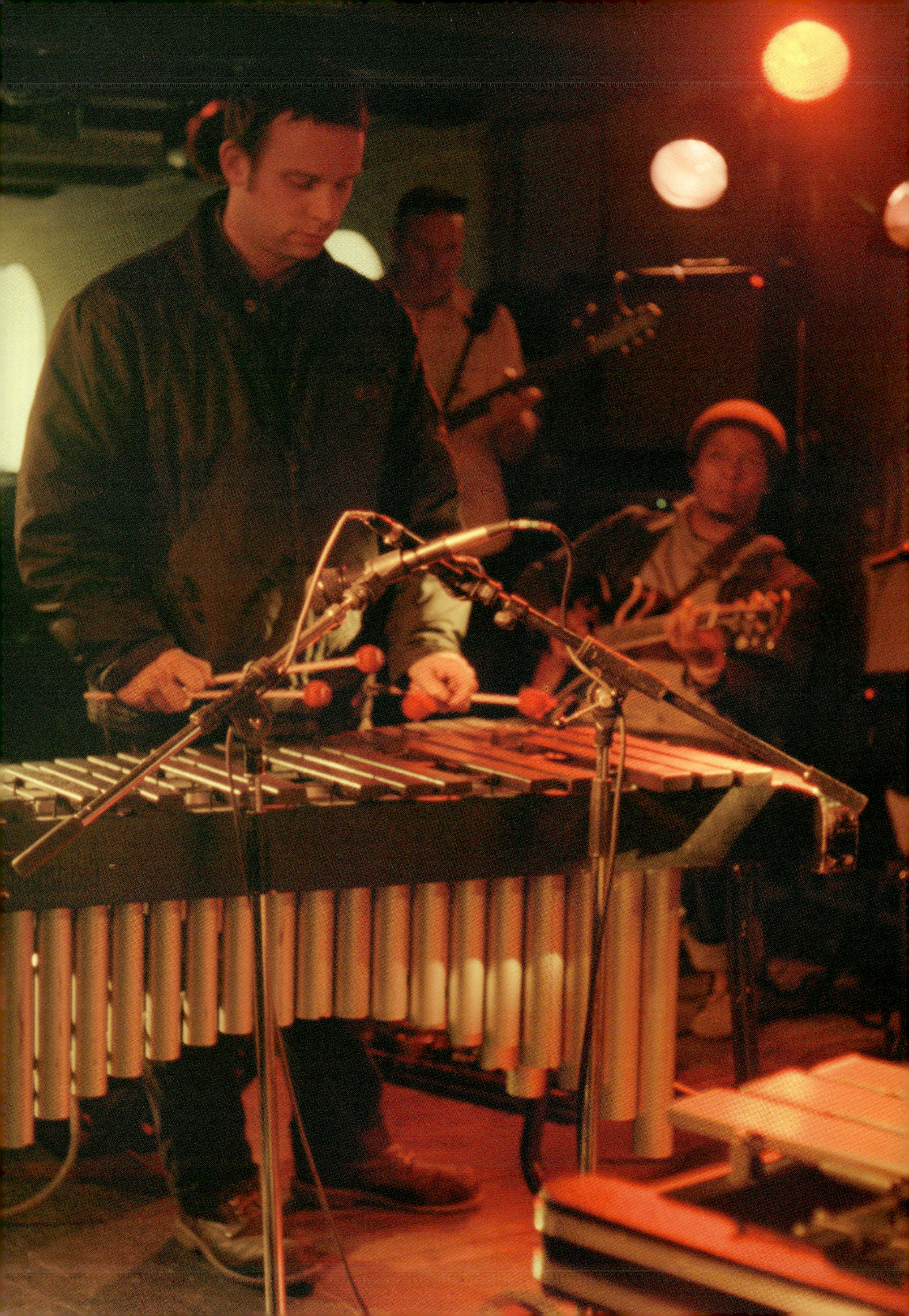

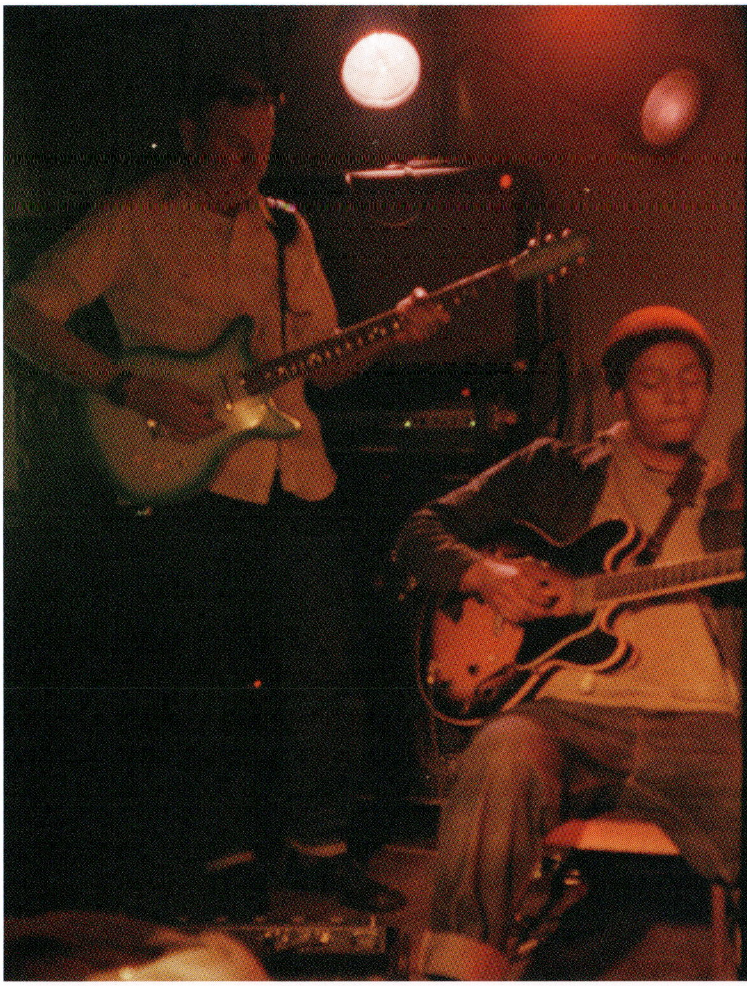

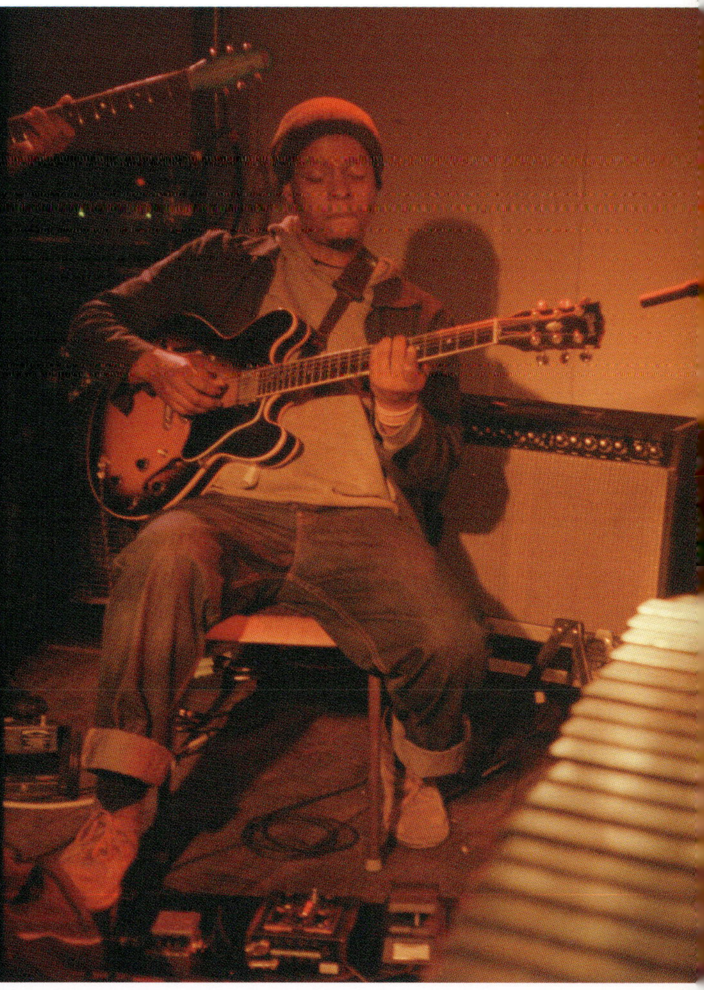

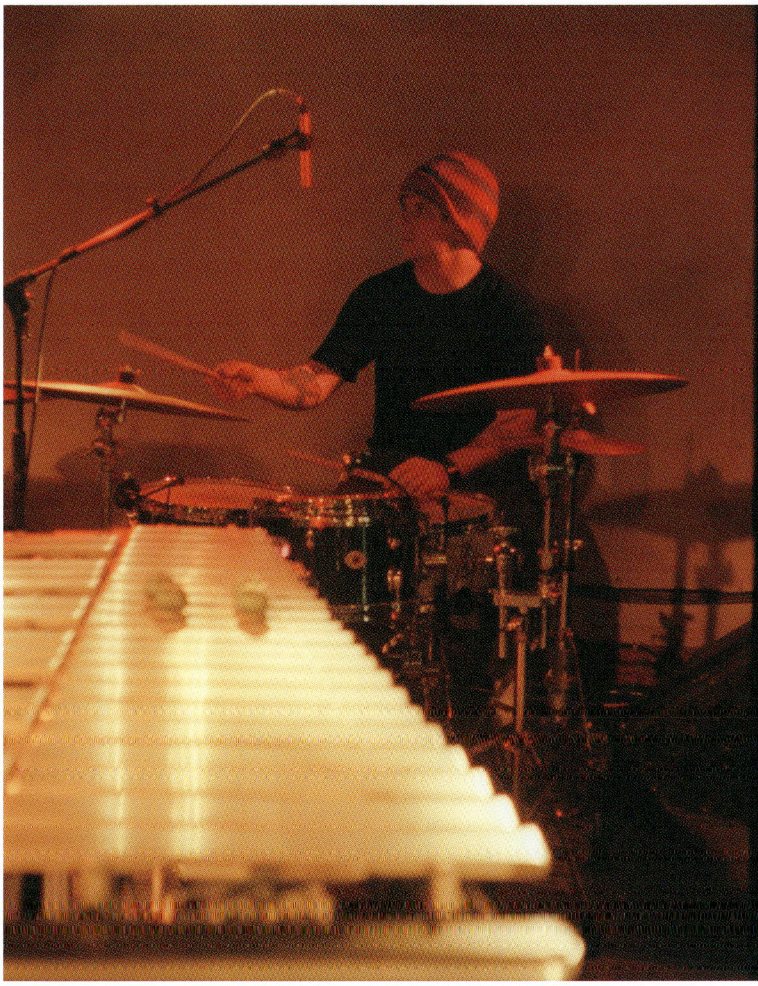

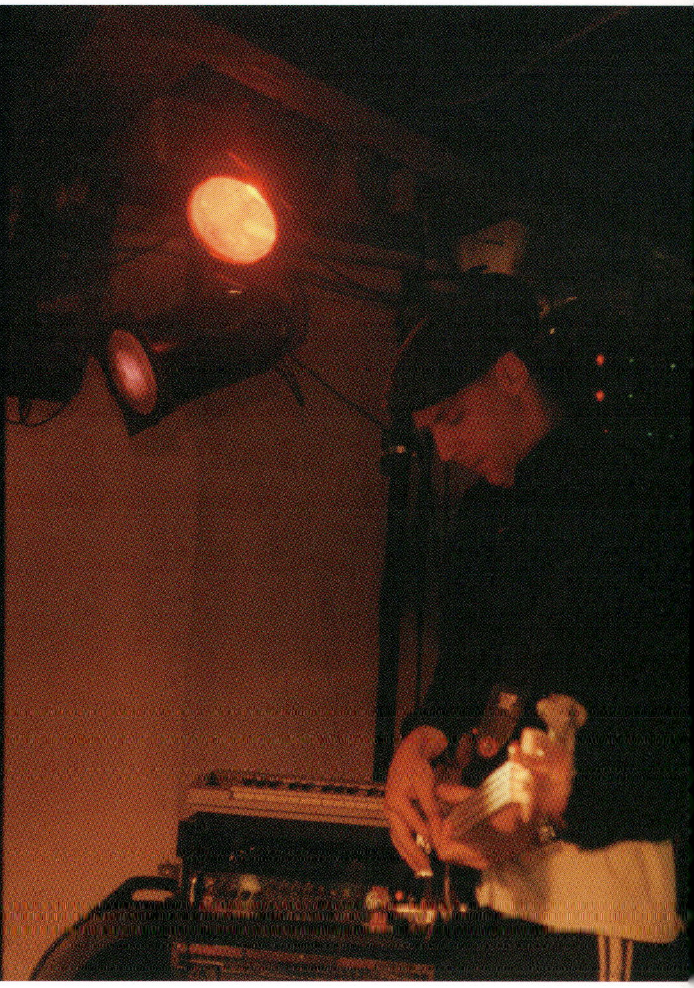

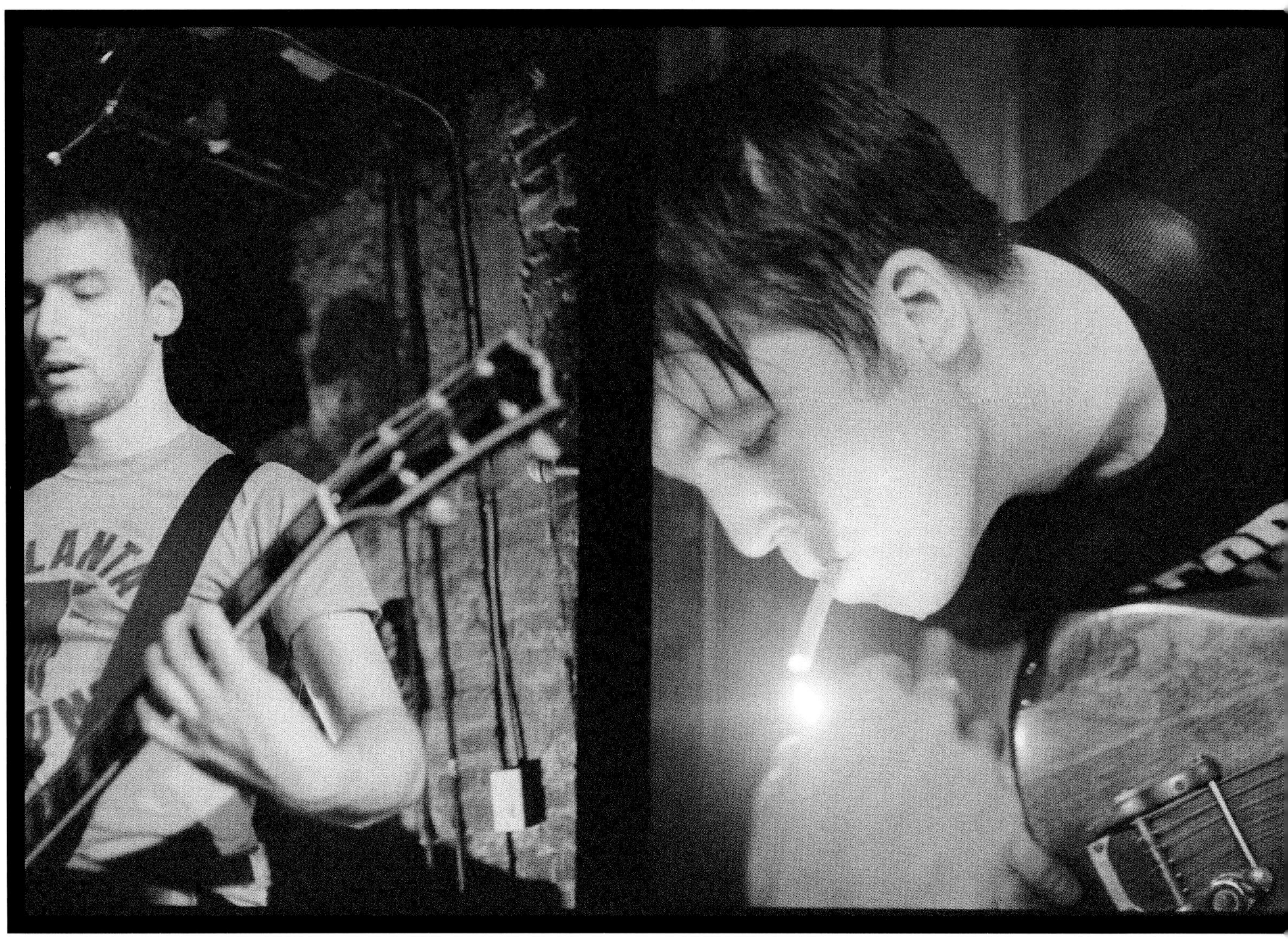

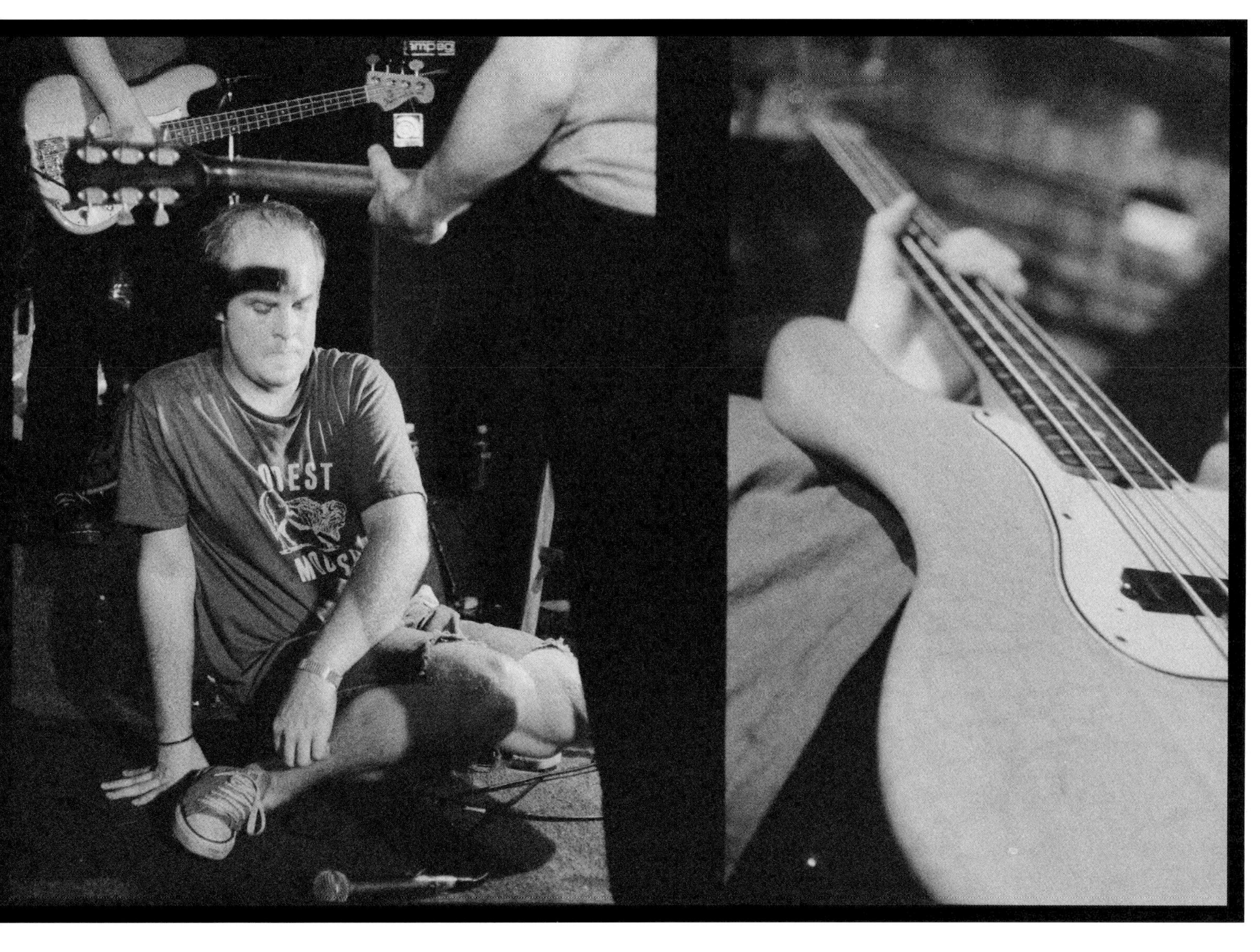

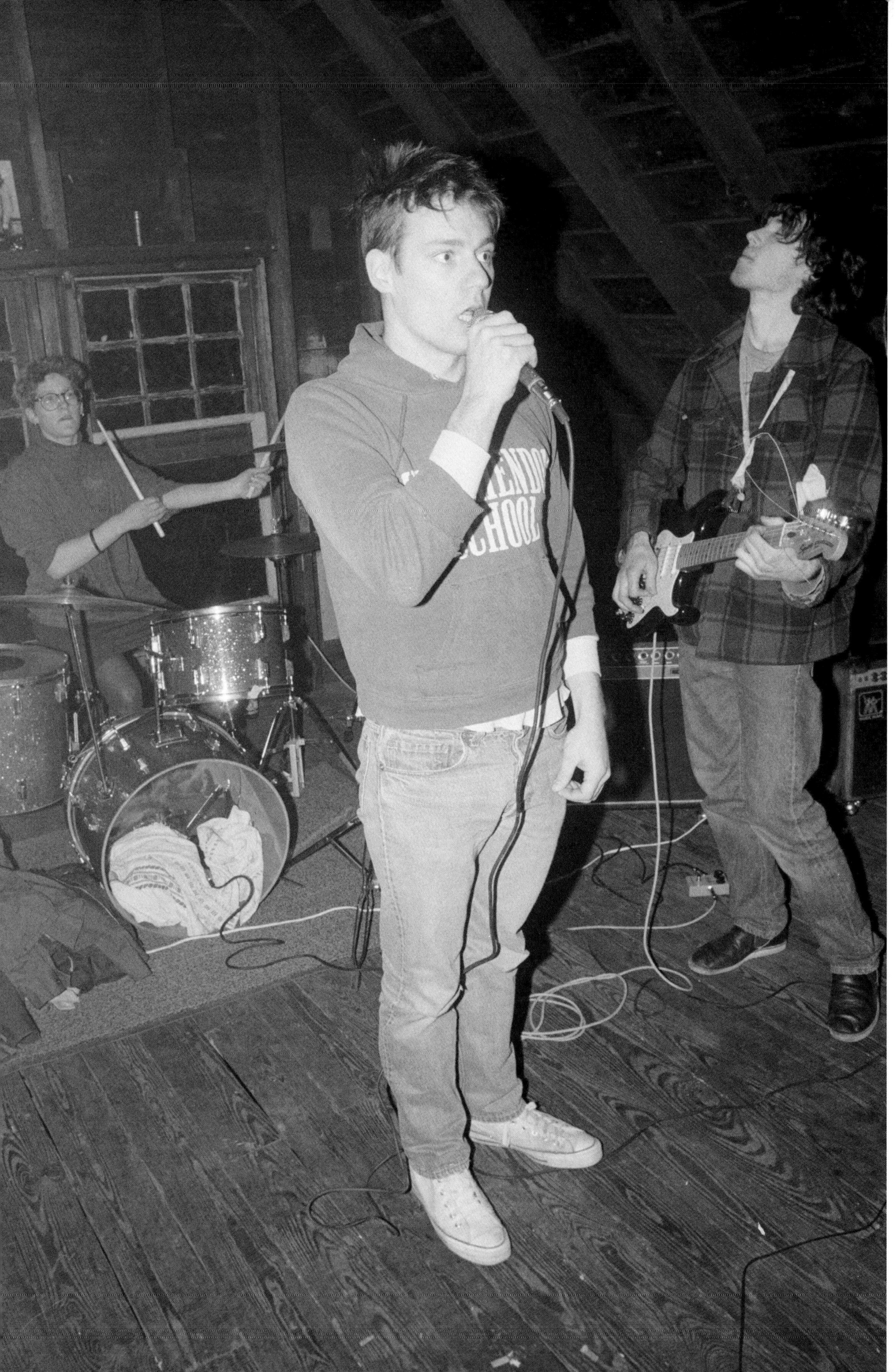
SCHOOL

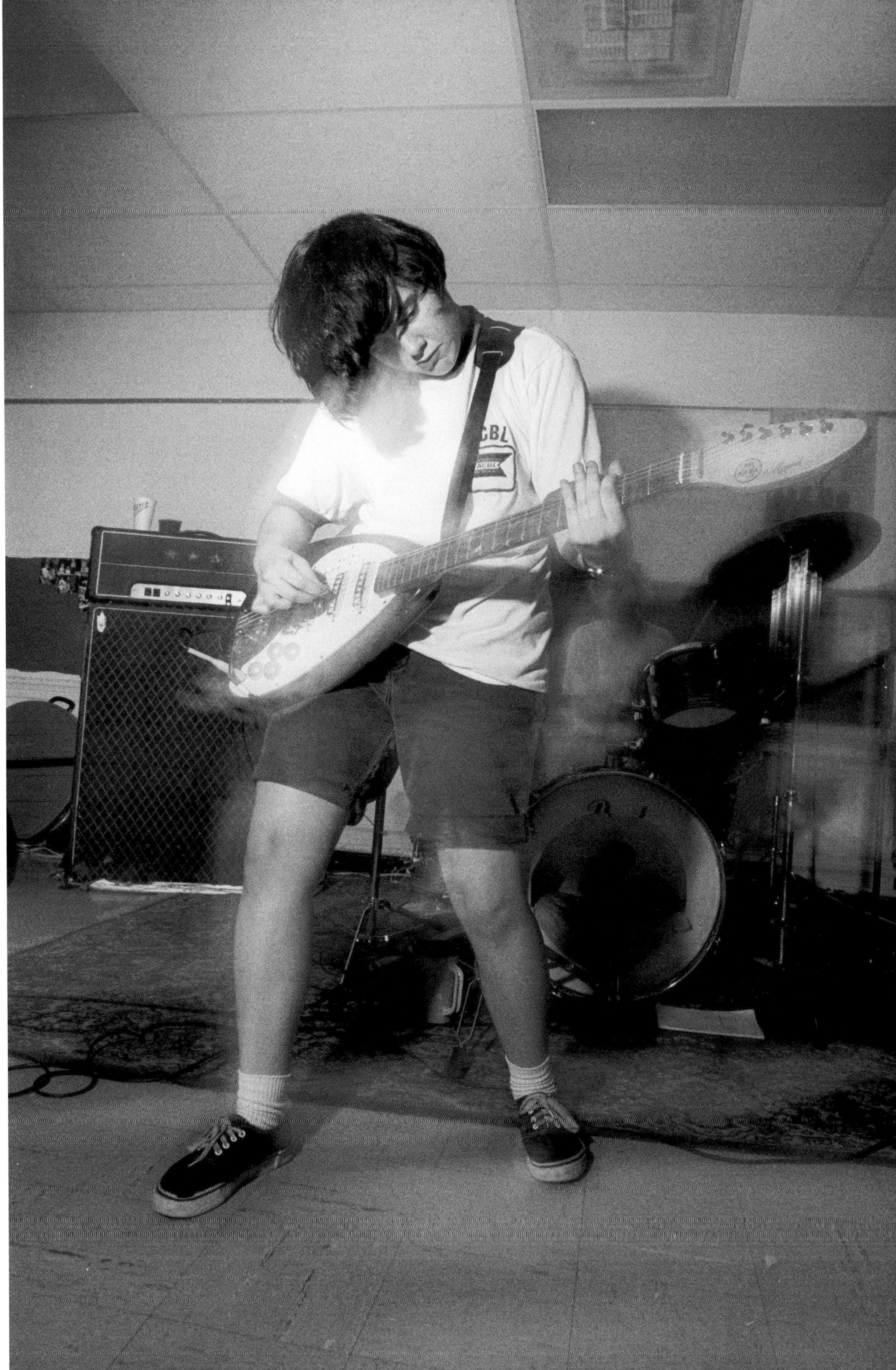

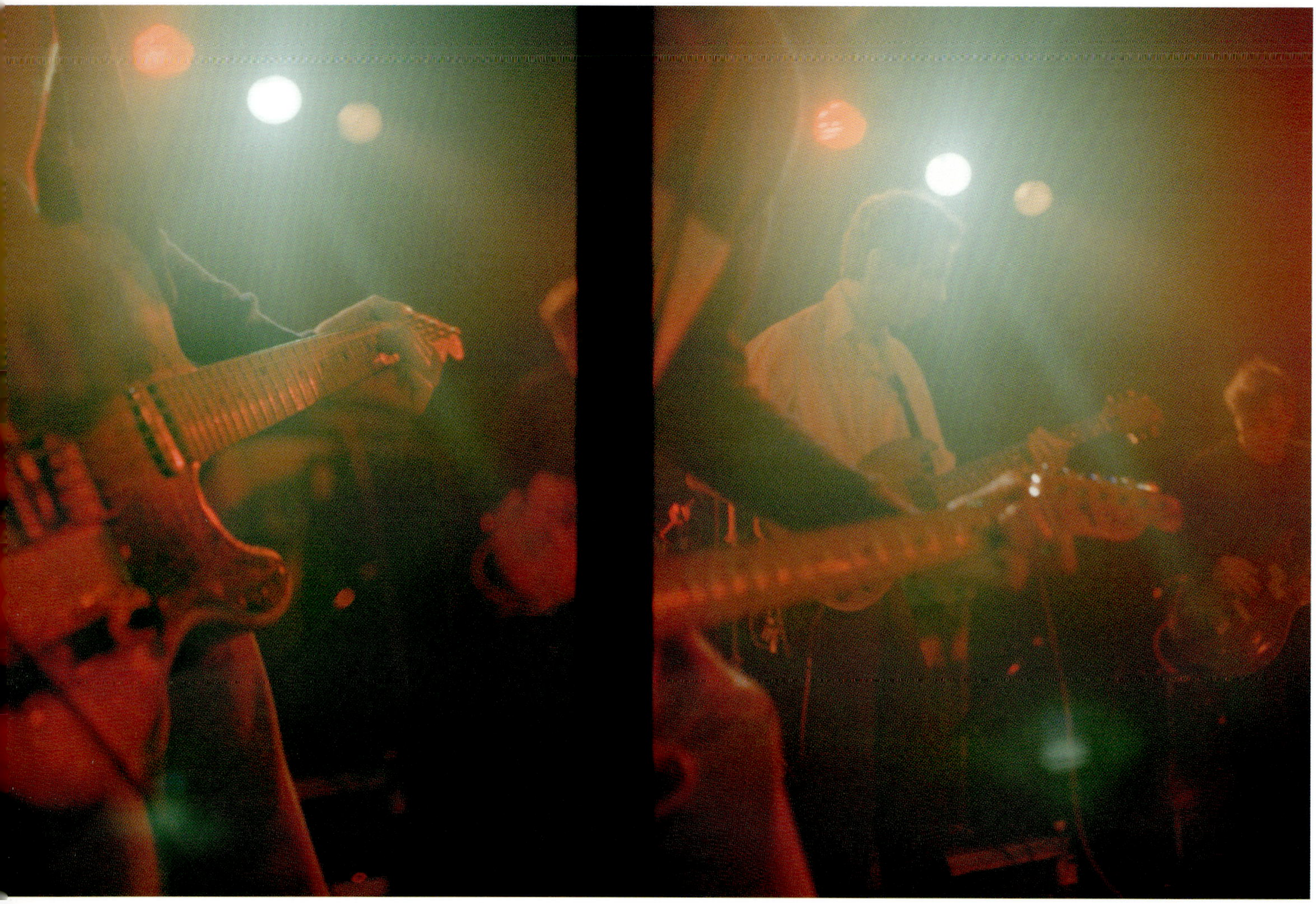

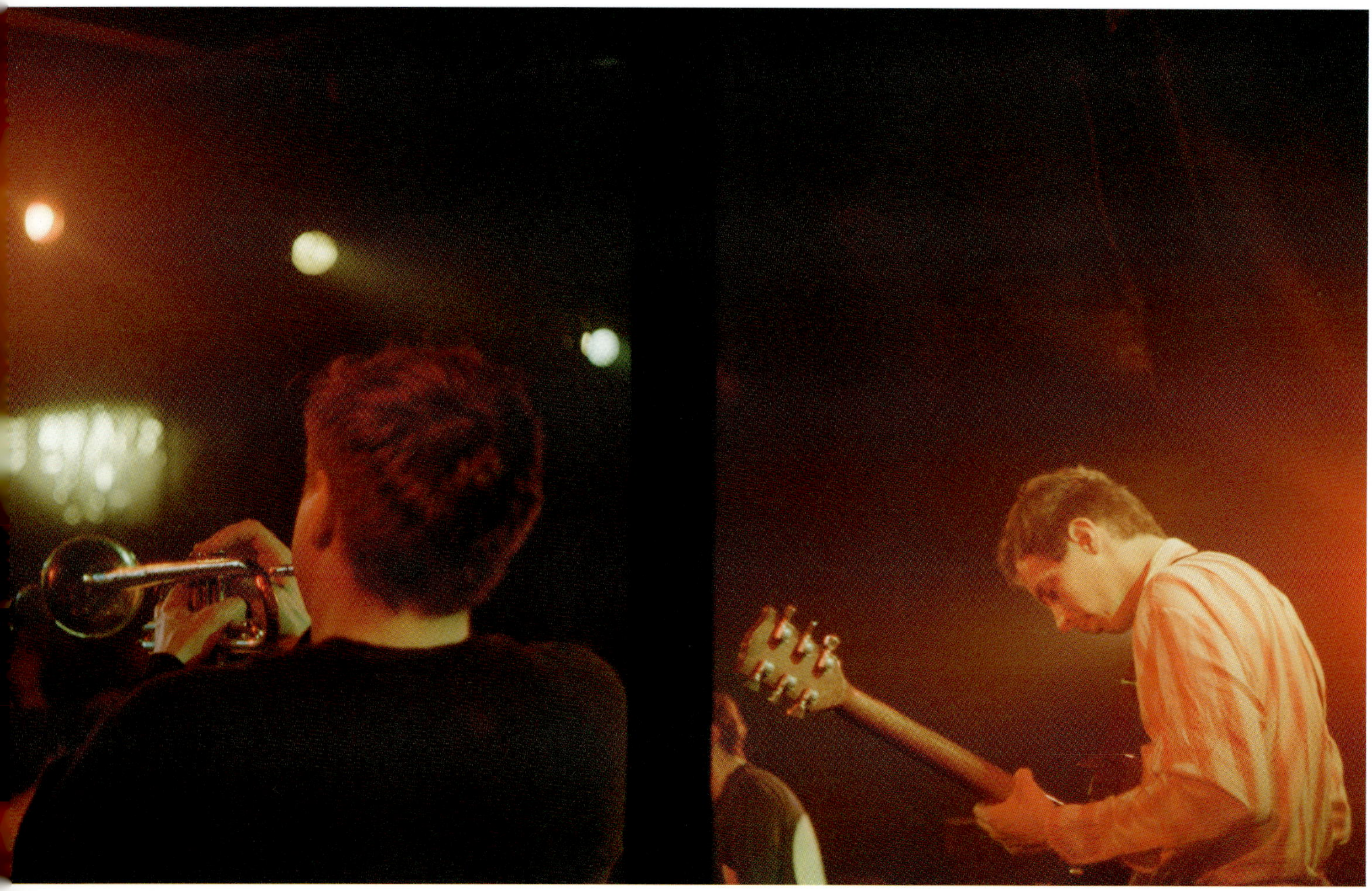

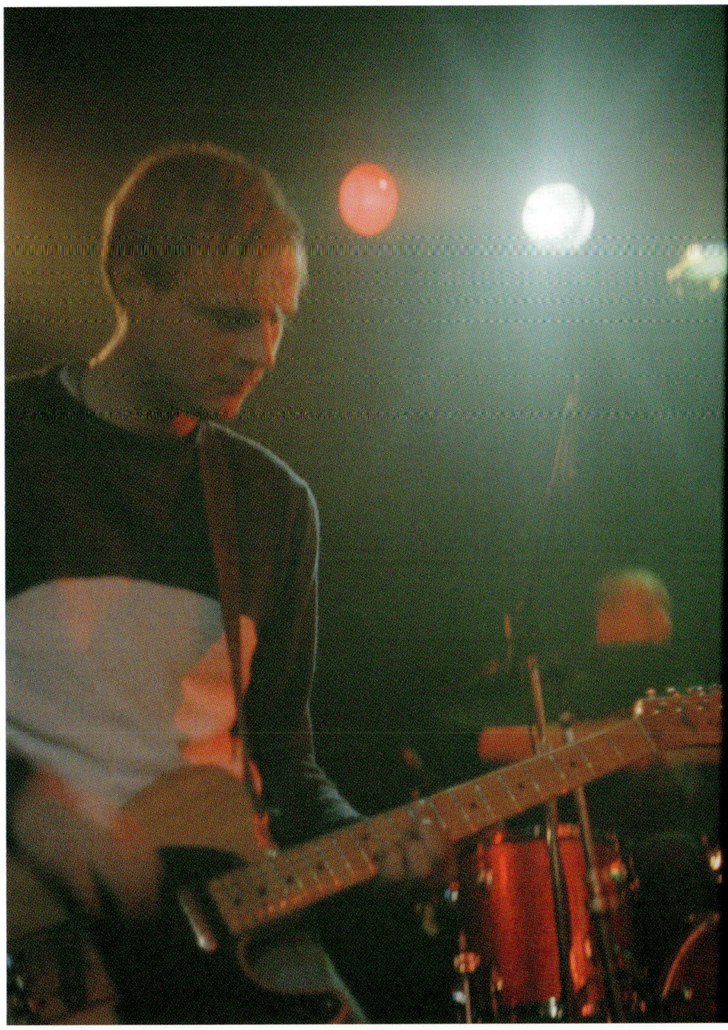

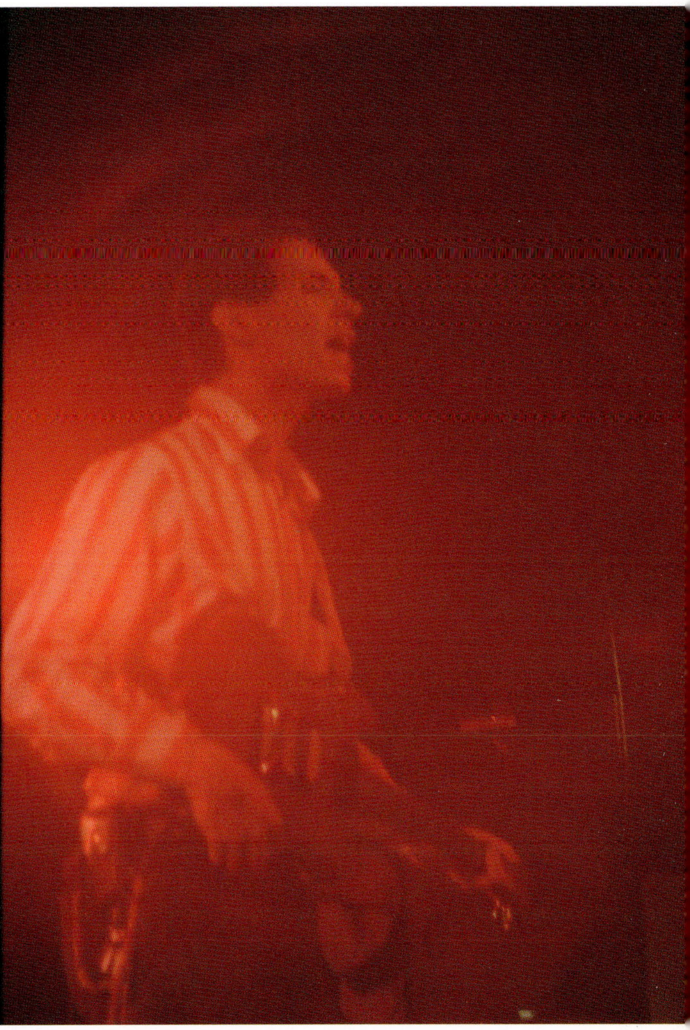

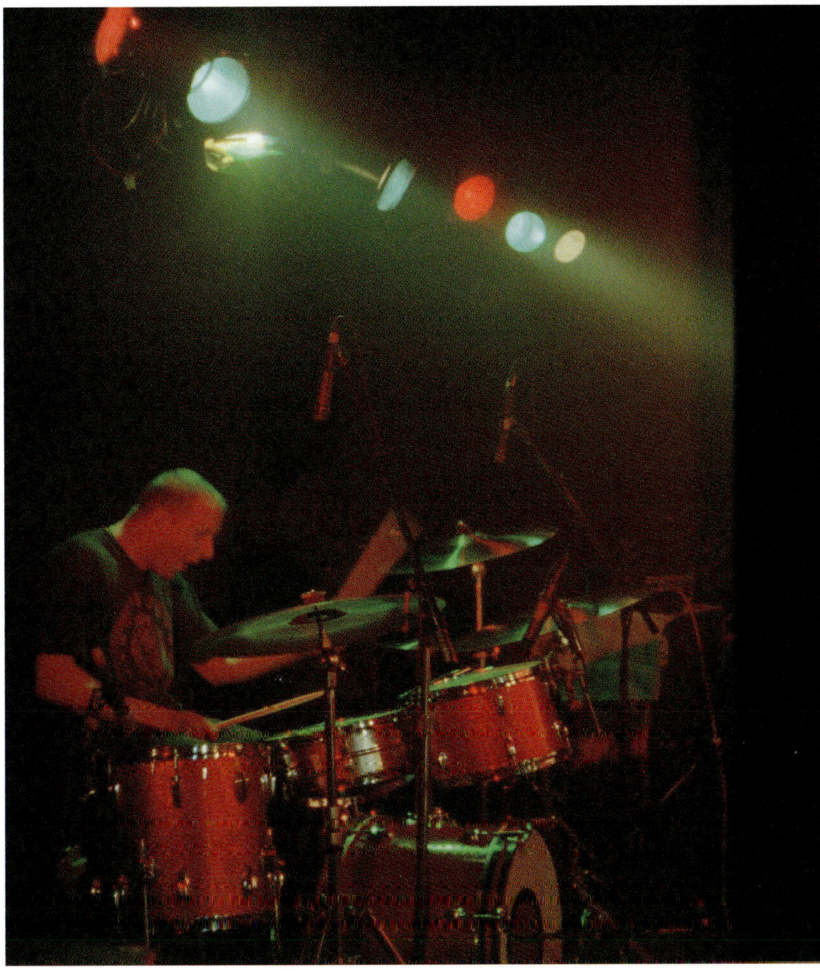

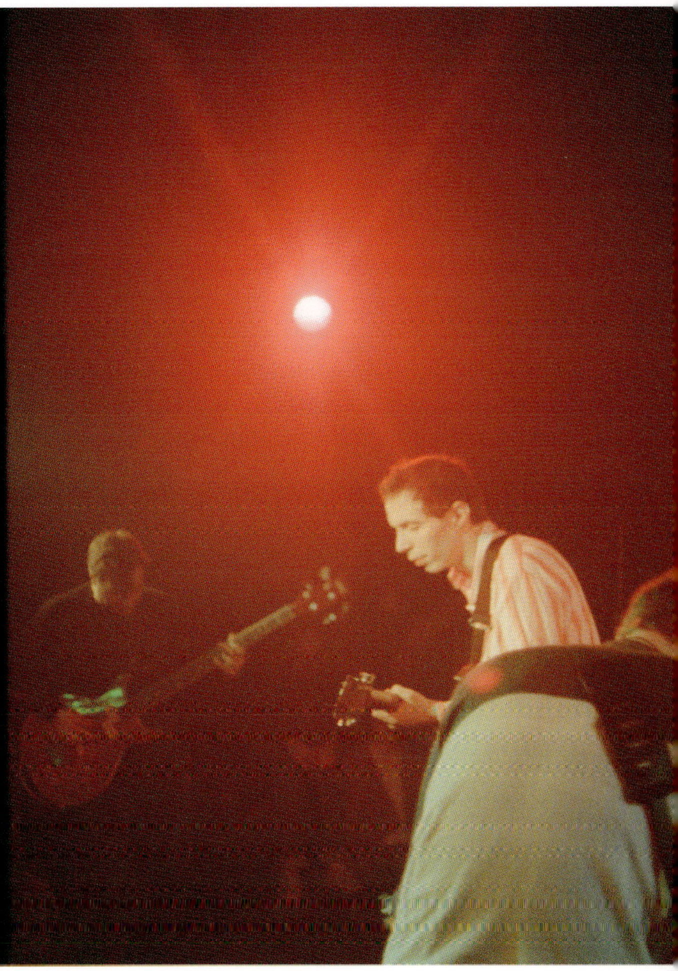

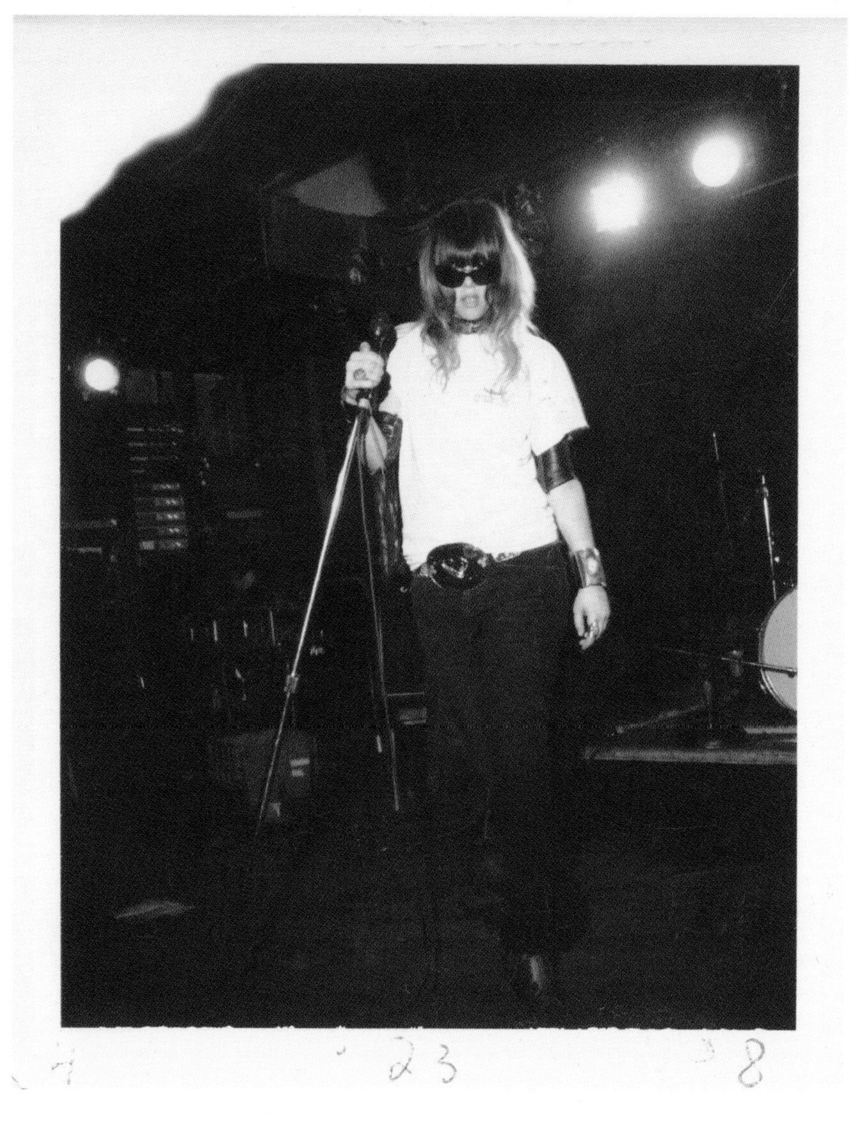
23

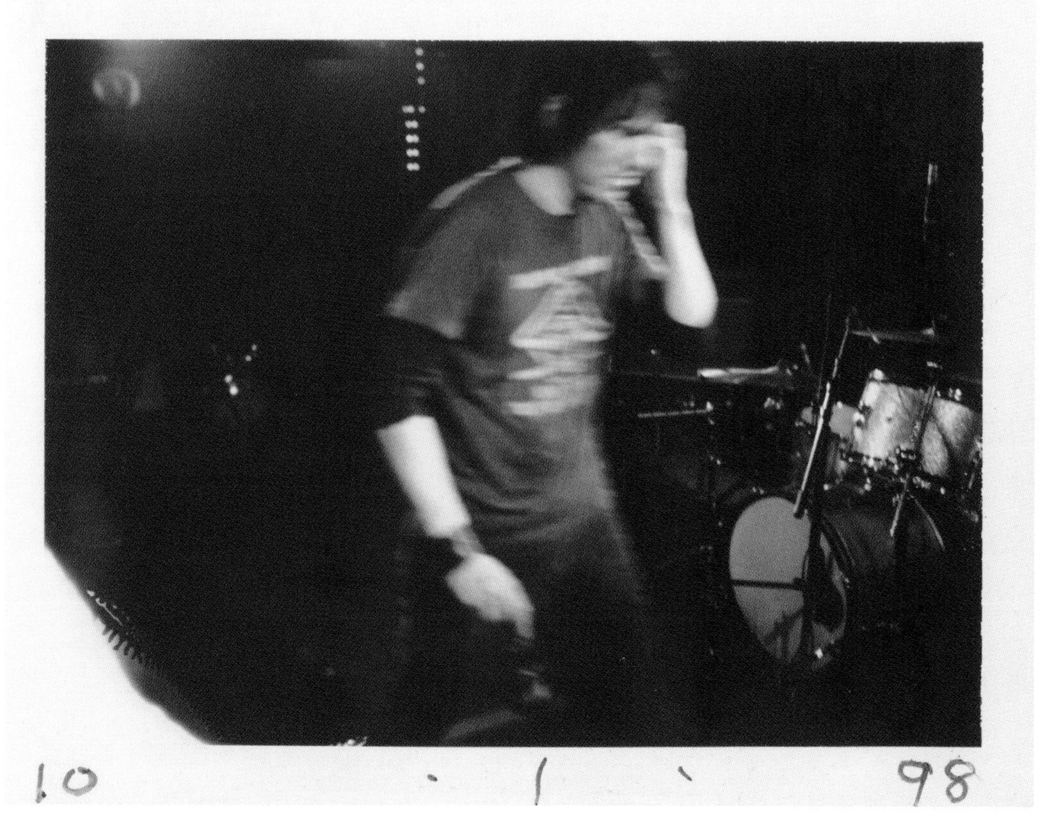
10 · 1 · 98

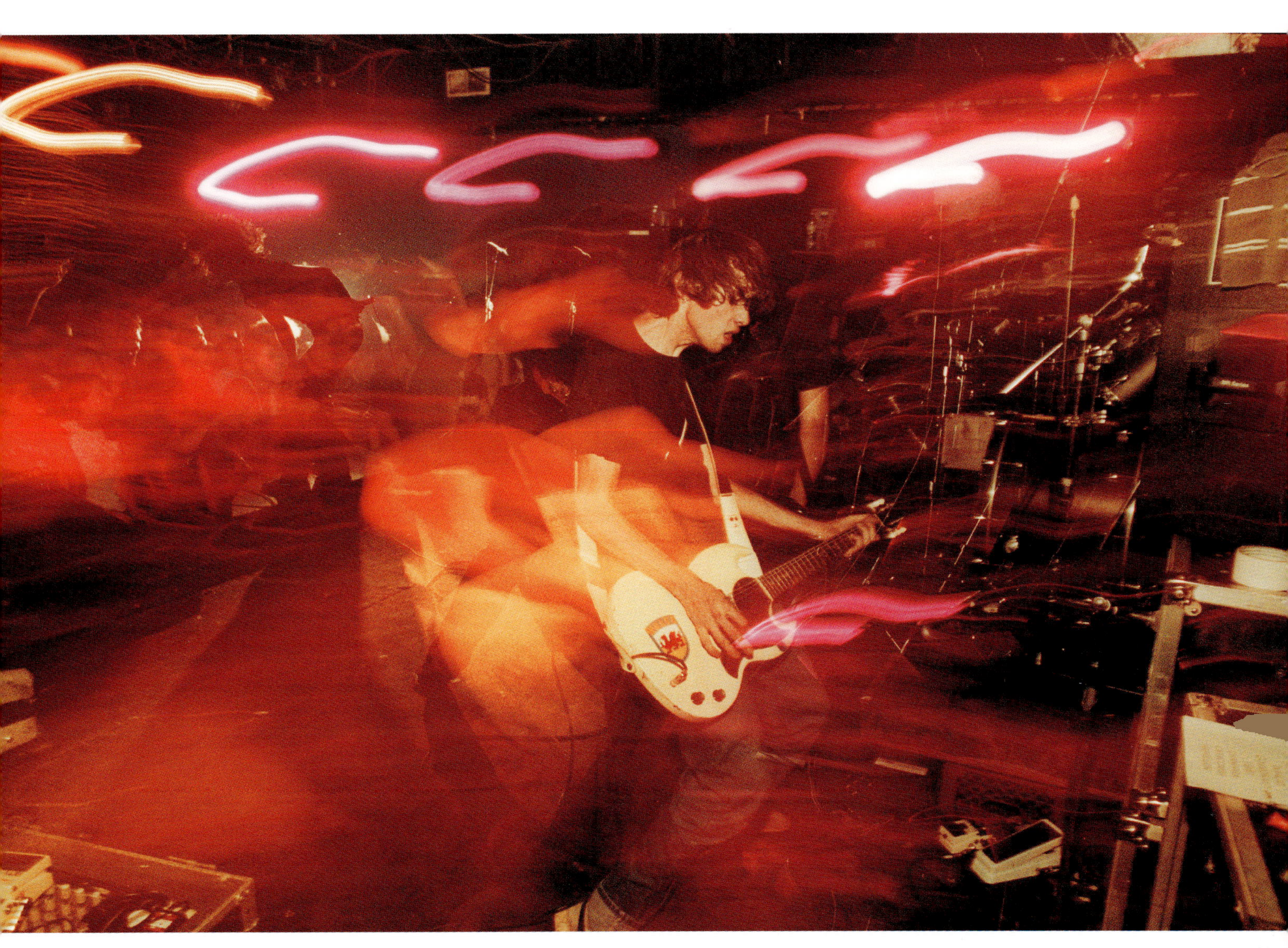

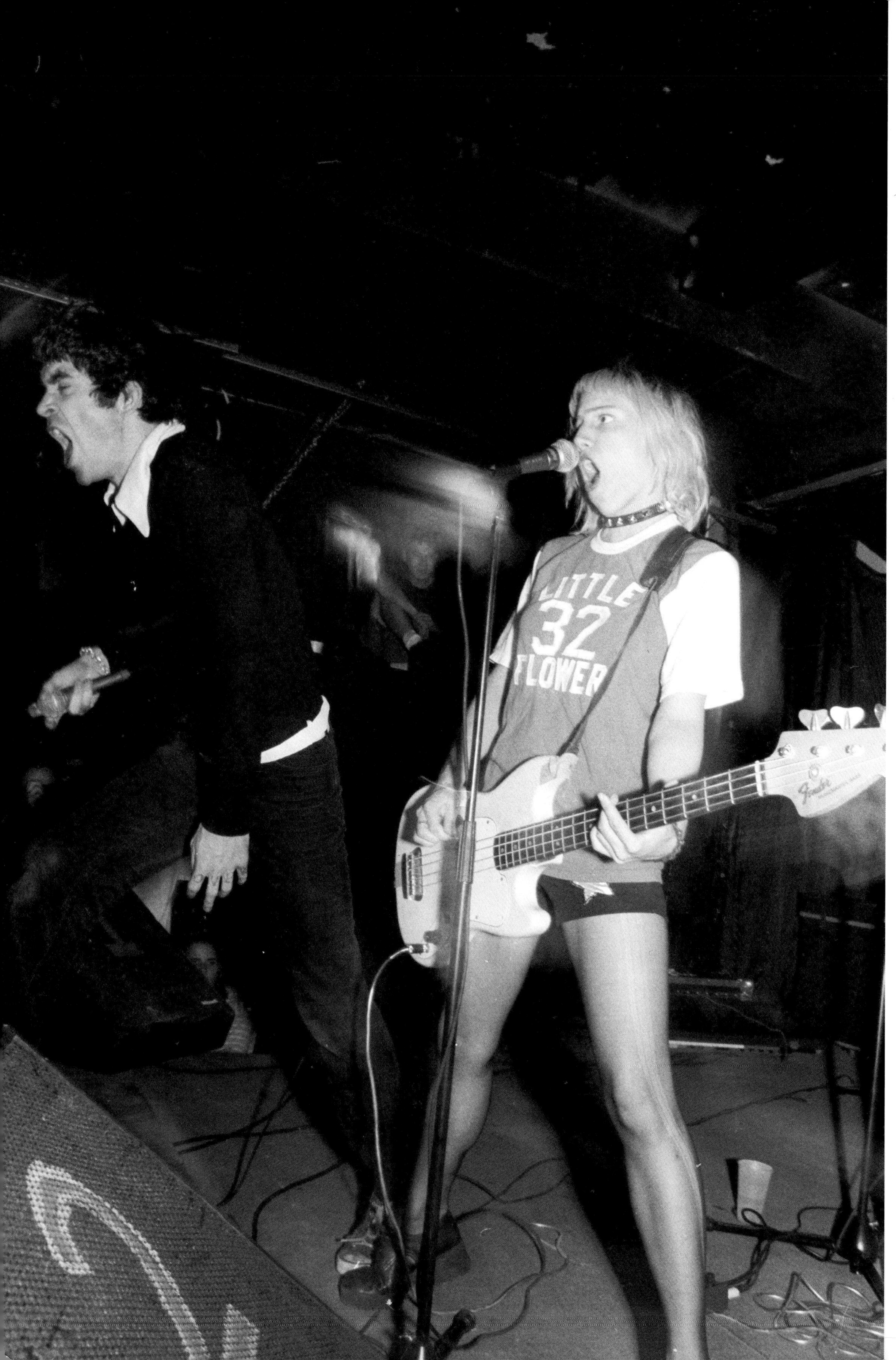
32

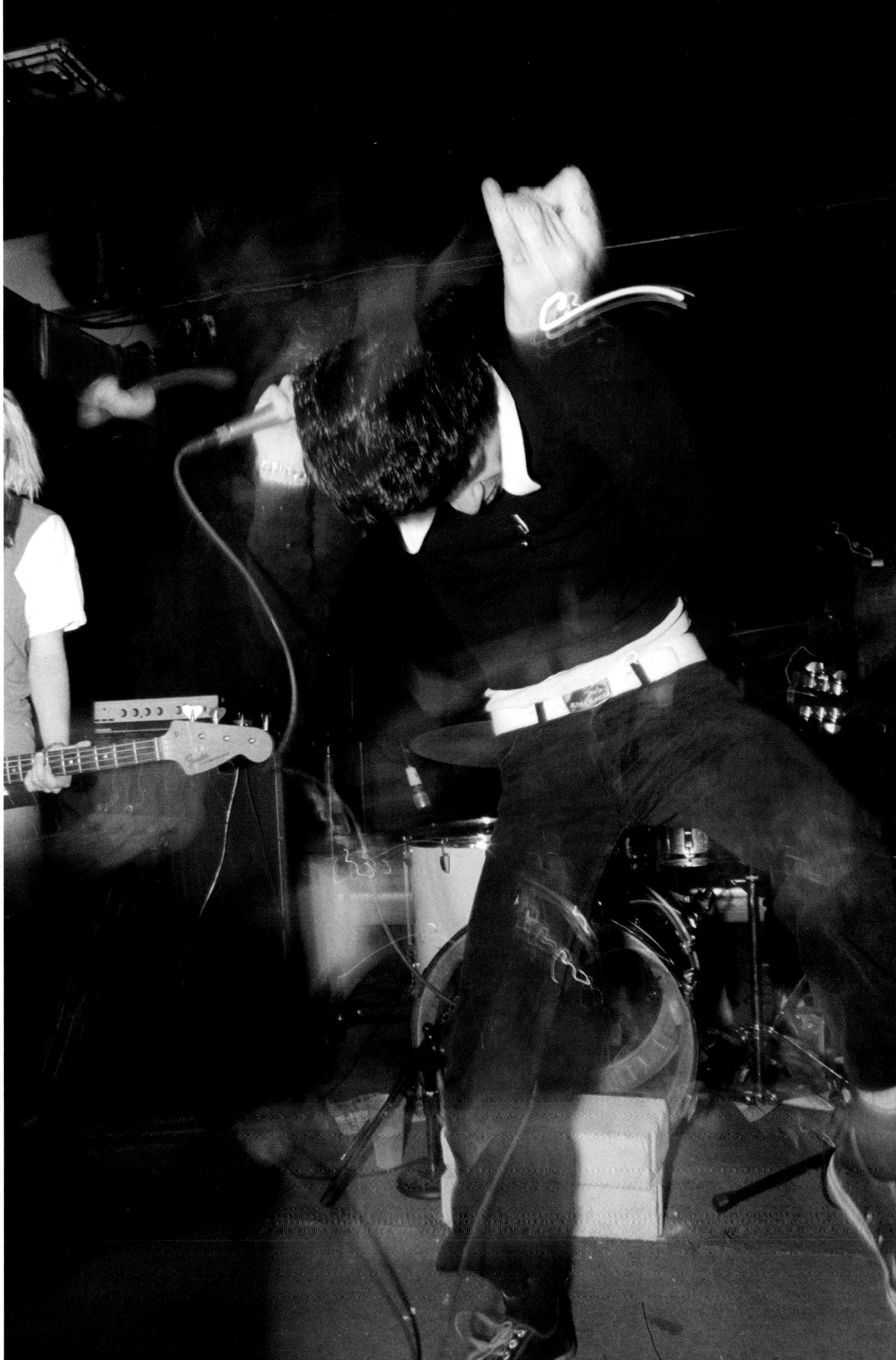

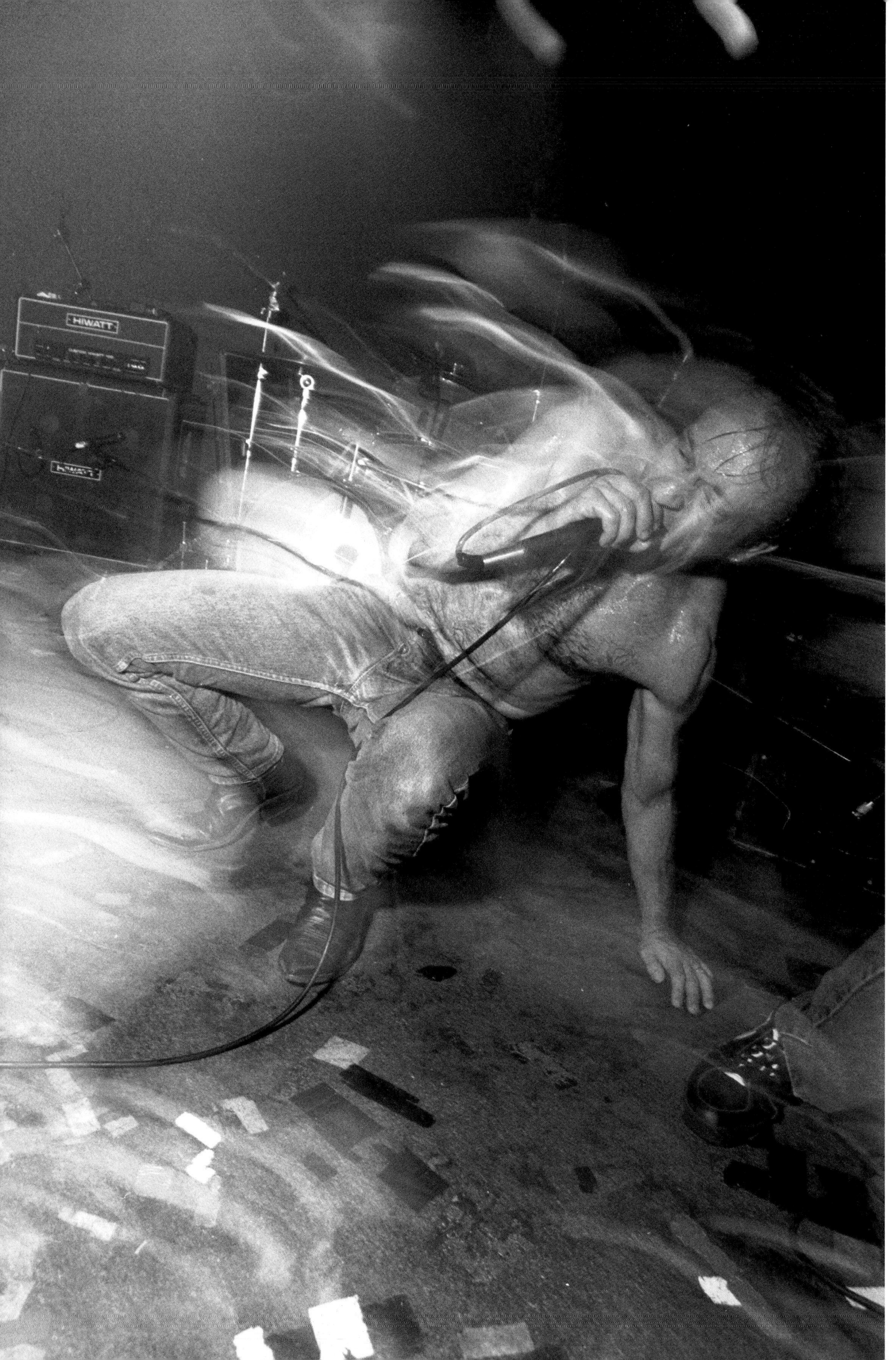
HIWATT

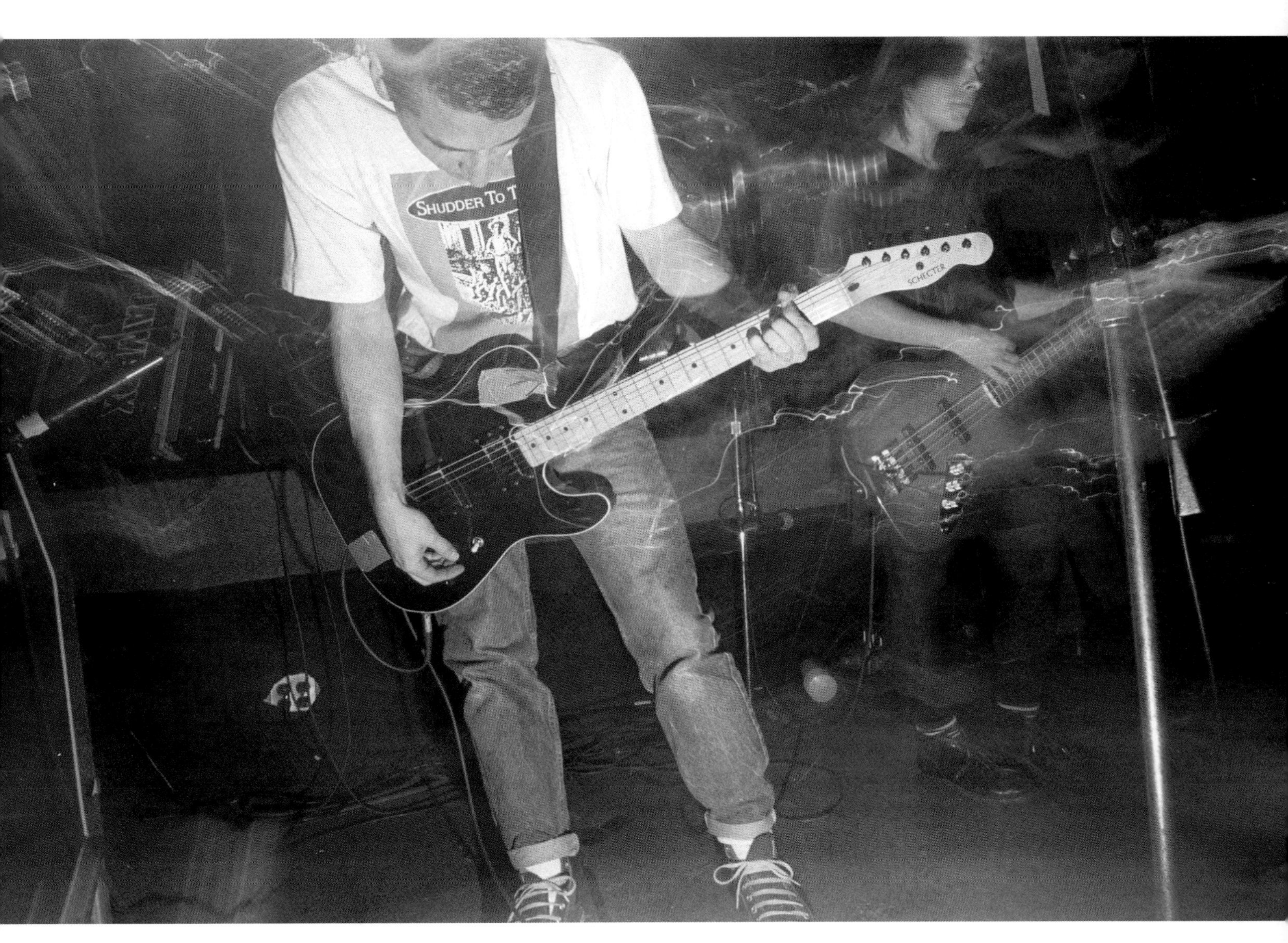
SHUDDER TO
SCHECTER

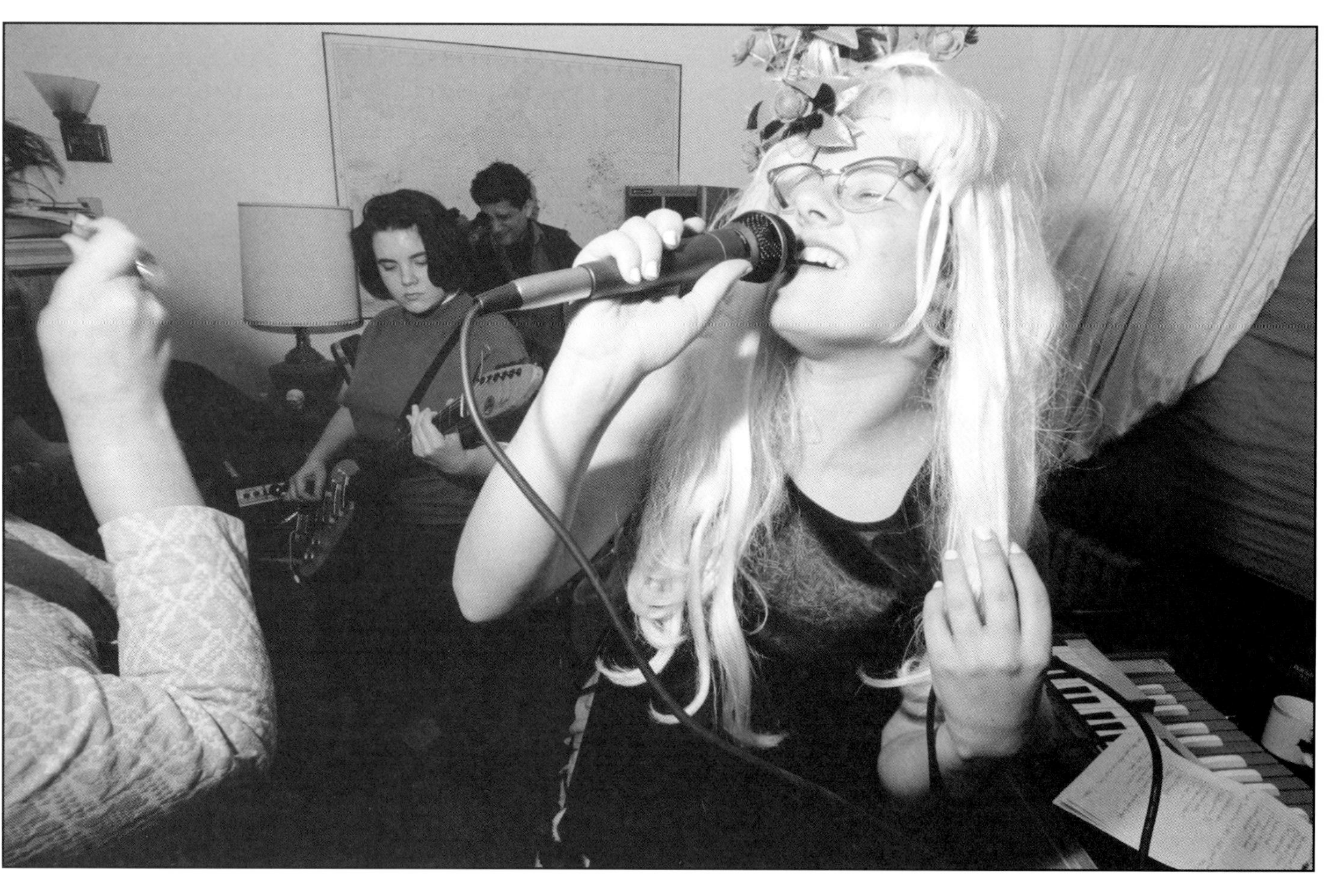

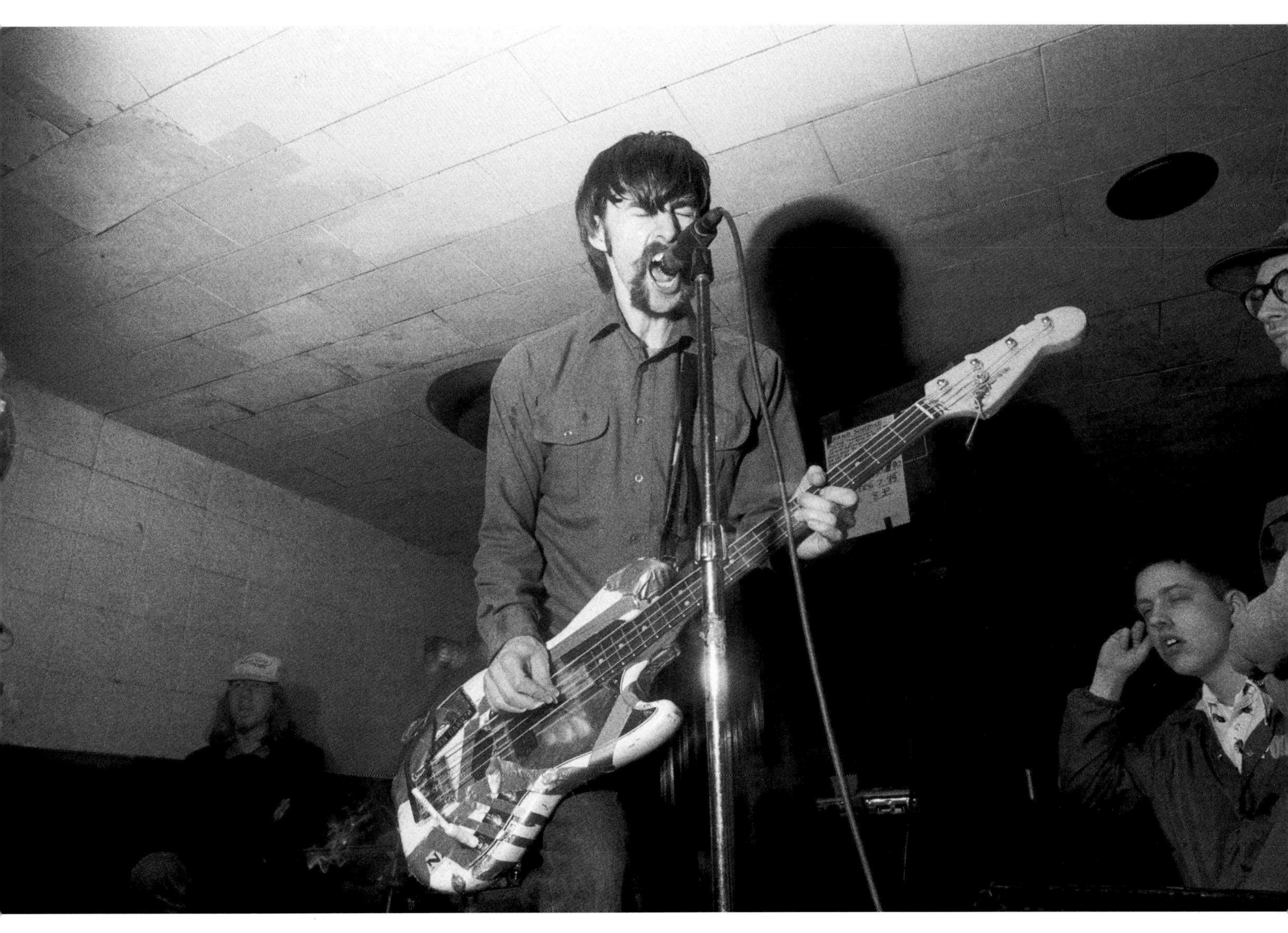

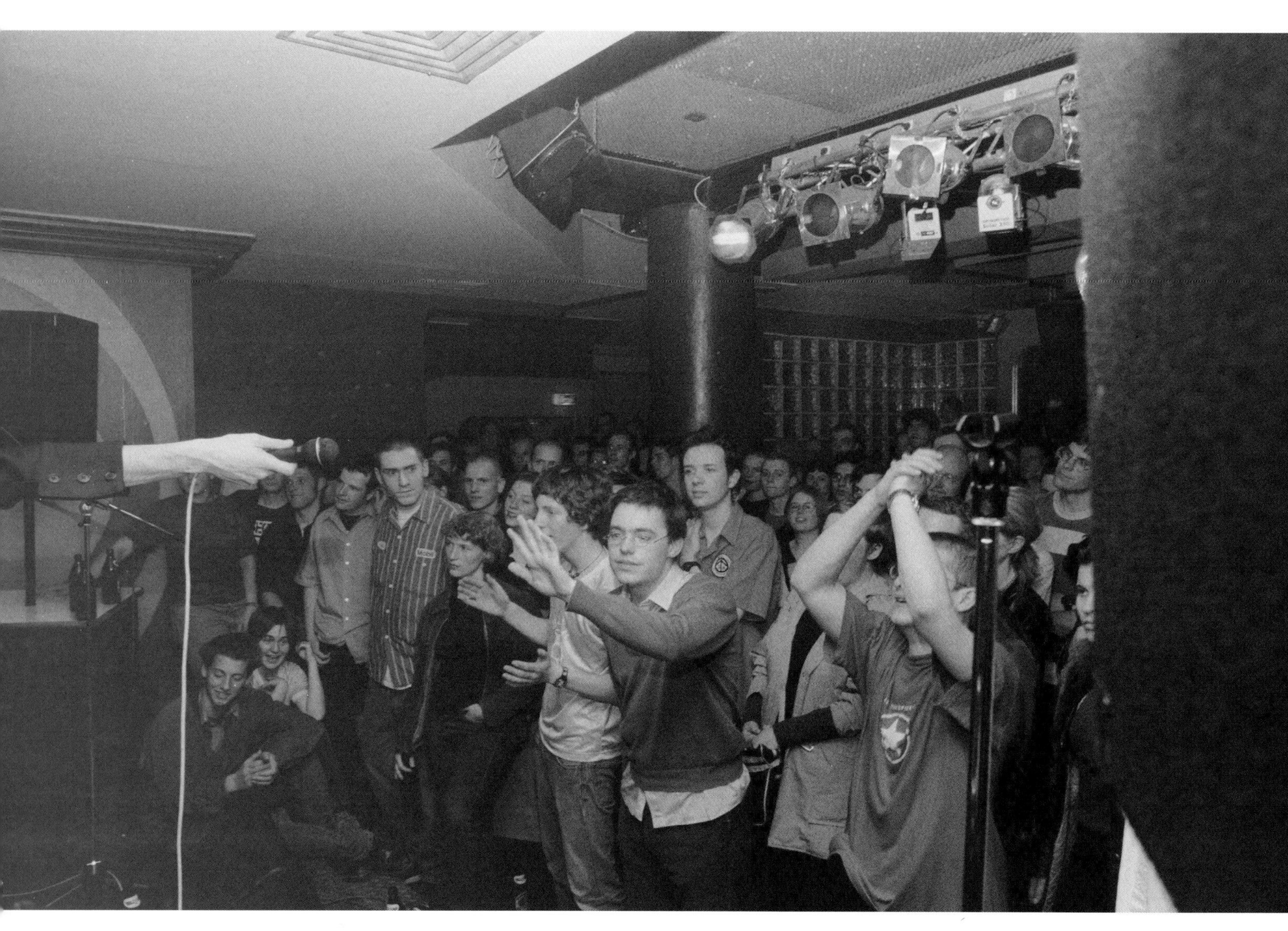

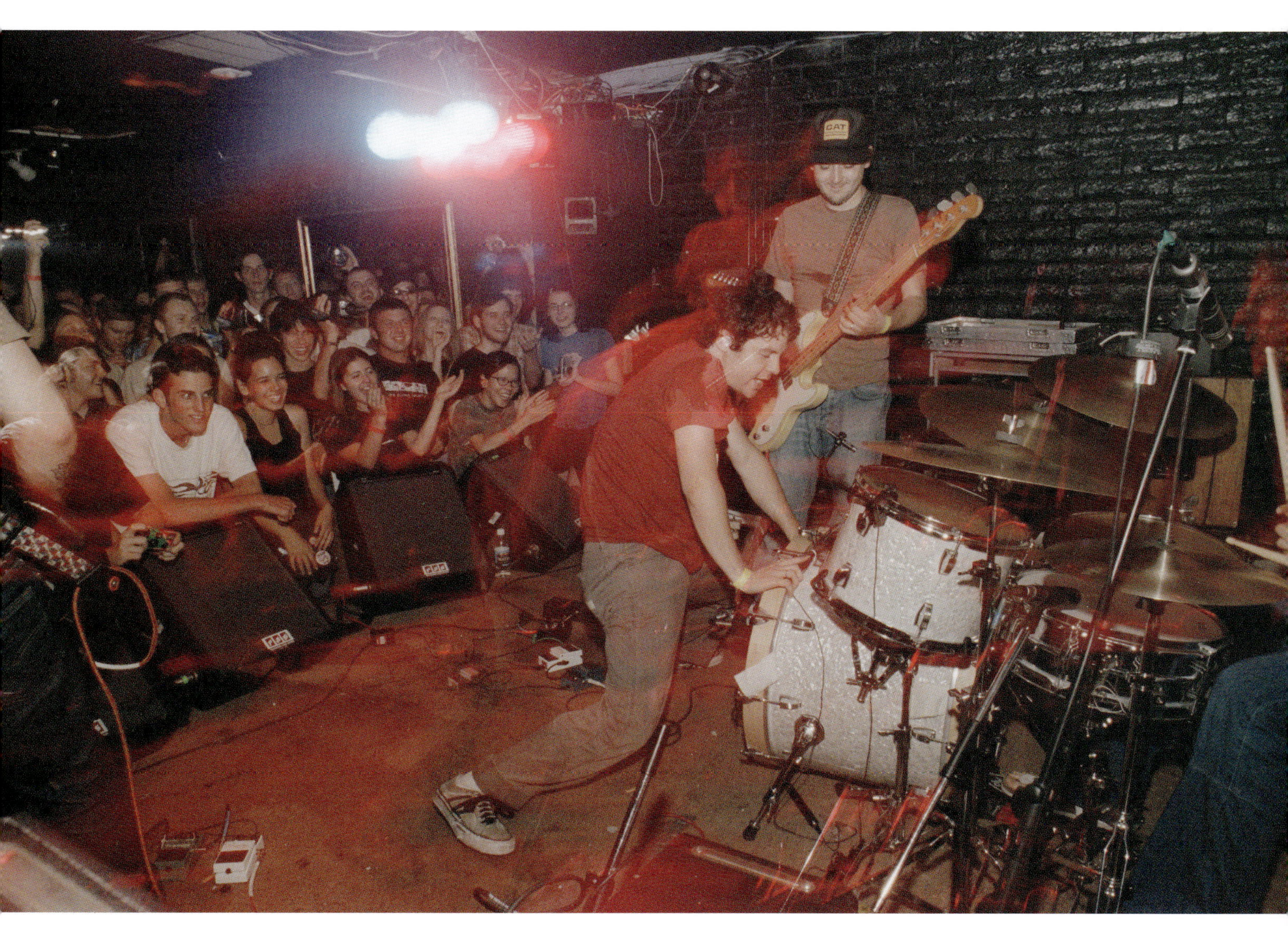
CAT

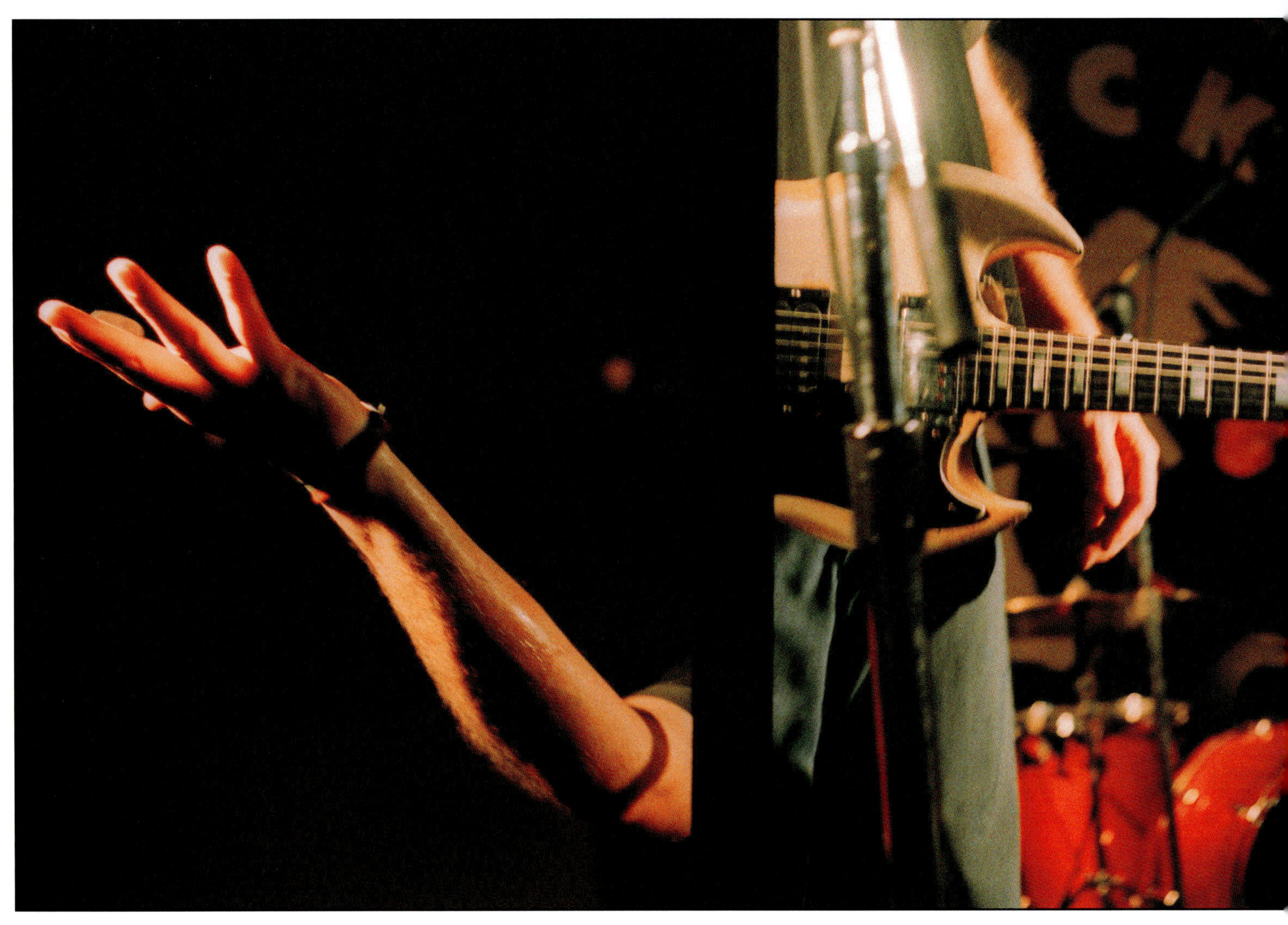

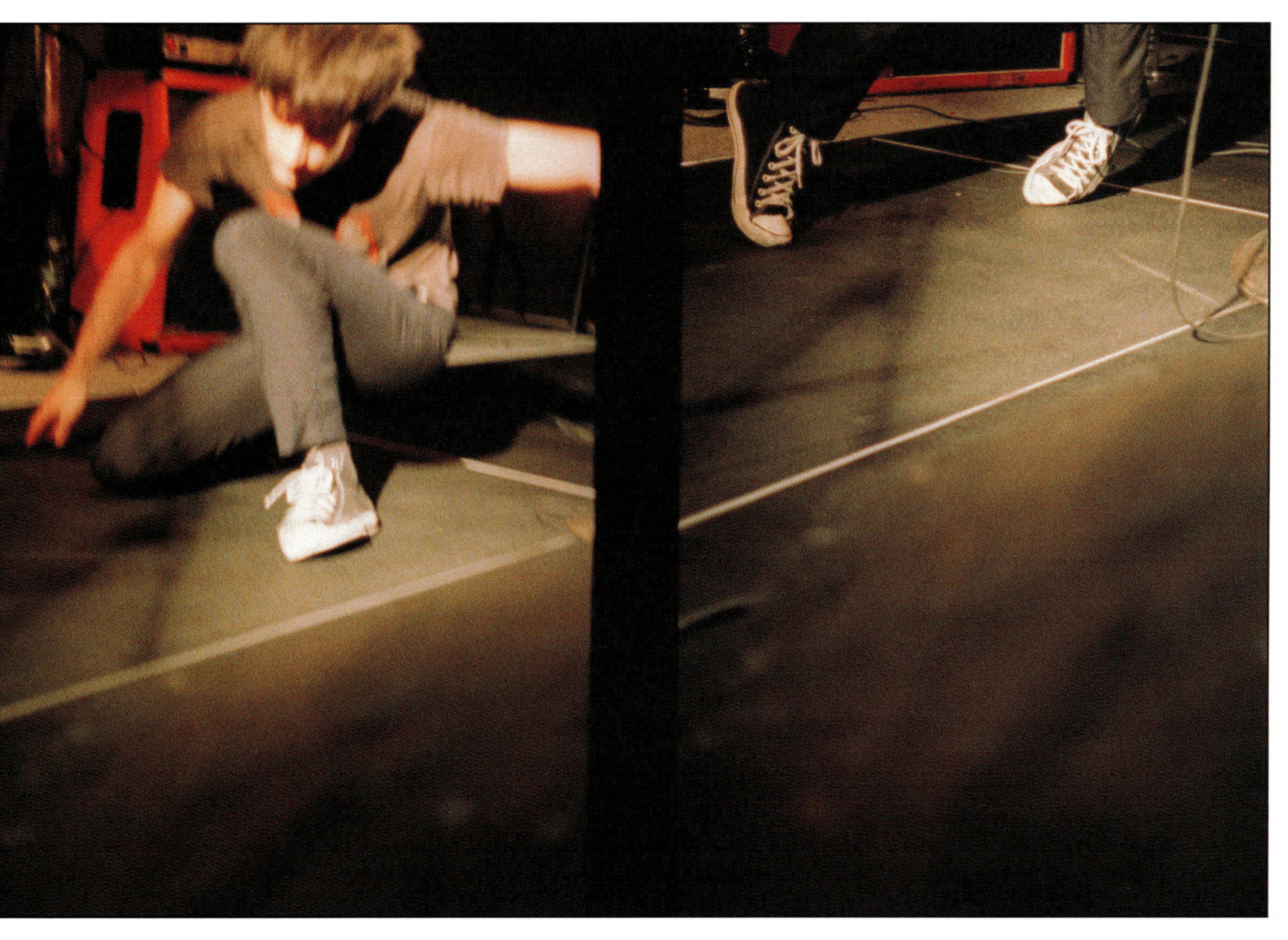

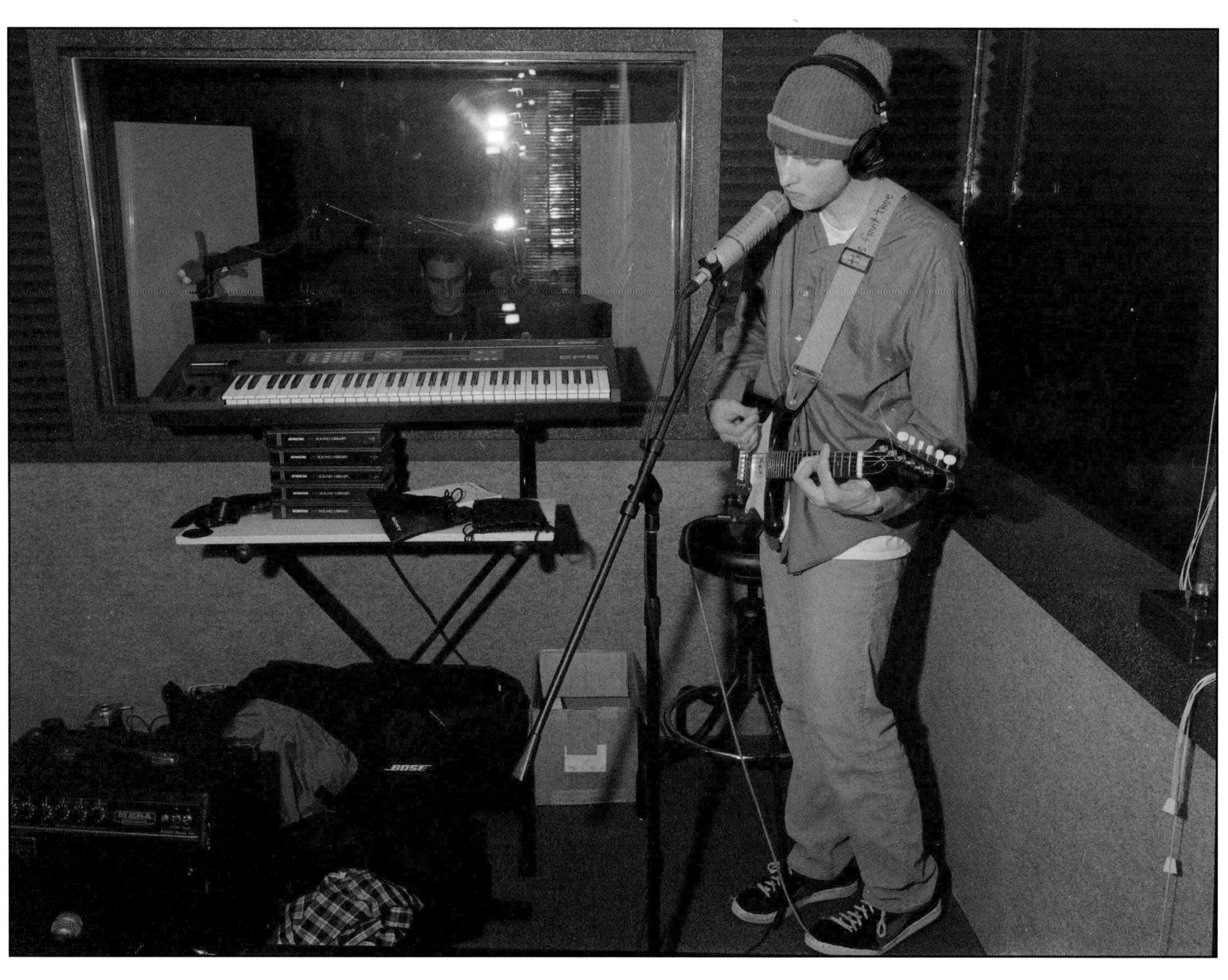
BOSE

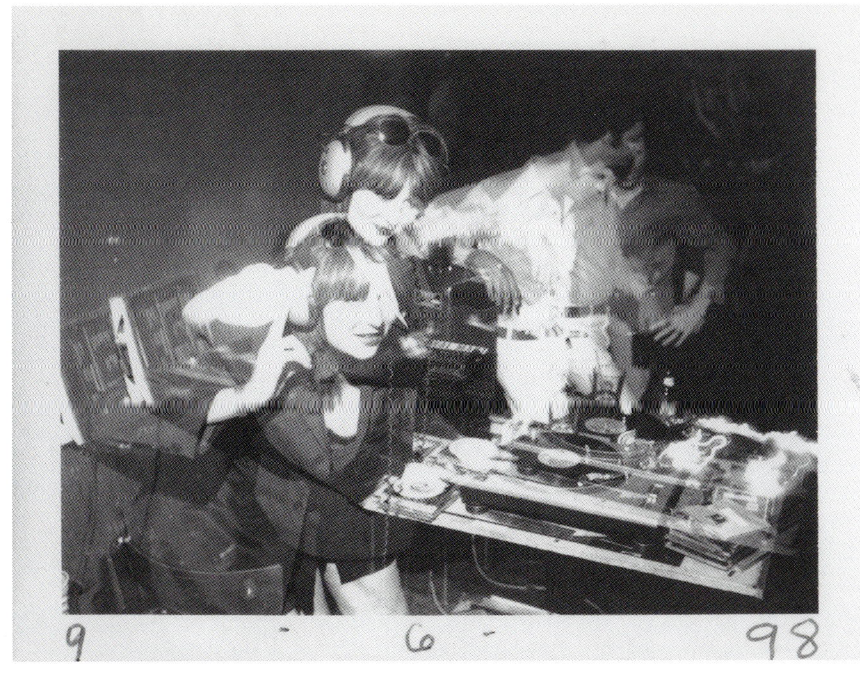
9 - 6 - 98

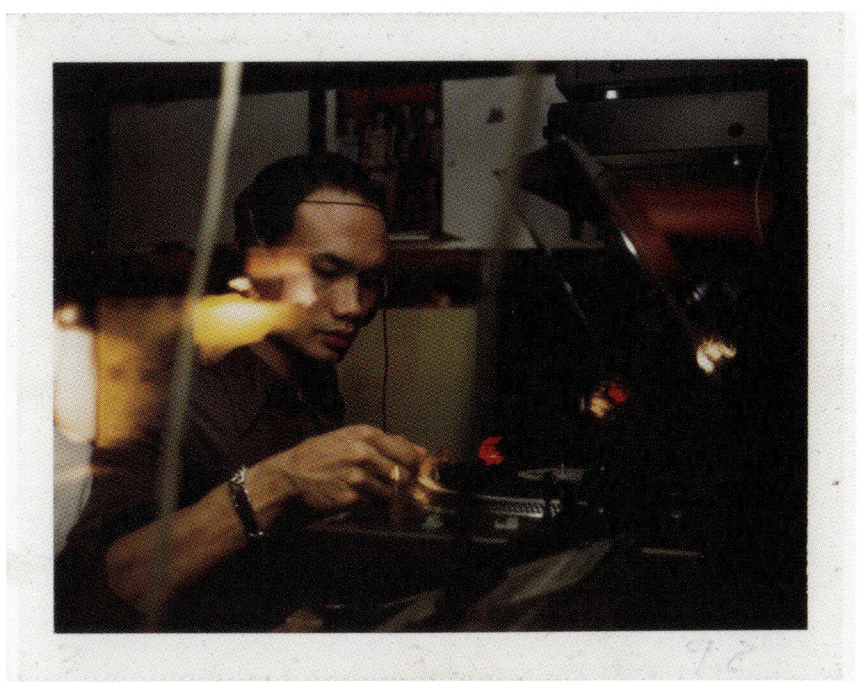

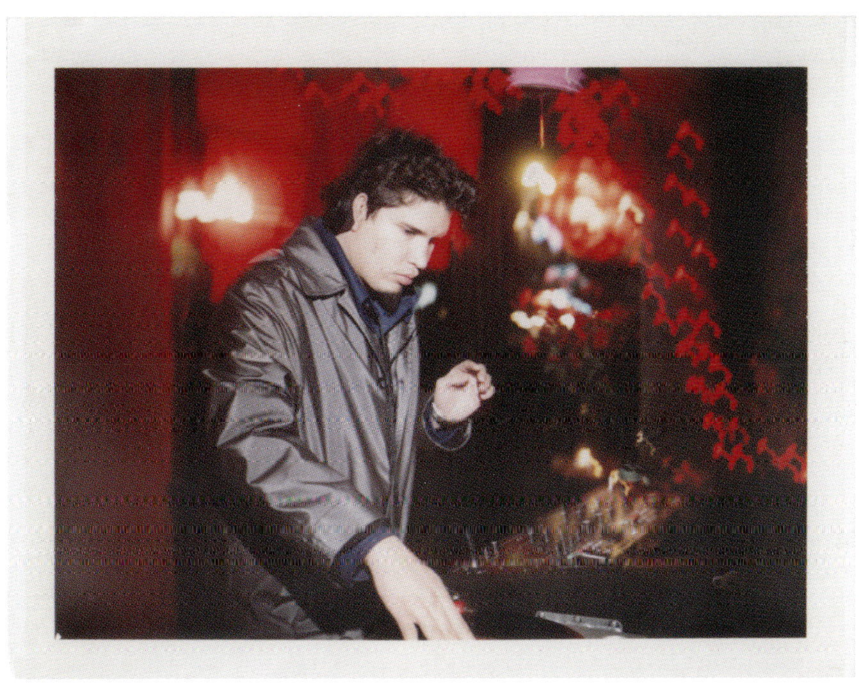

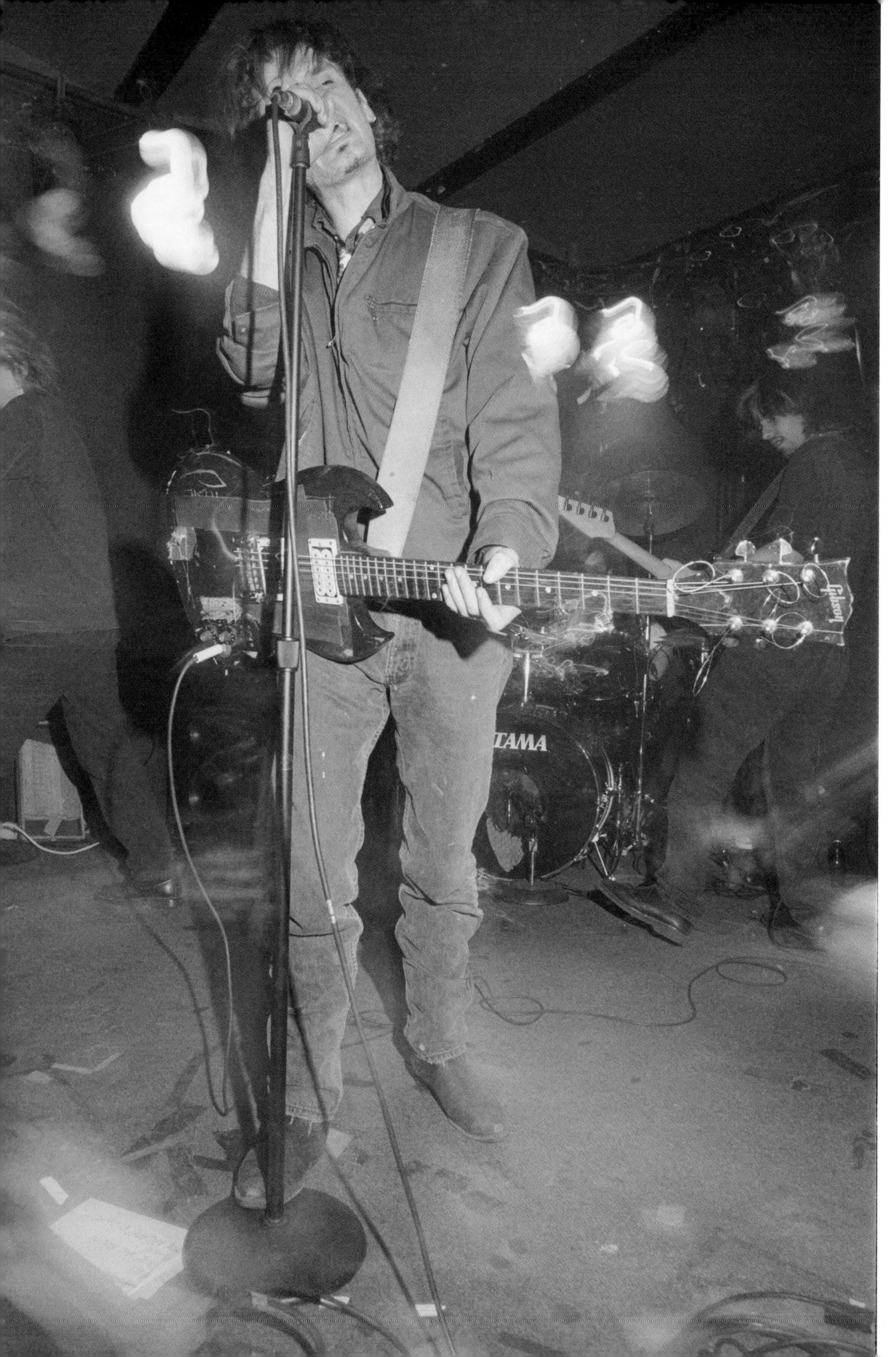
TAMA
Gibson

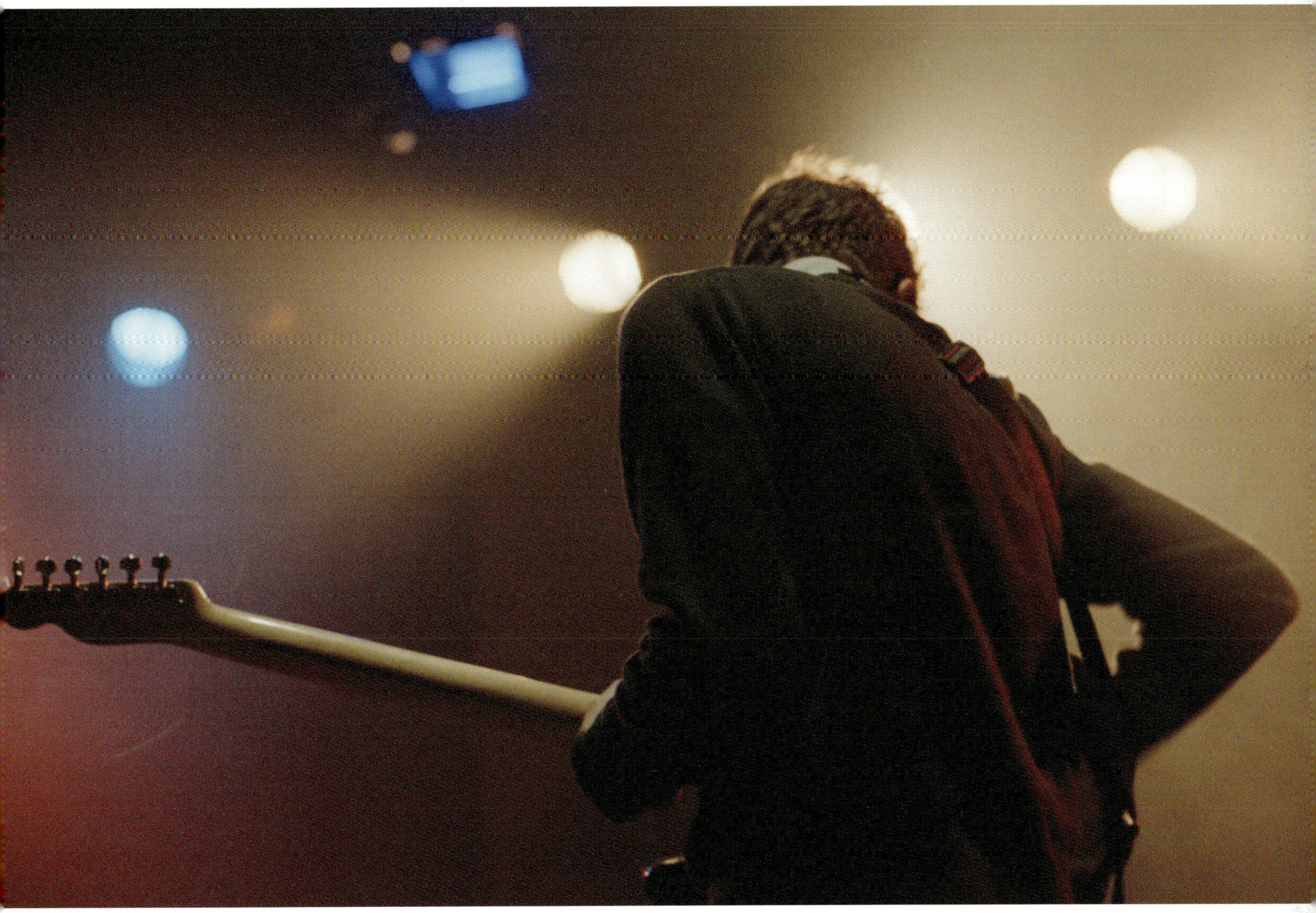

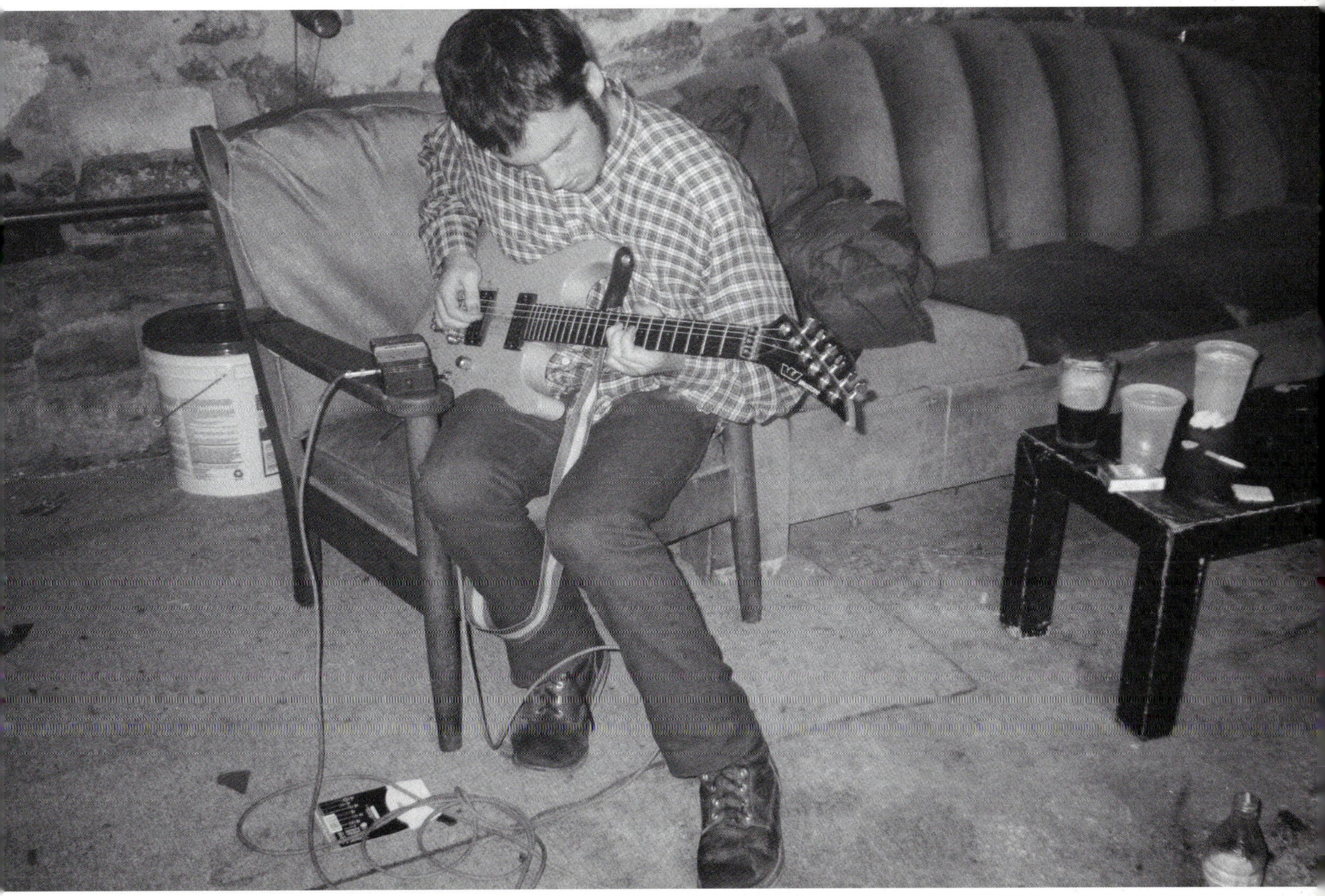

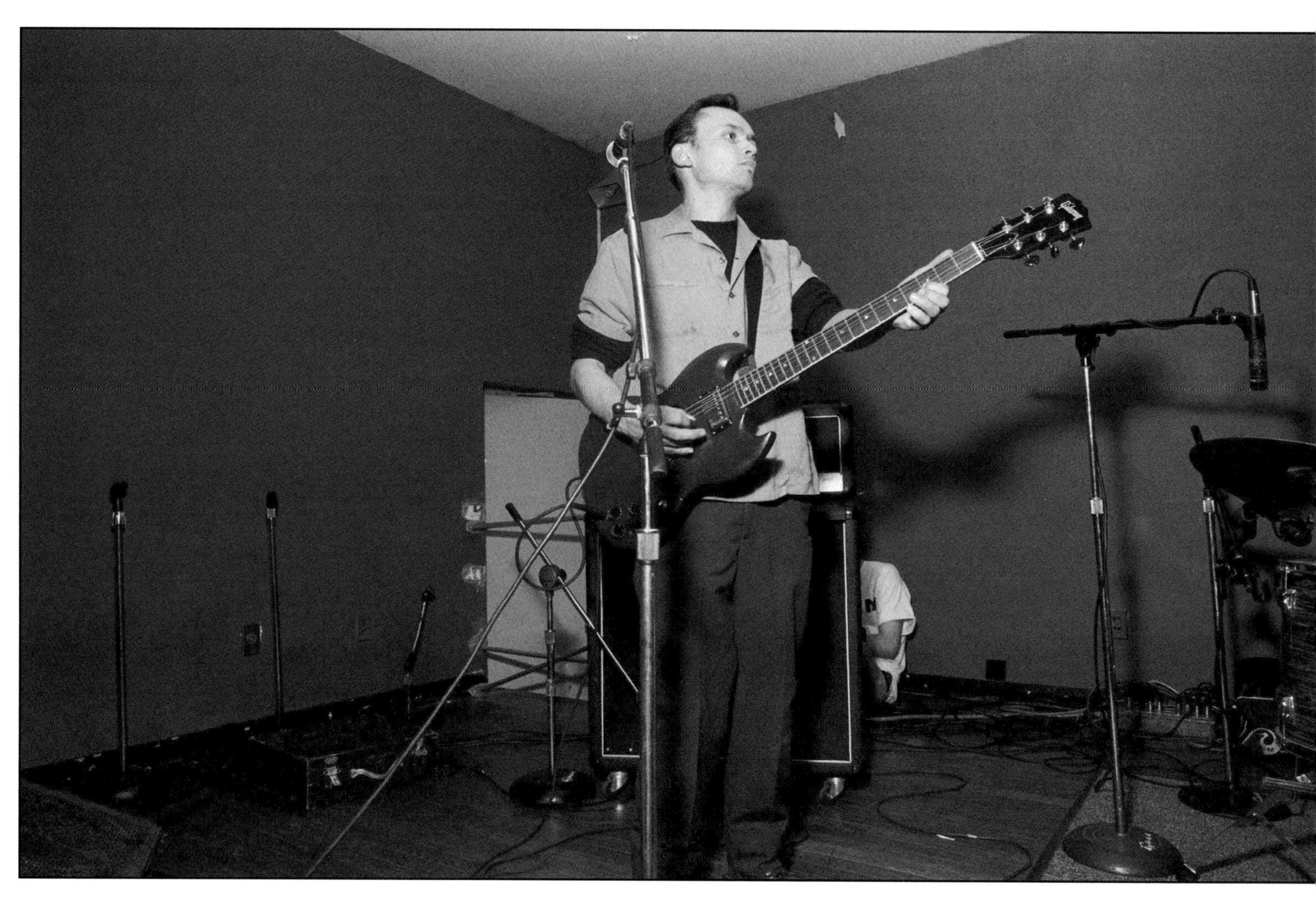

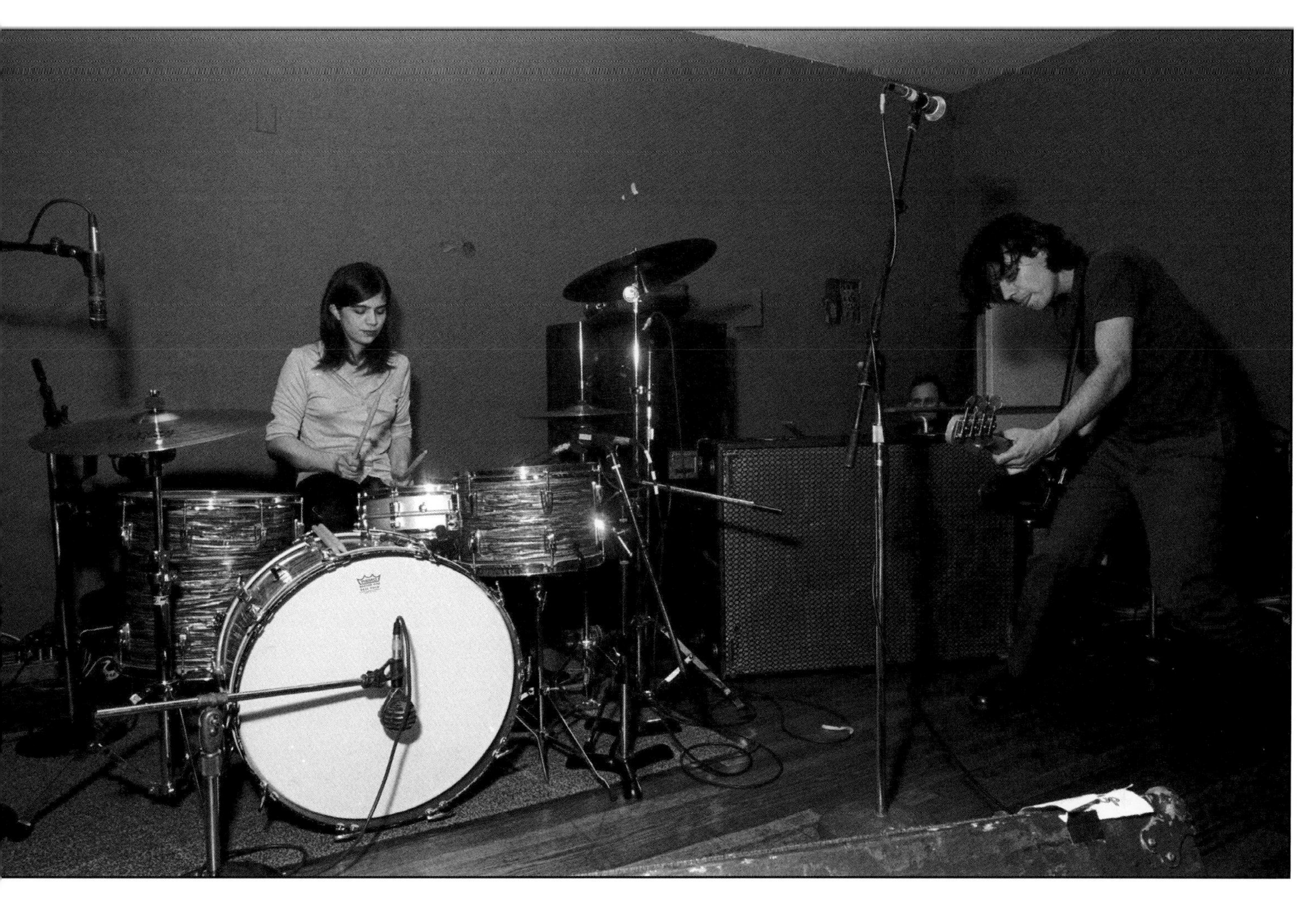

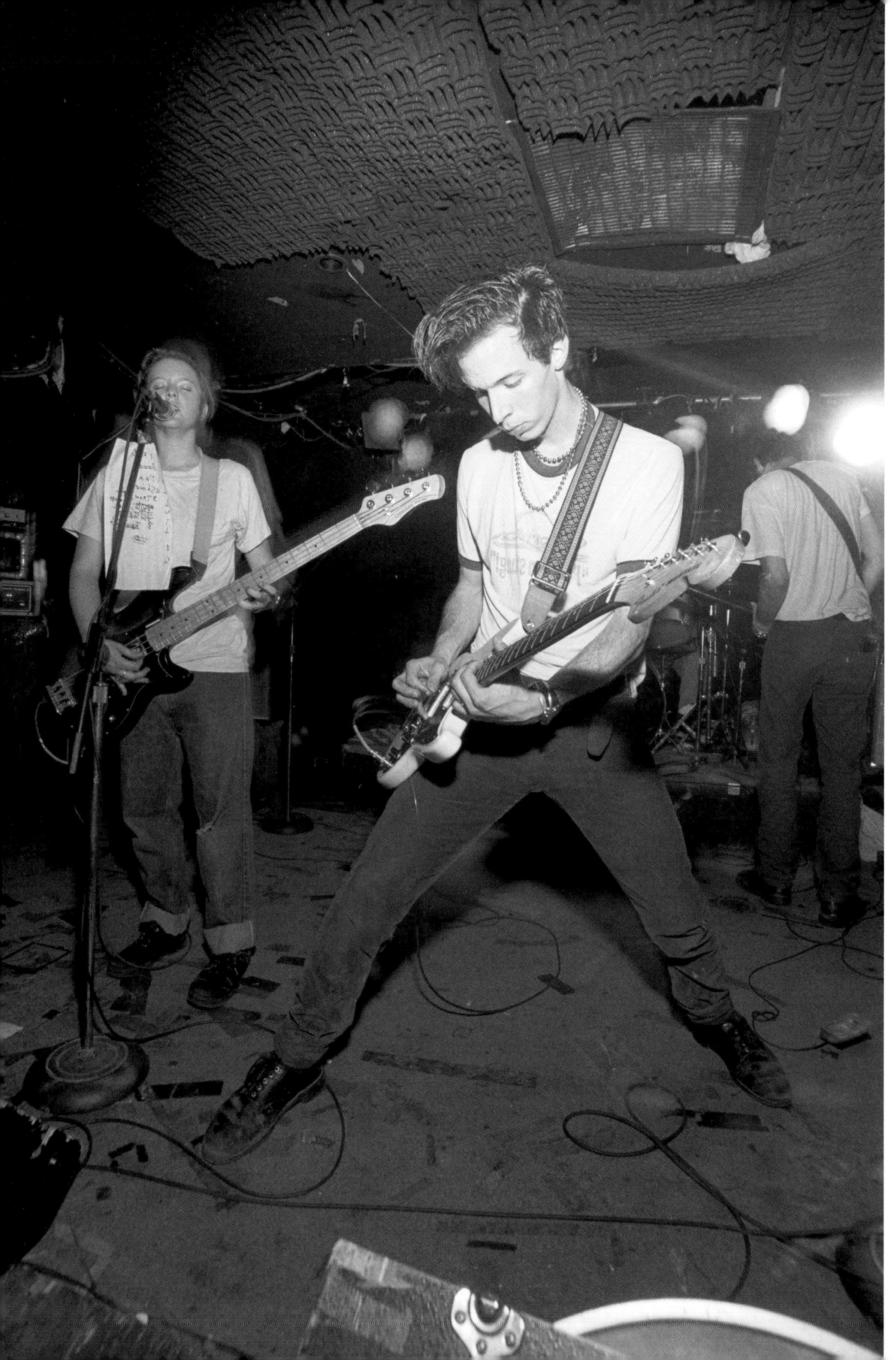

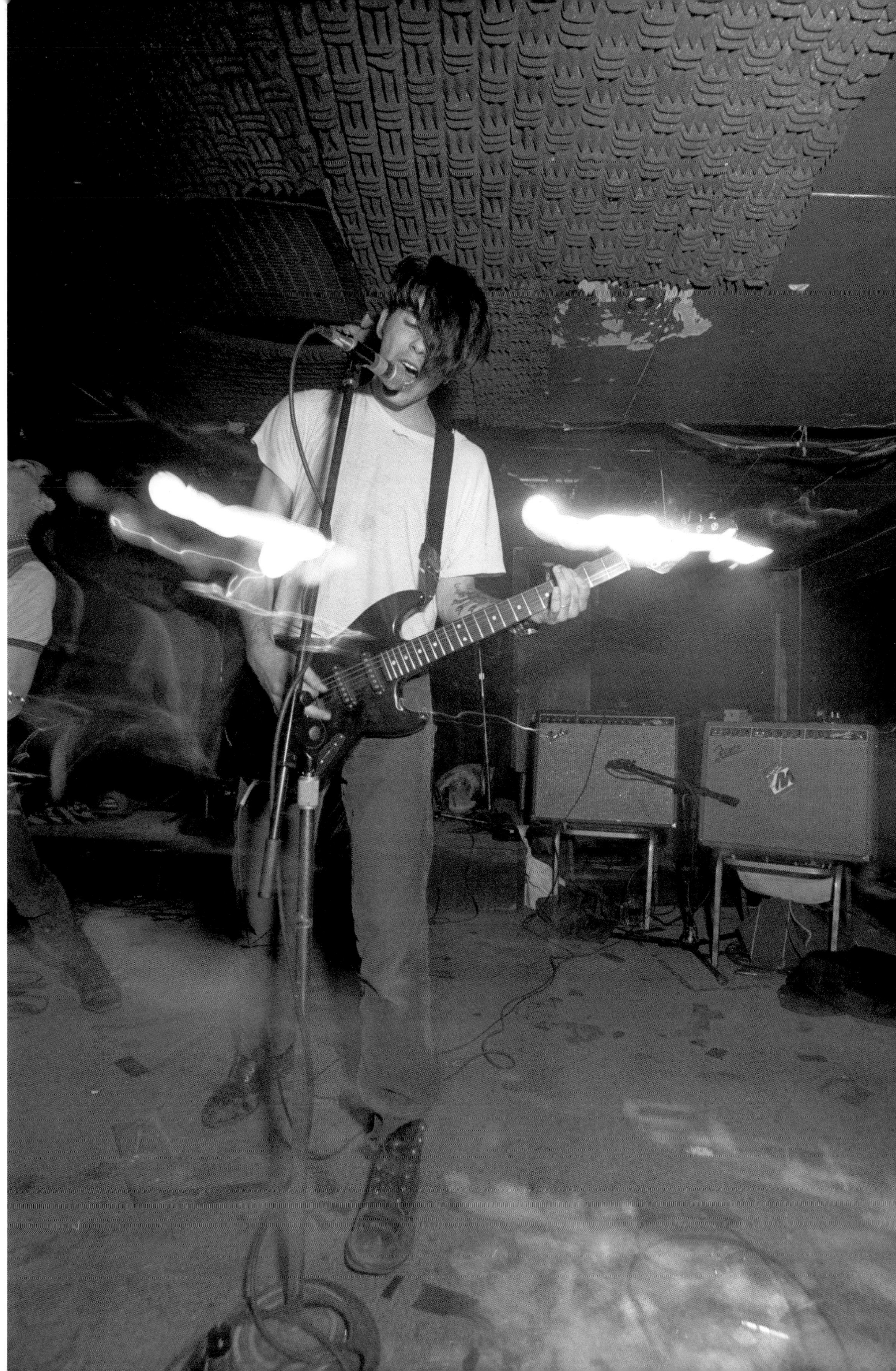

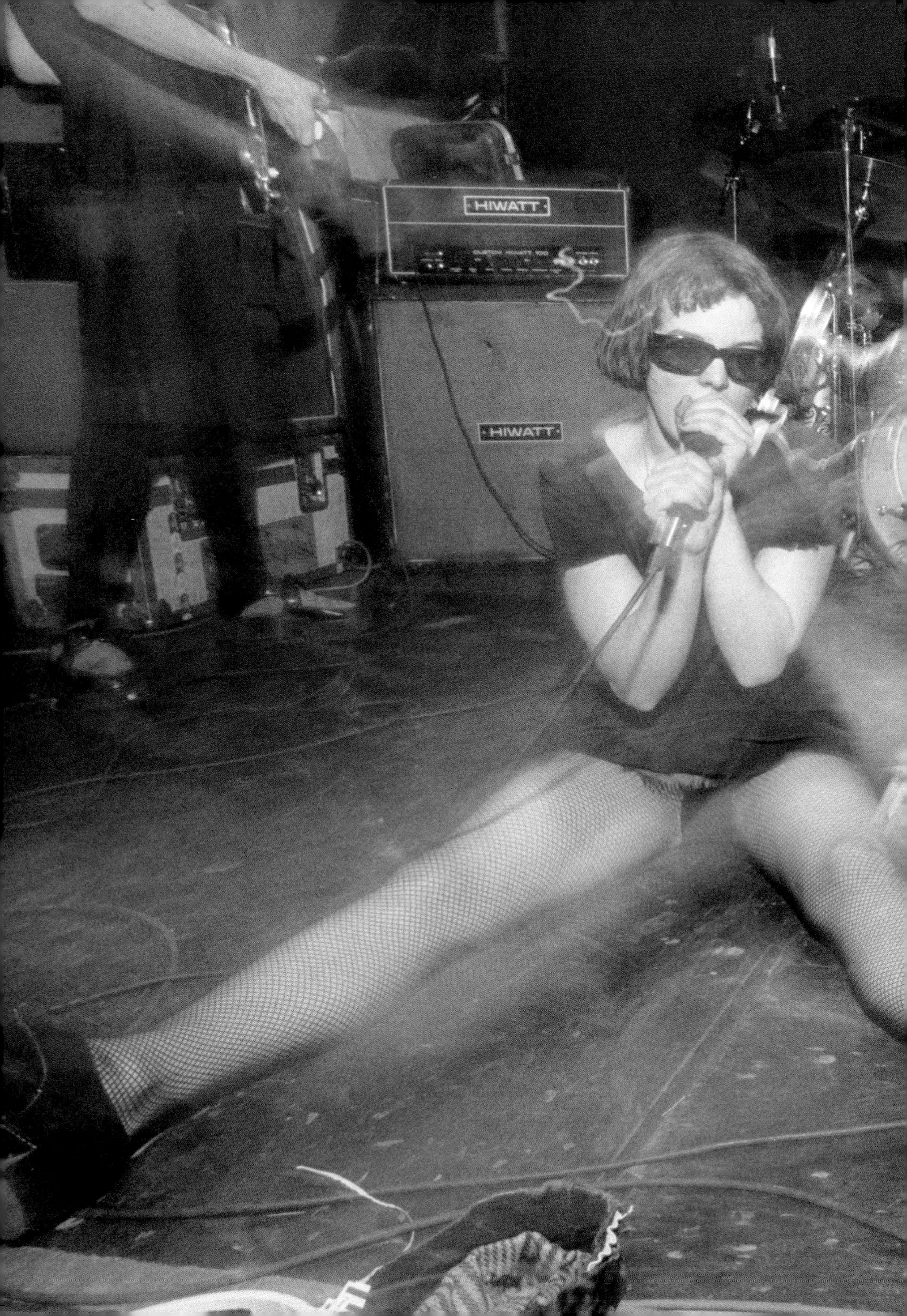
HIWATT
HIWATT

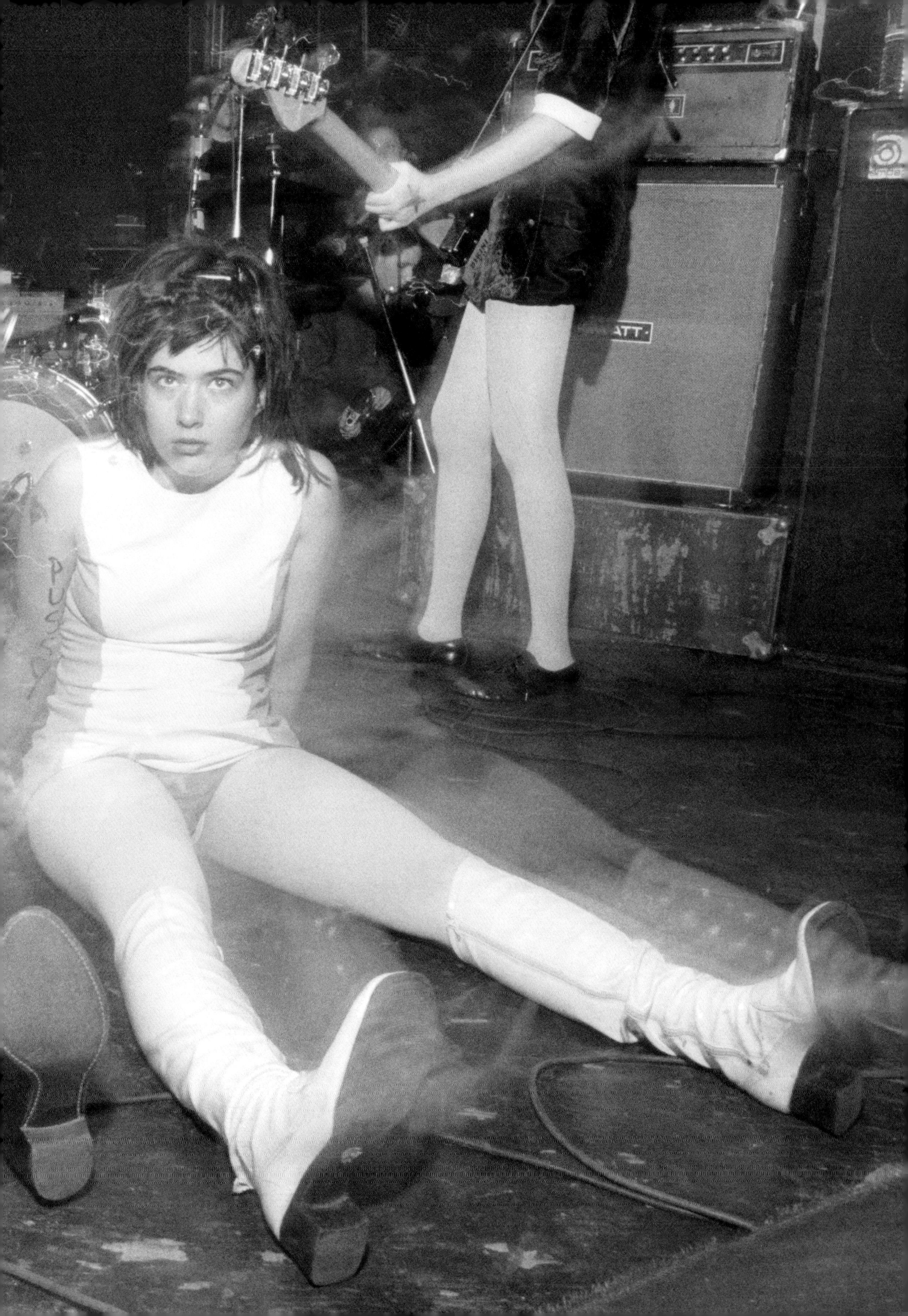

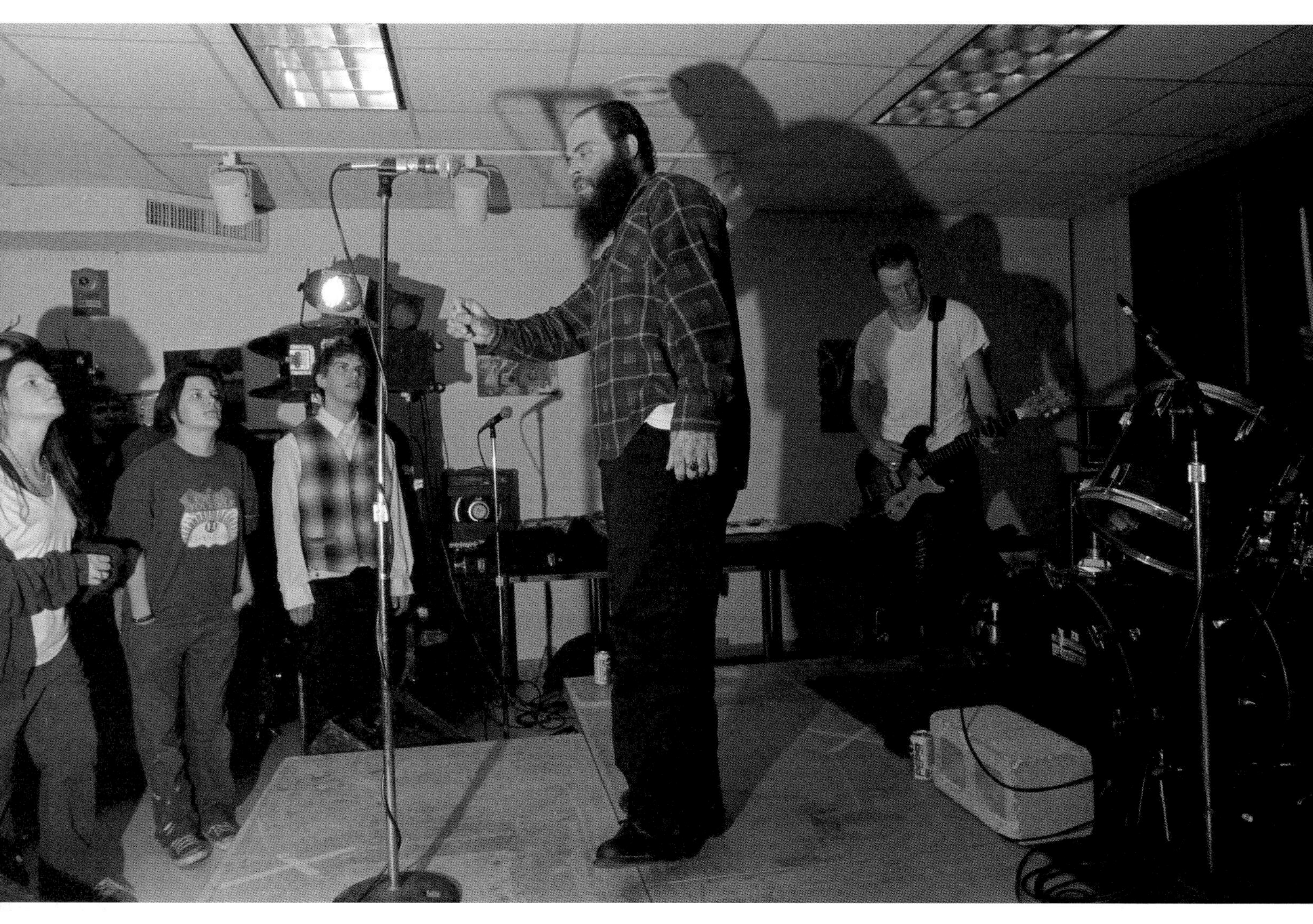

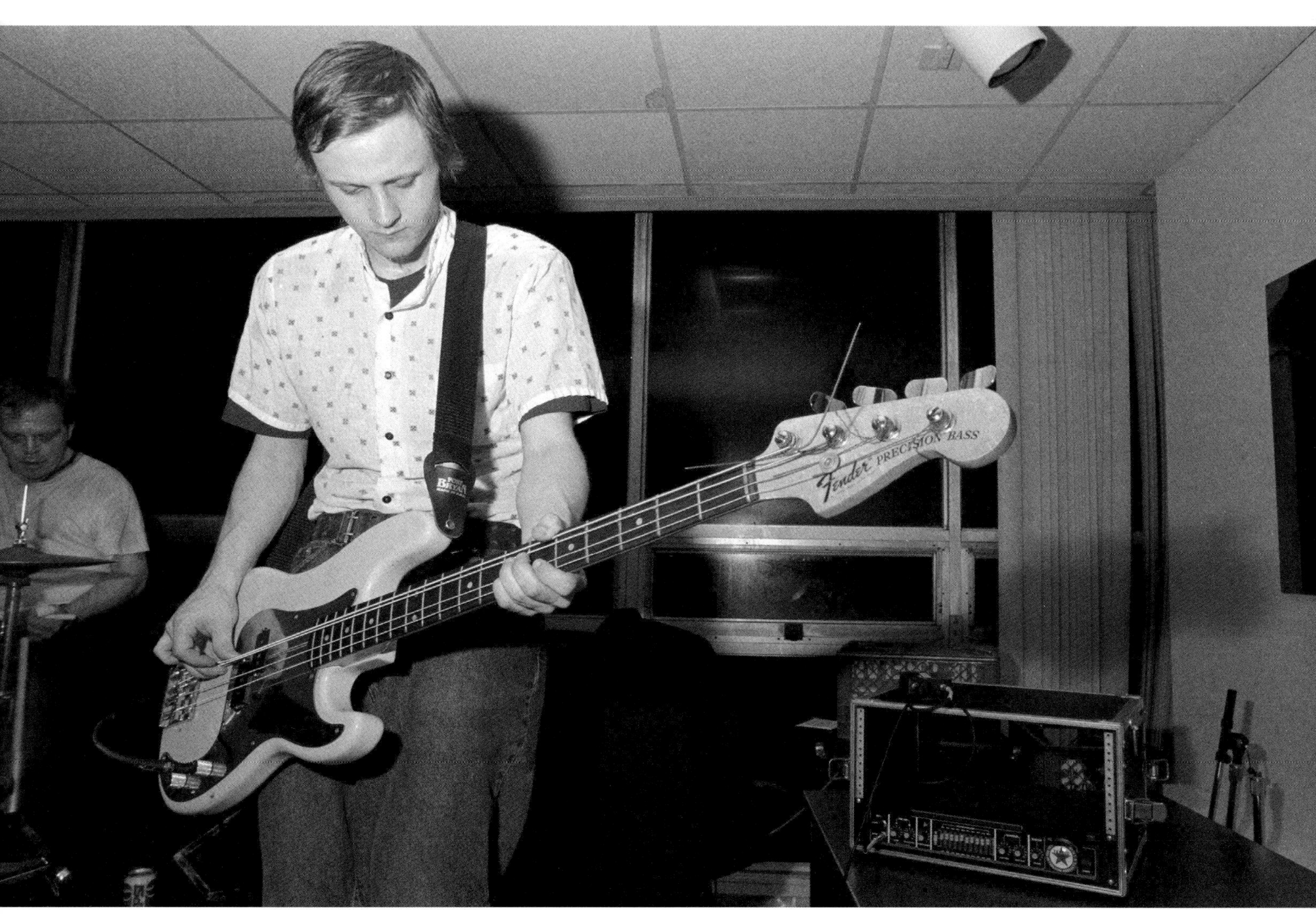
Fender PRECISION BASS

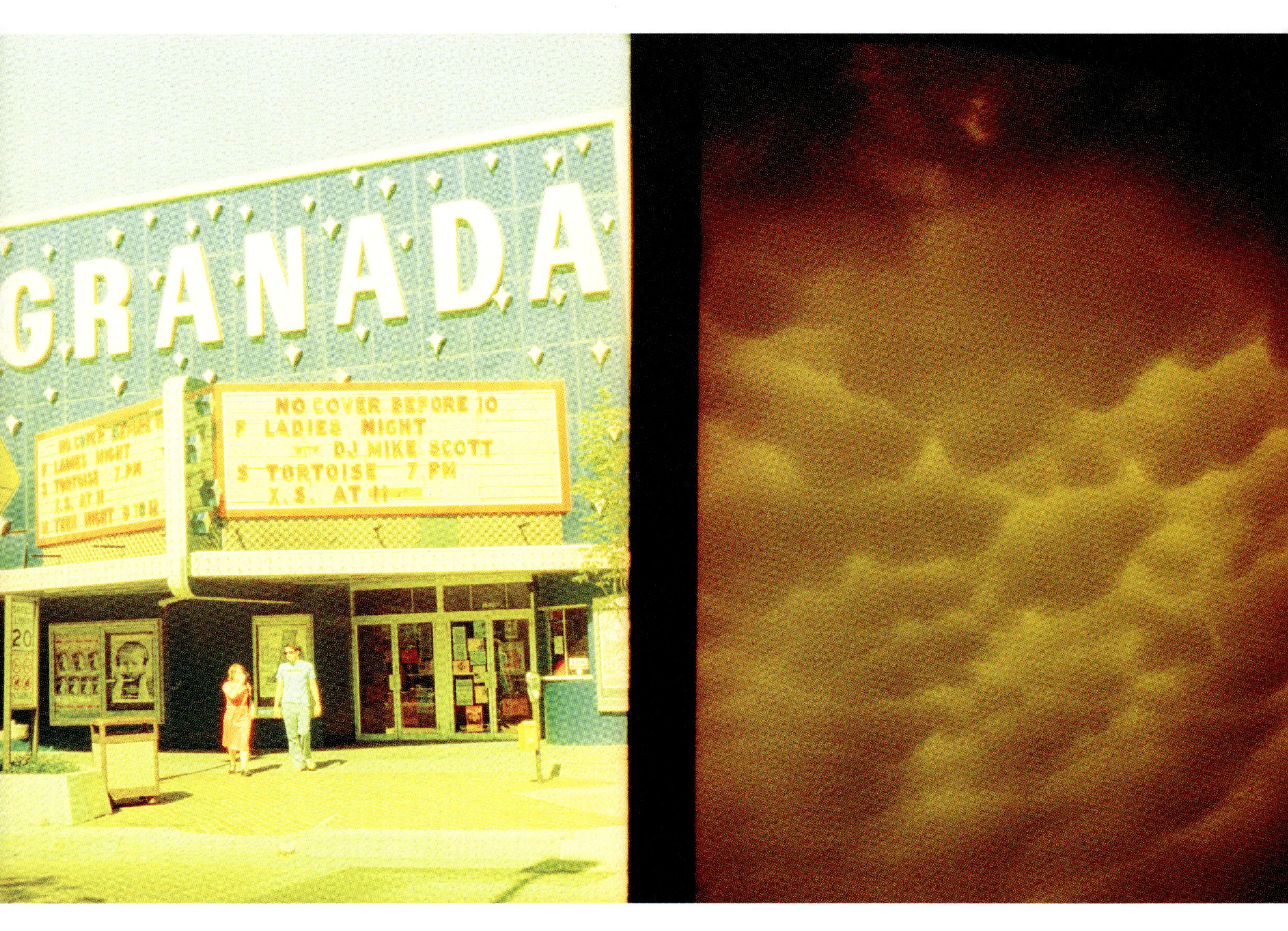
GRANADA
NO COVER BEFORE 10
F LADIES NIGHT
DJ MIKE SCOTT
S TORTOISE 7 PM
X.S. AT 11

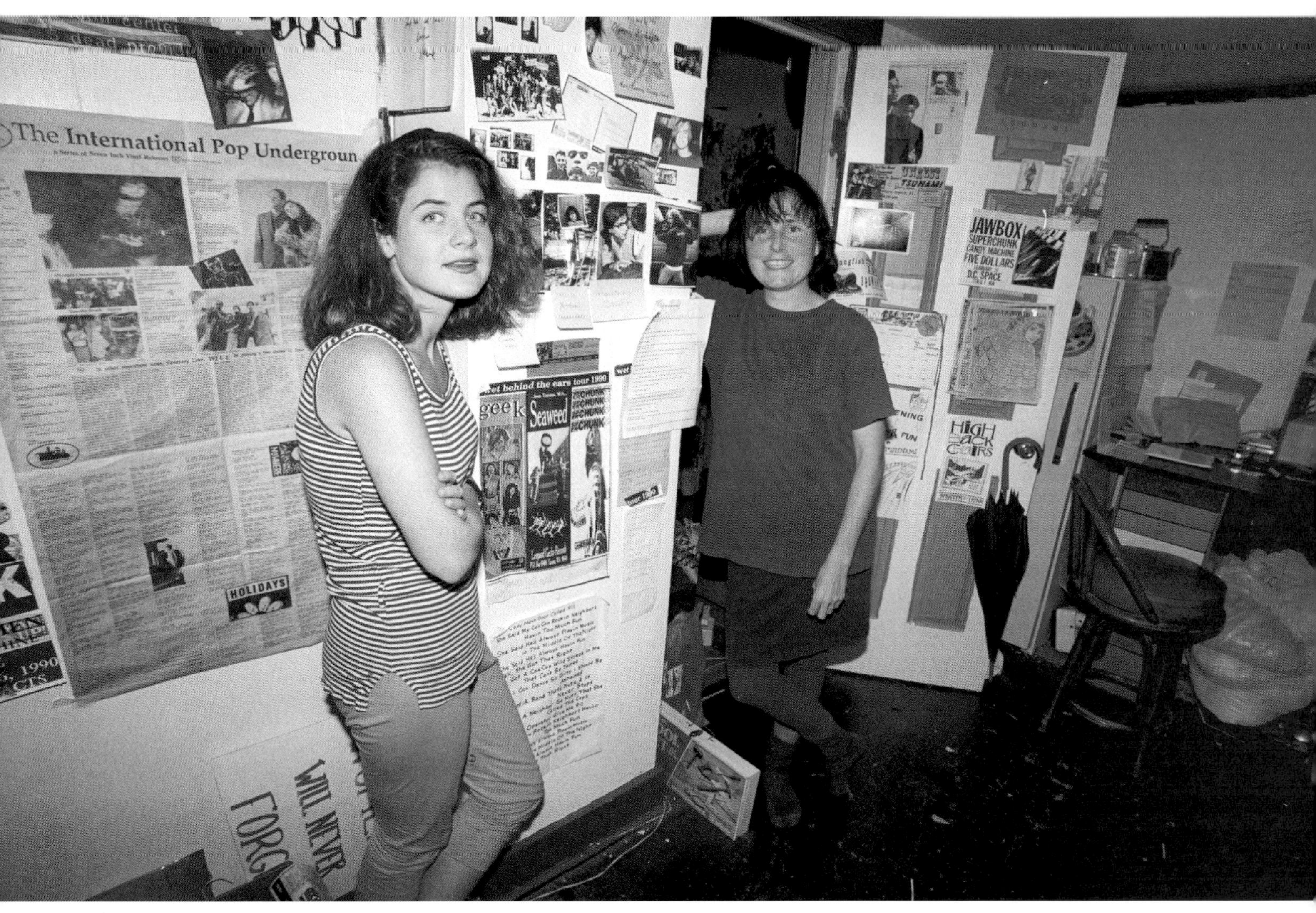

The International Pop Undergroun
wet behind the ears tour 1990
Seaweed
HOLIDAYS
WILL NEVER
TSUNAMI
JAWBOX
SUPERCHUNK
CANDY MACHINE
FIVE DOLLARS
D.C. SPACE

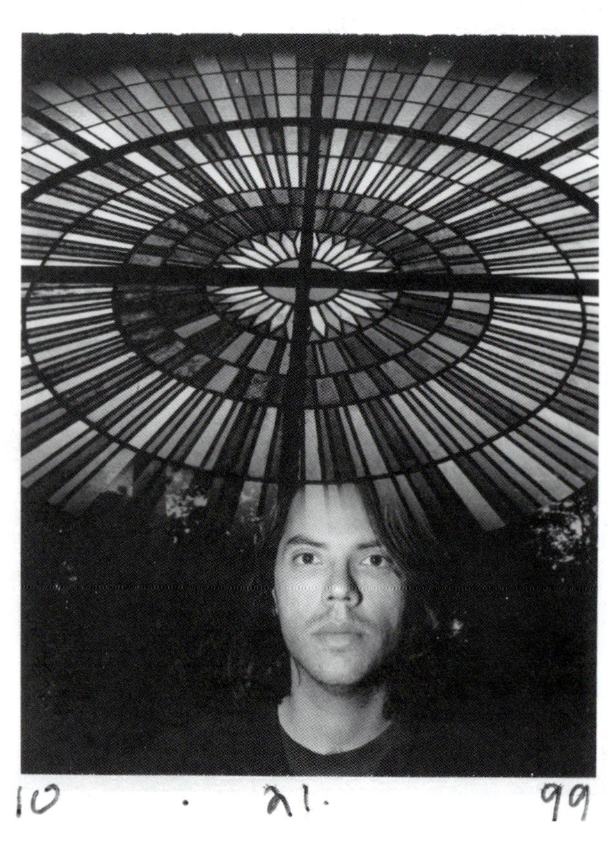
10 · 21 · 99

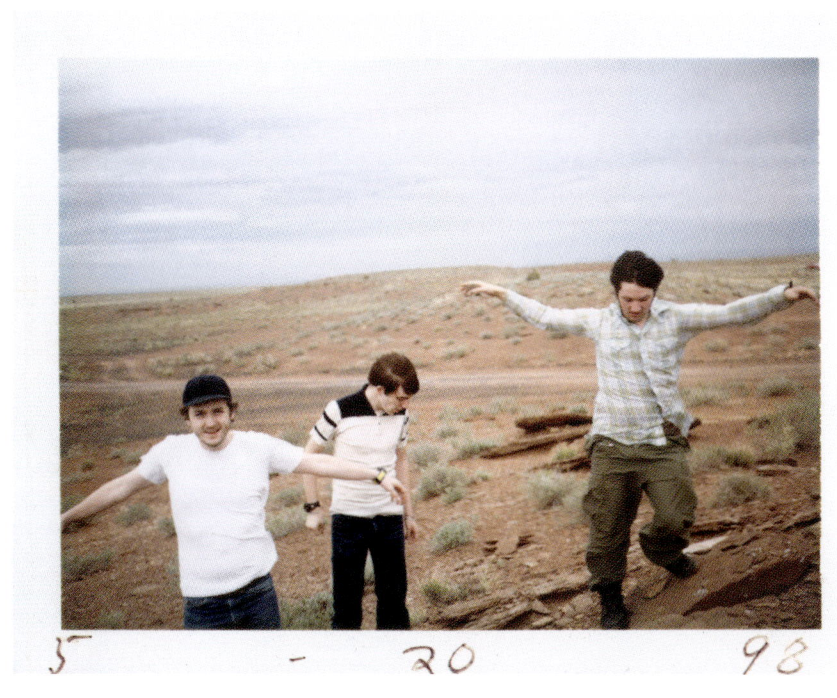
5 - 20 98

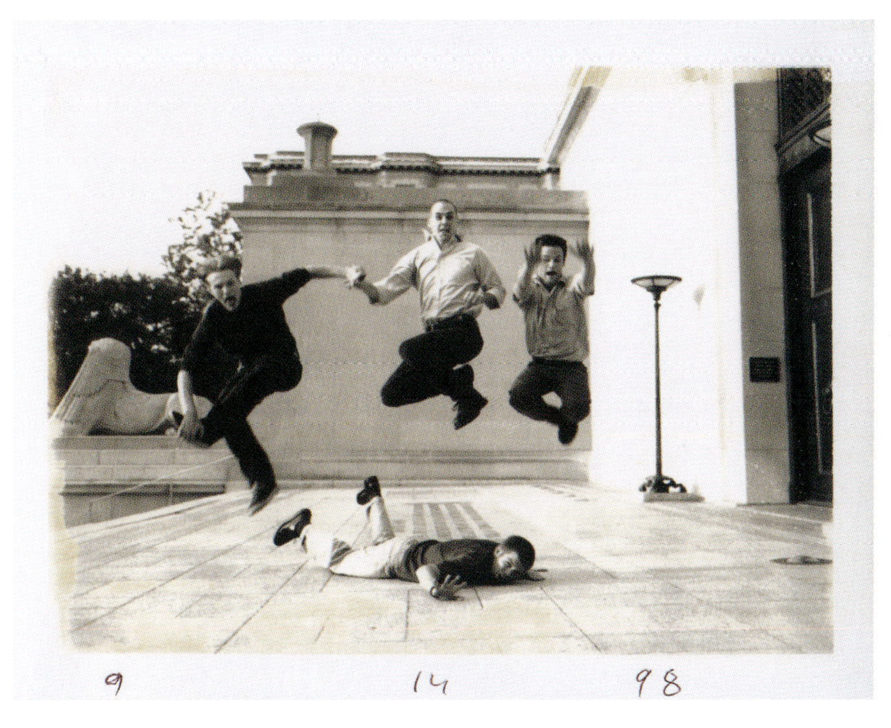
9 14 98

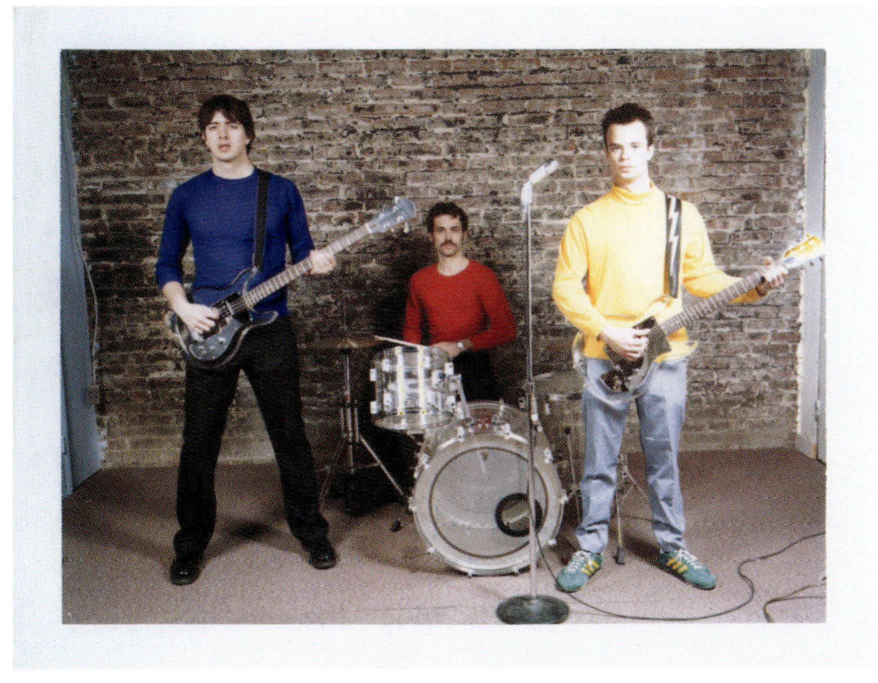

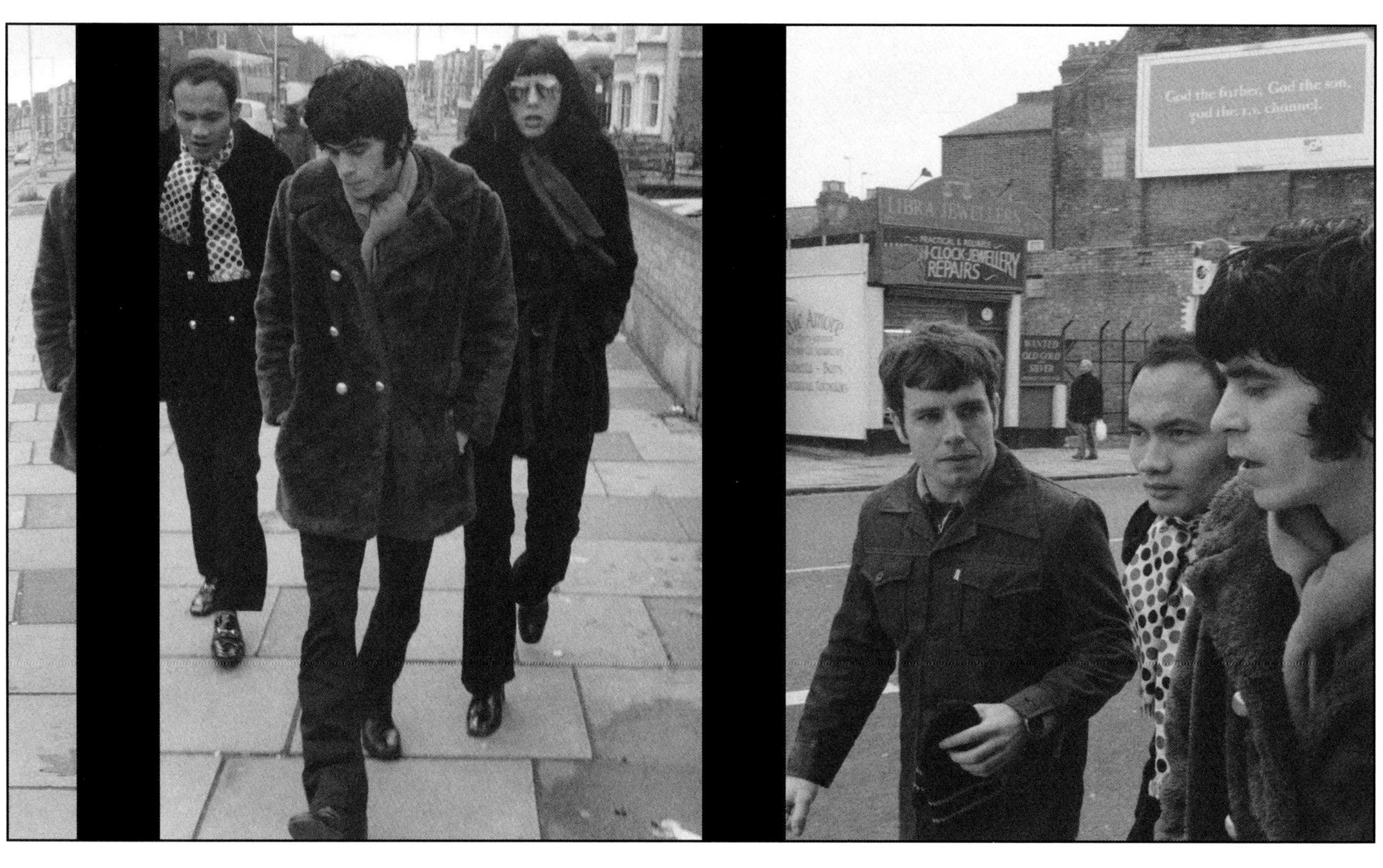
CLOCK-JEWELLERY
REPAIRS

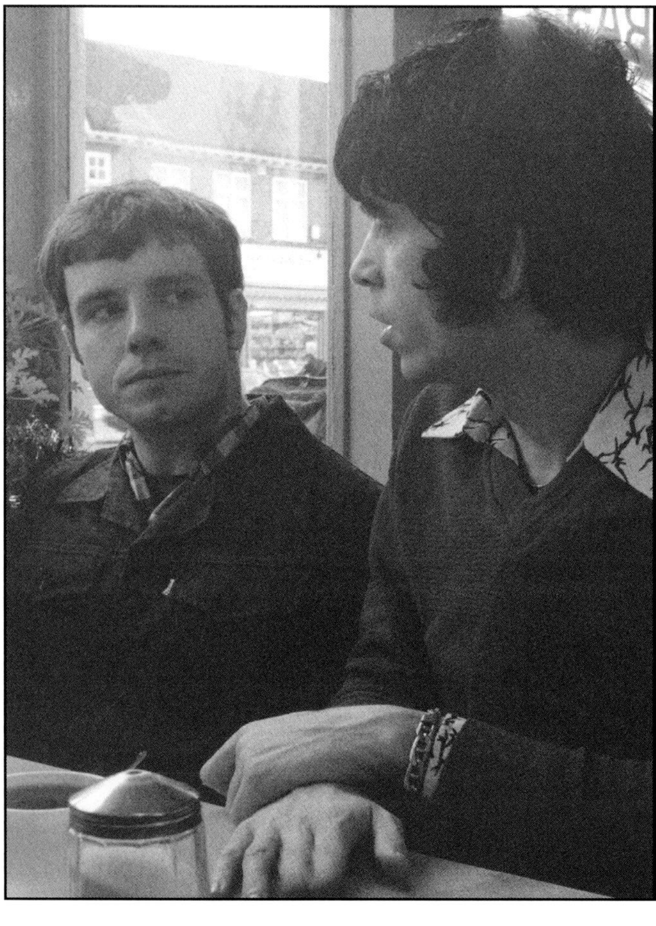

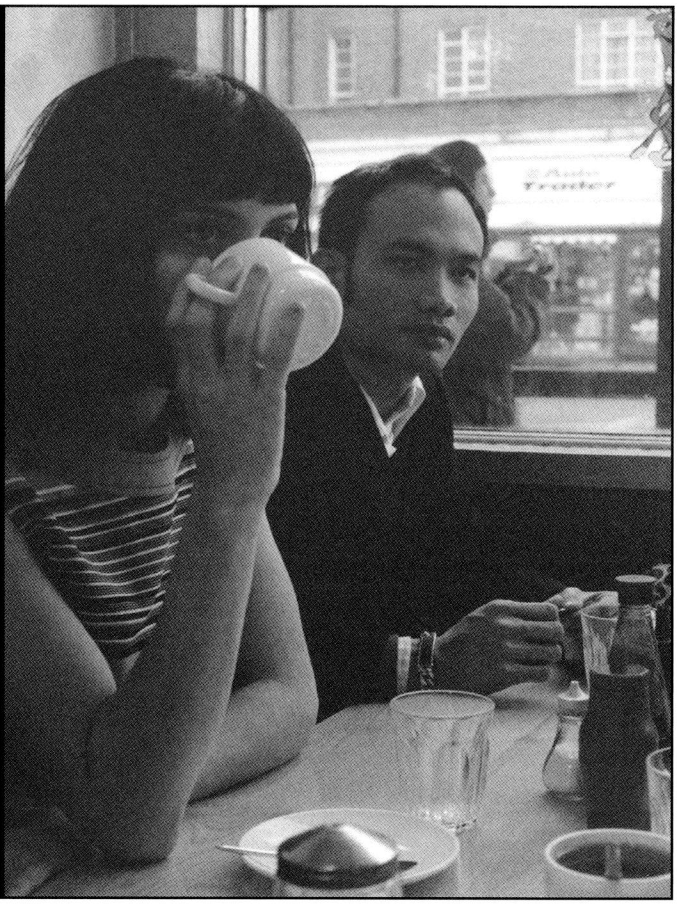

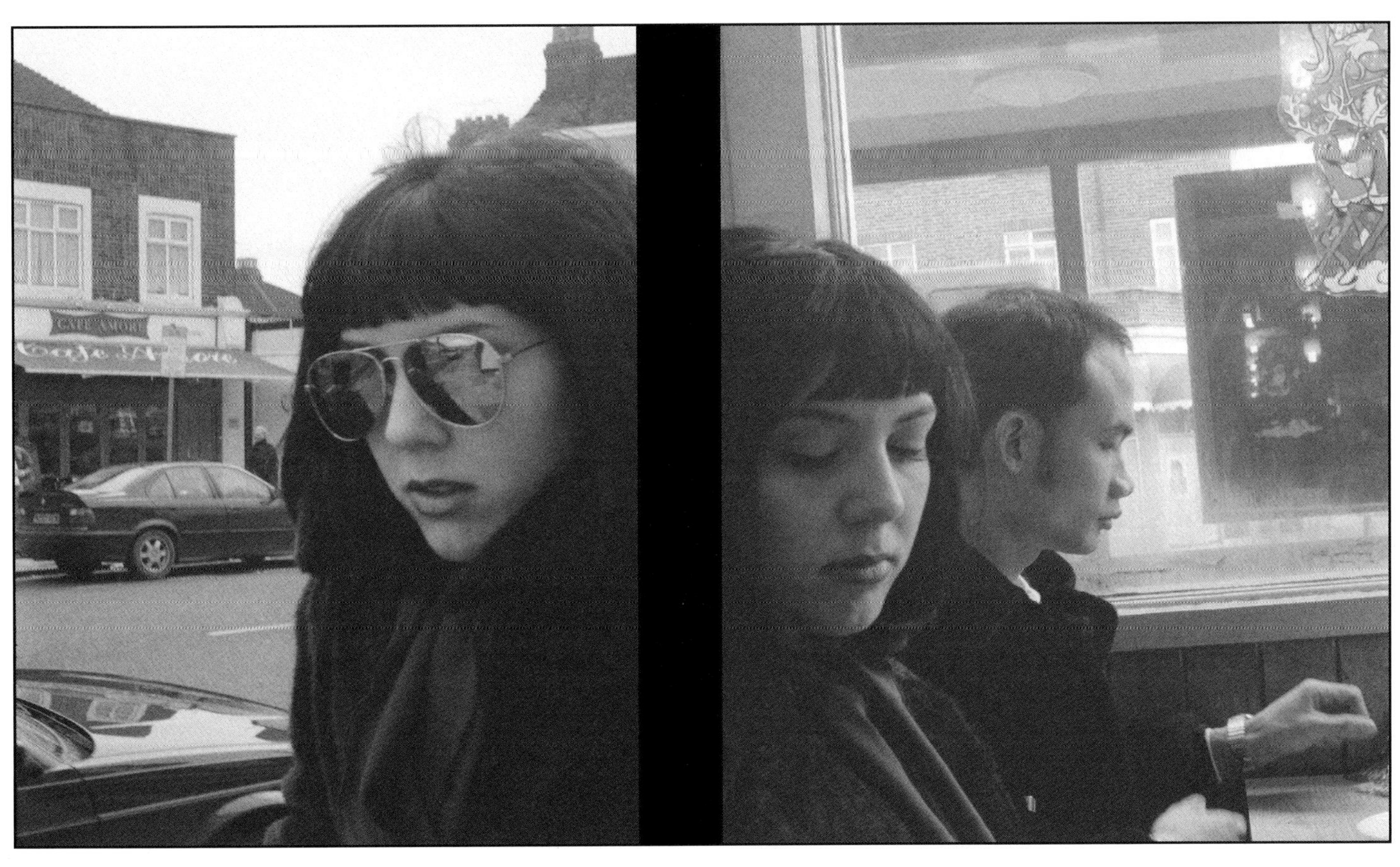

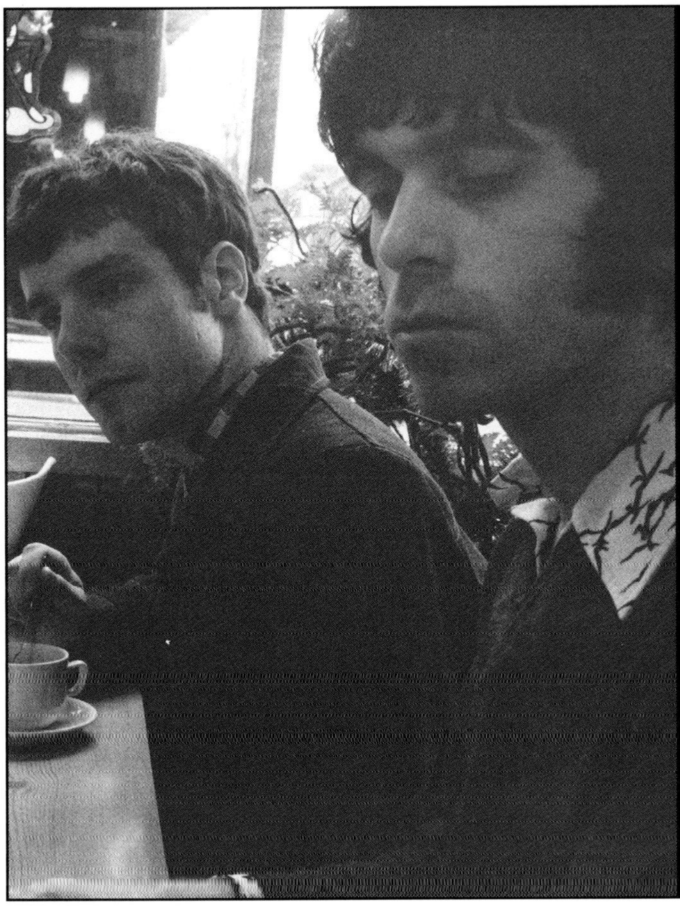

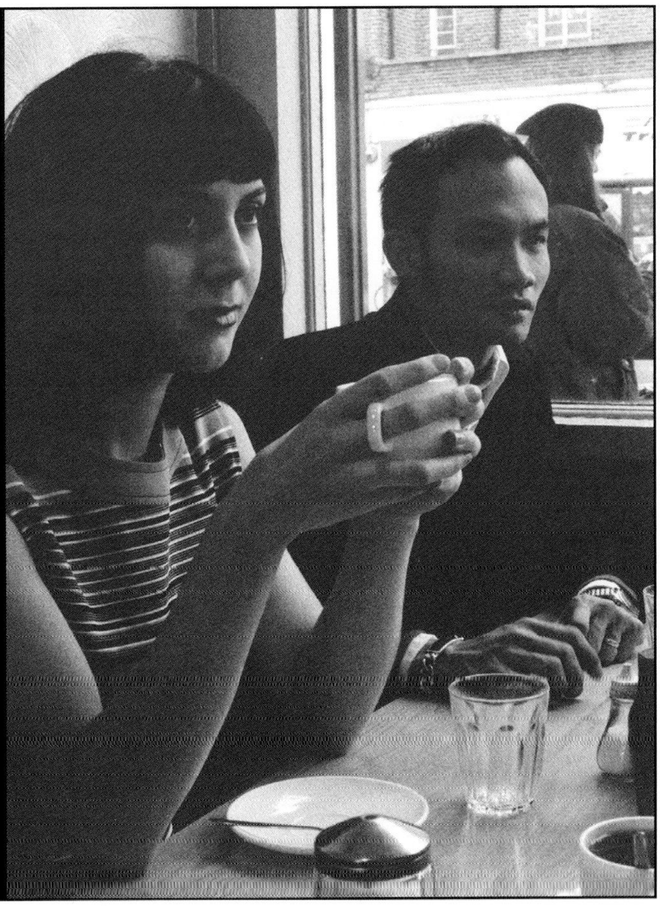

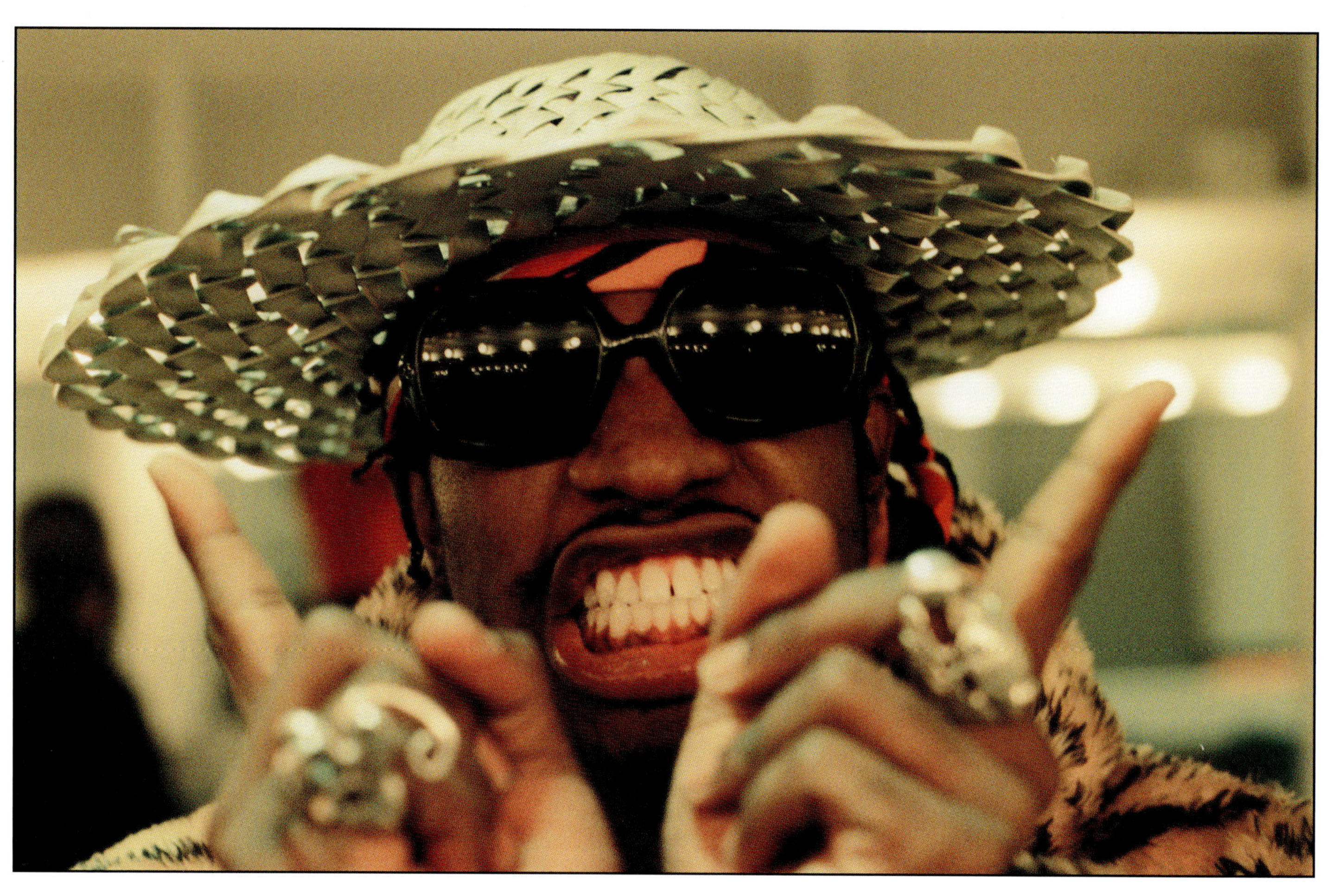

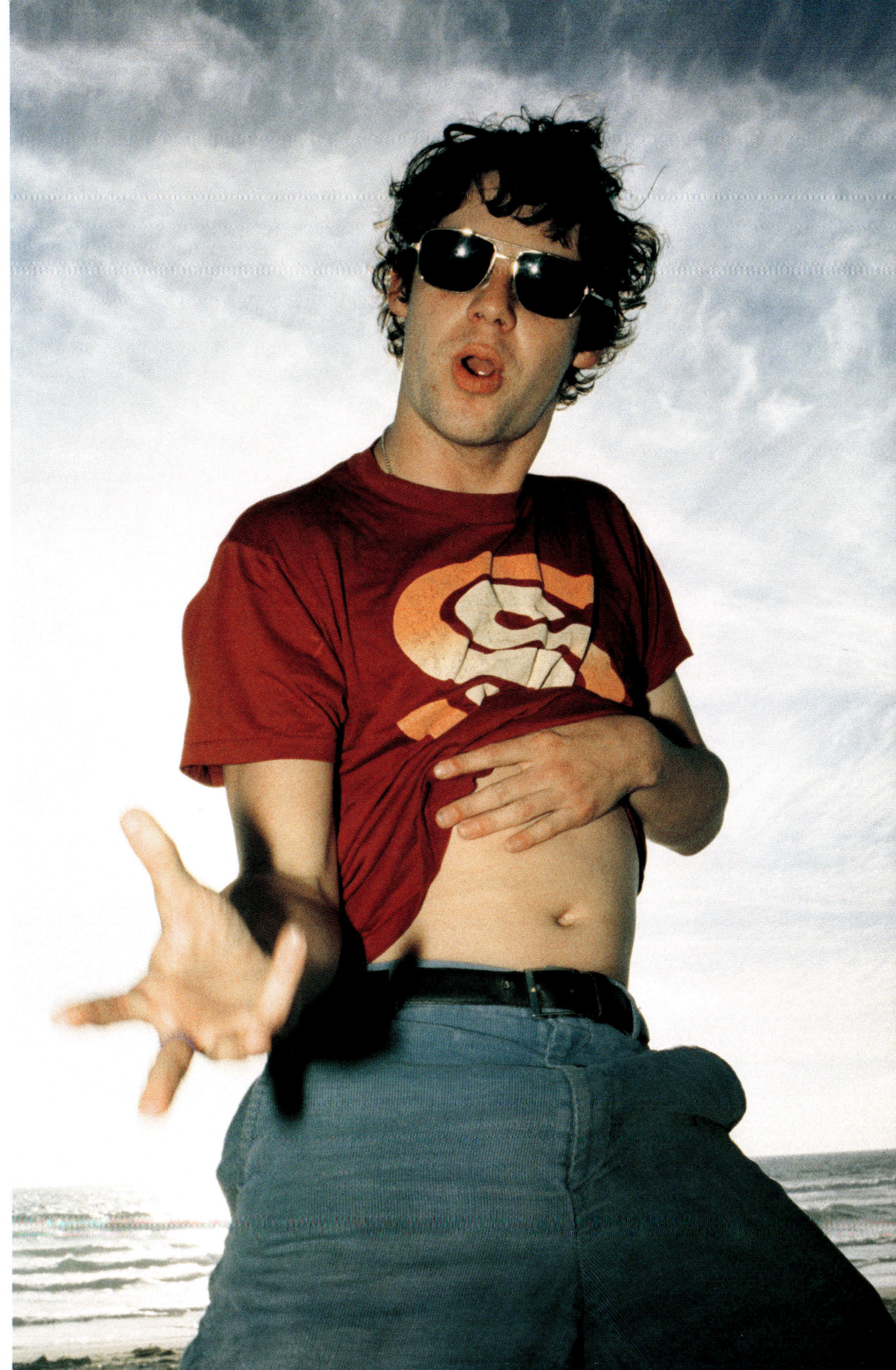

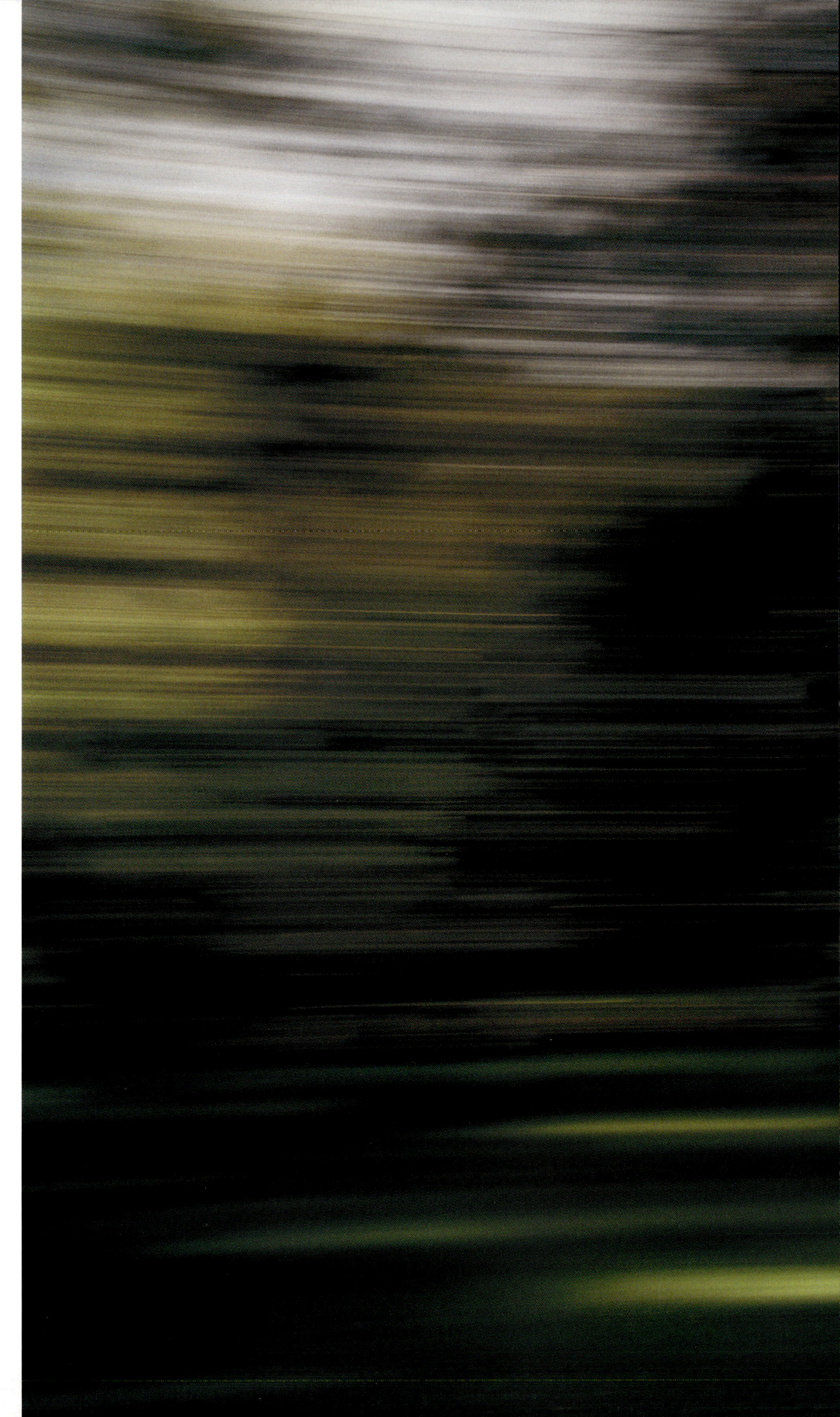

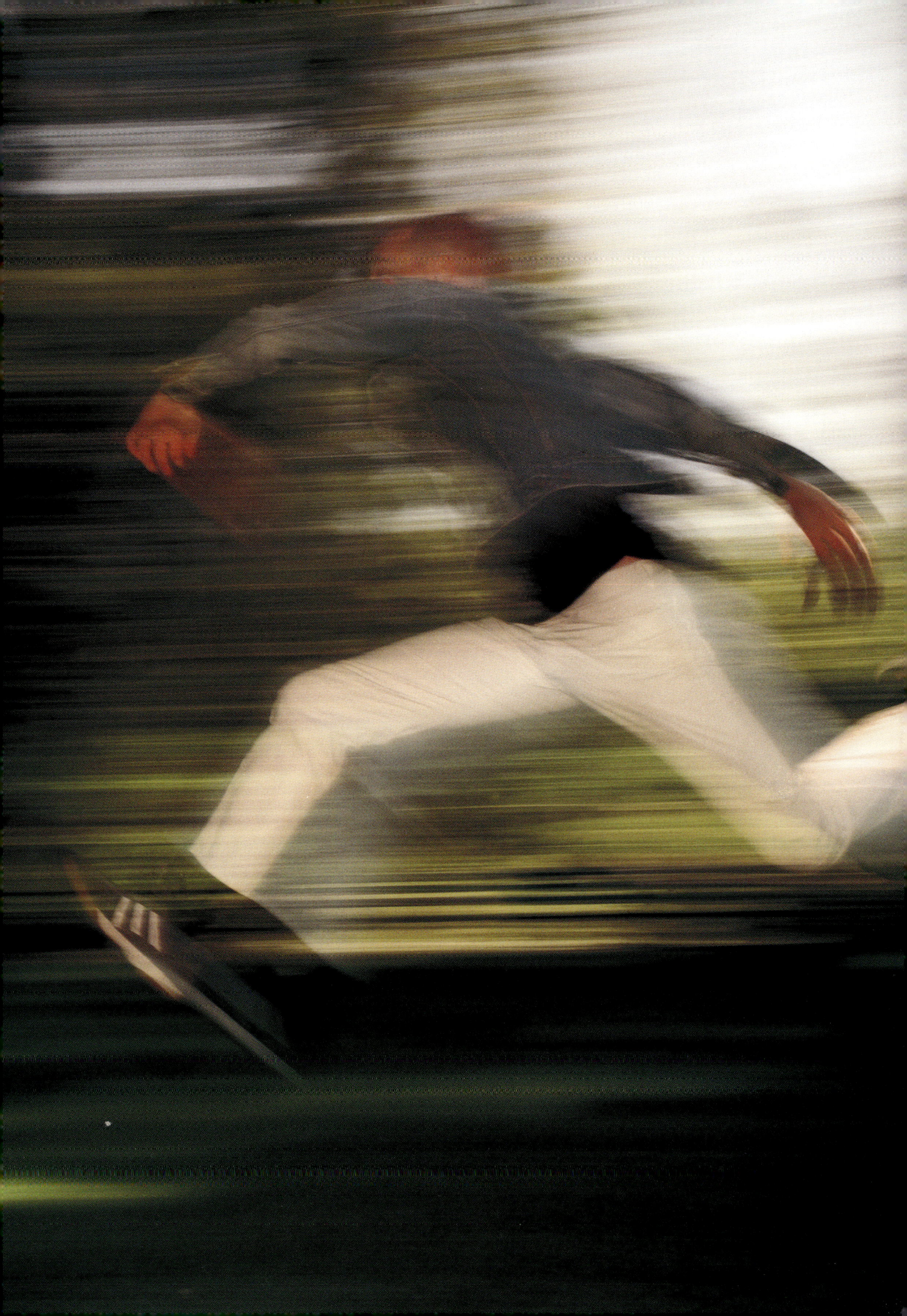

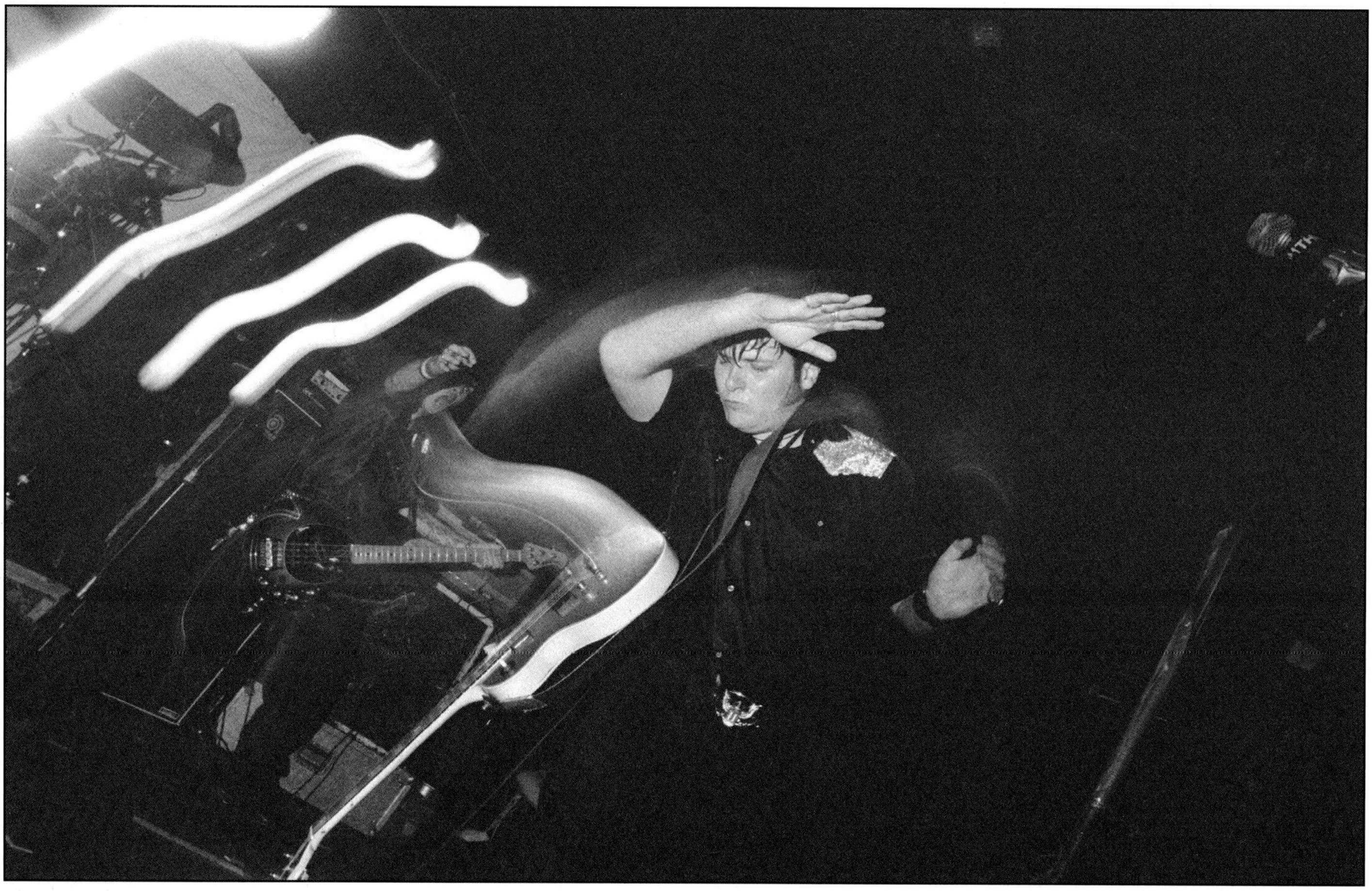

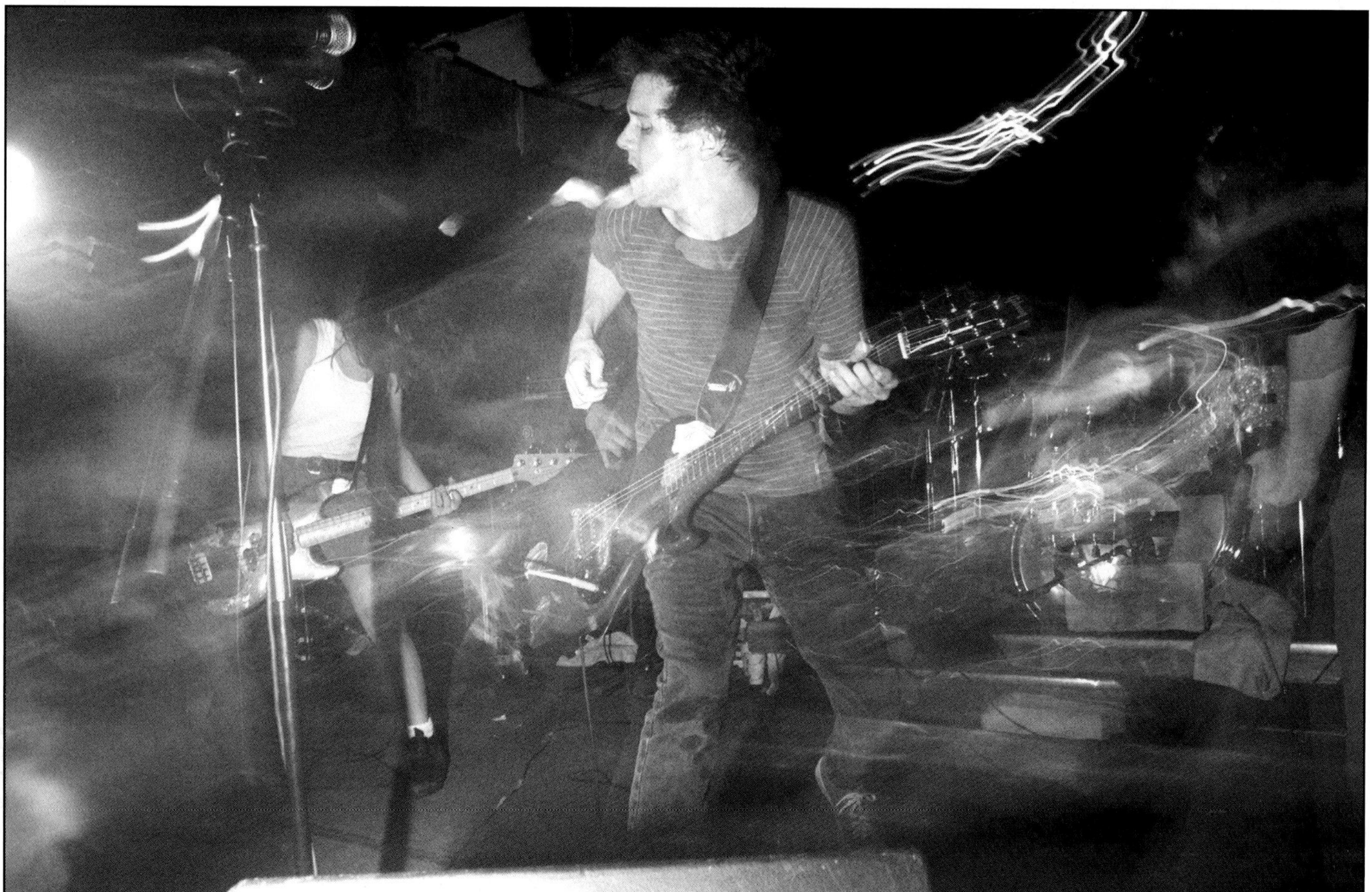

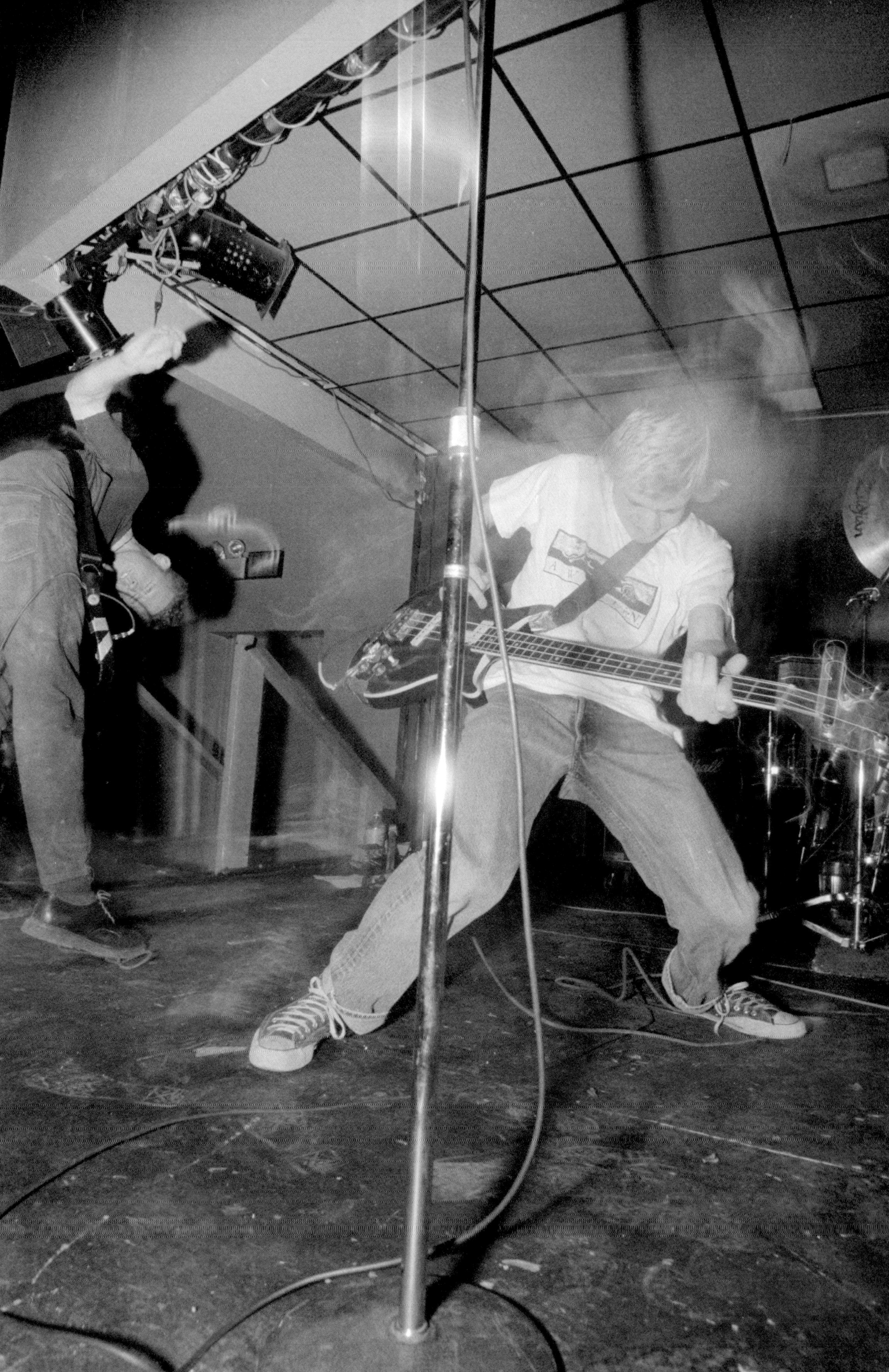

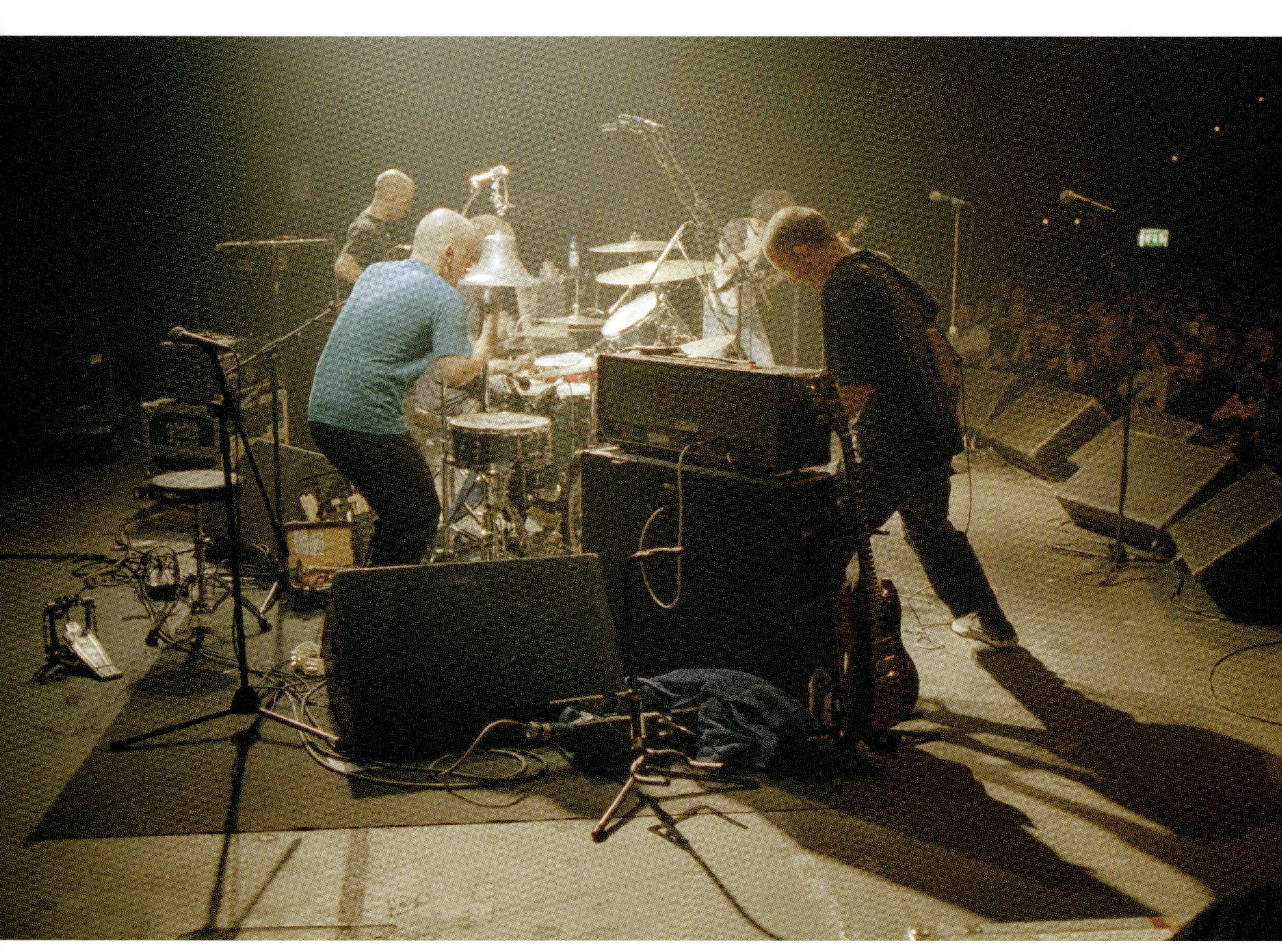

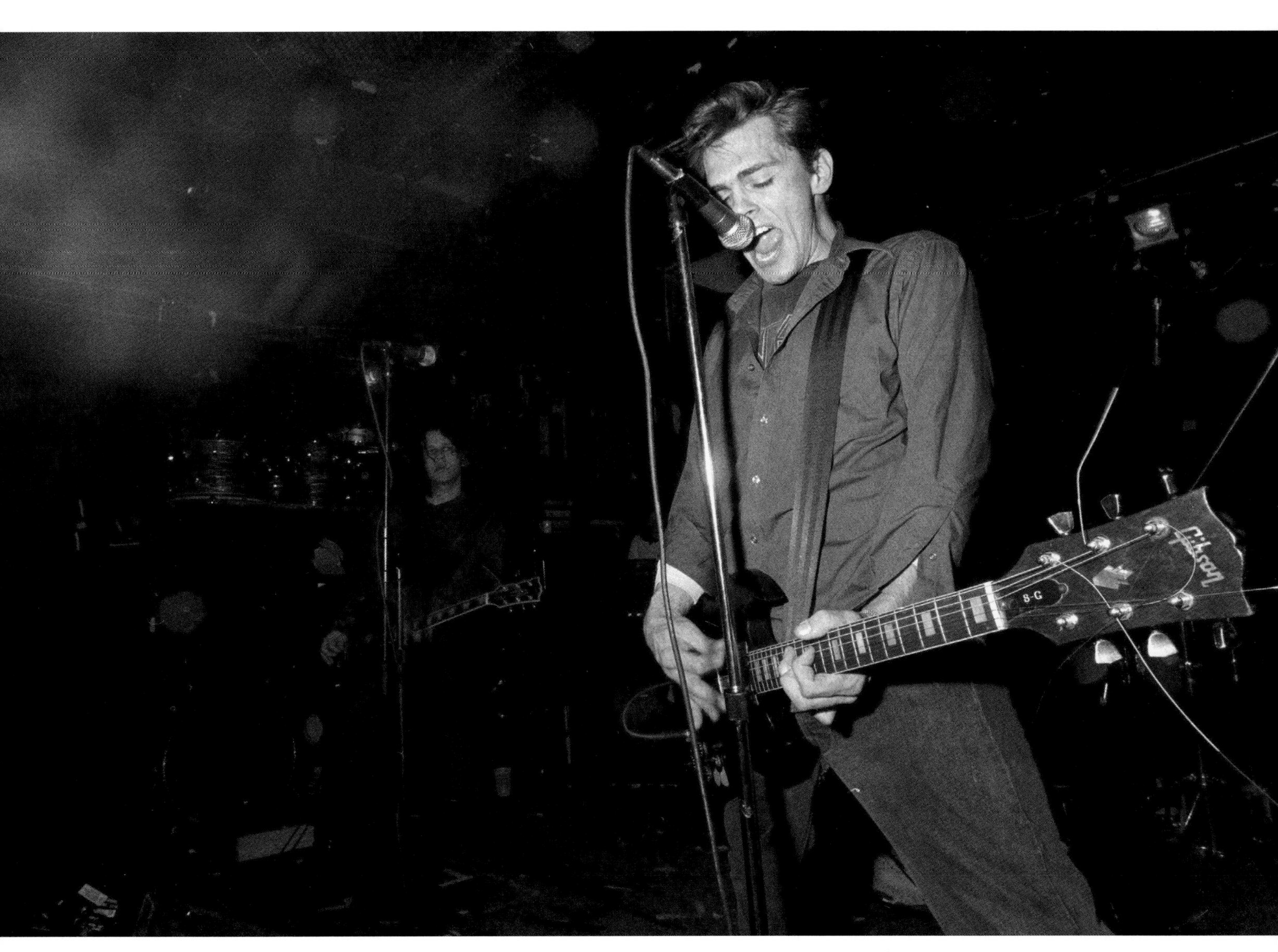
Gibson
S-G

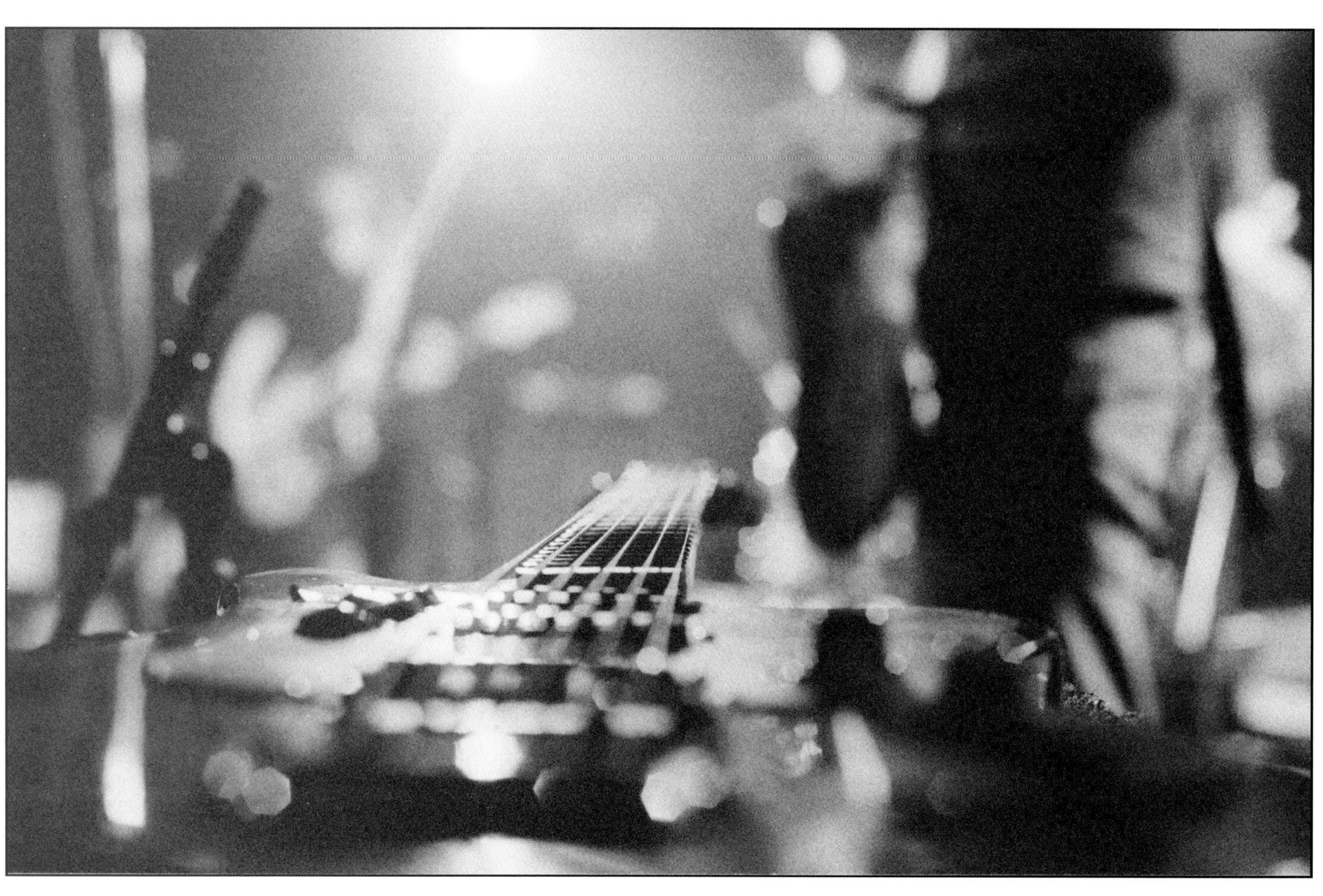

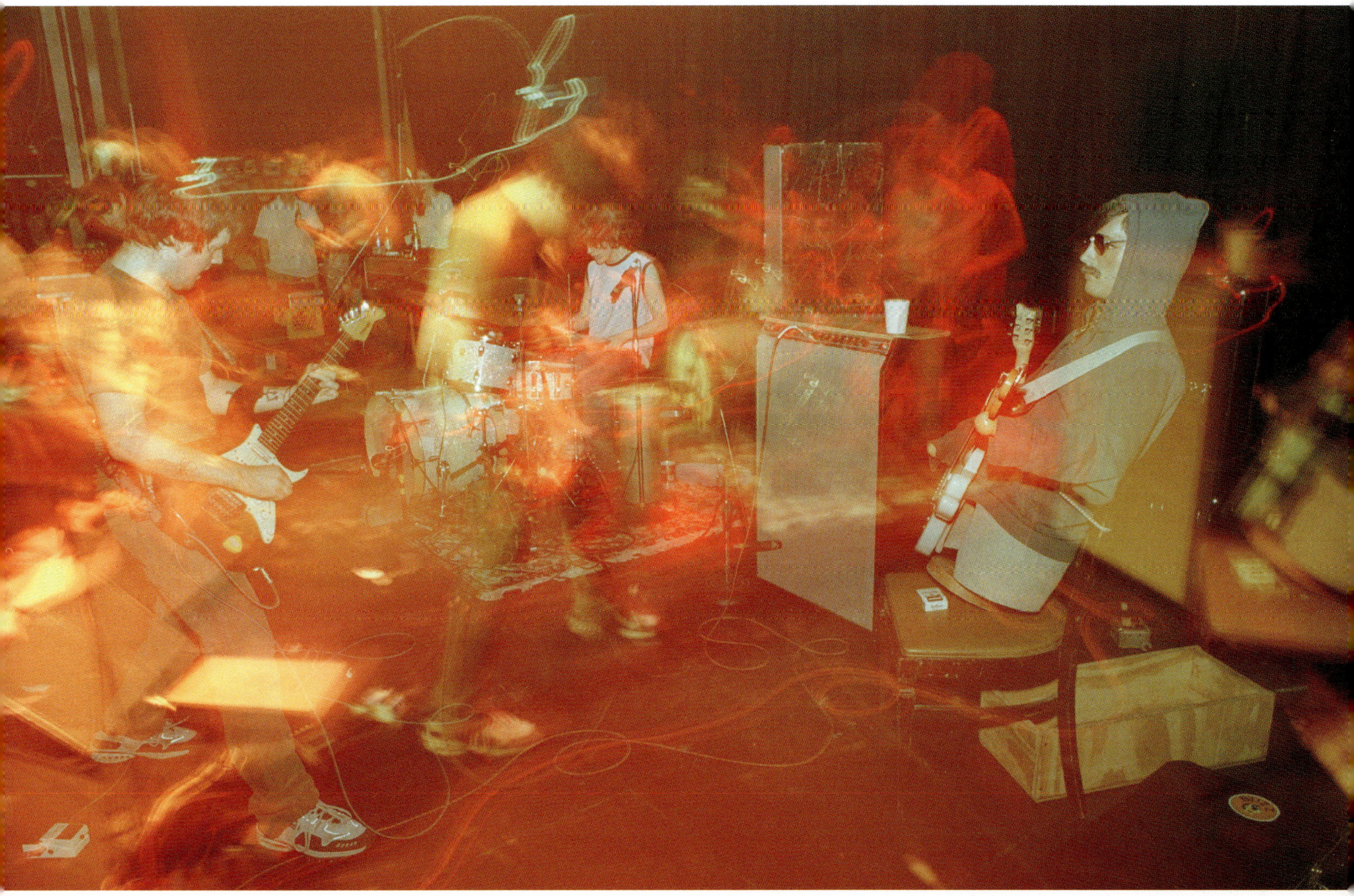

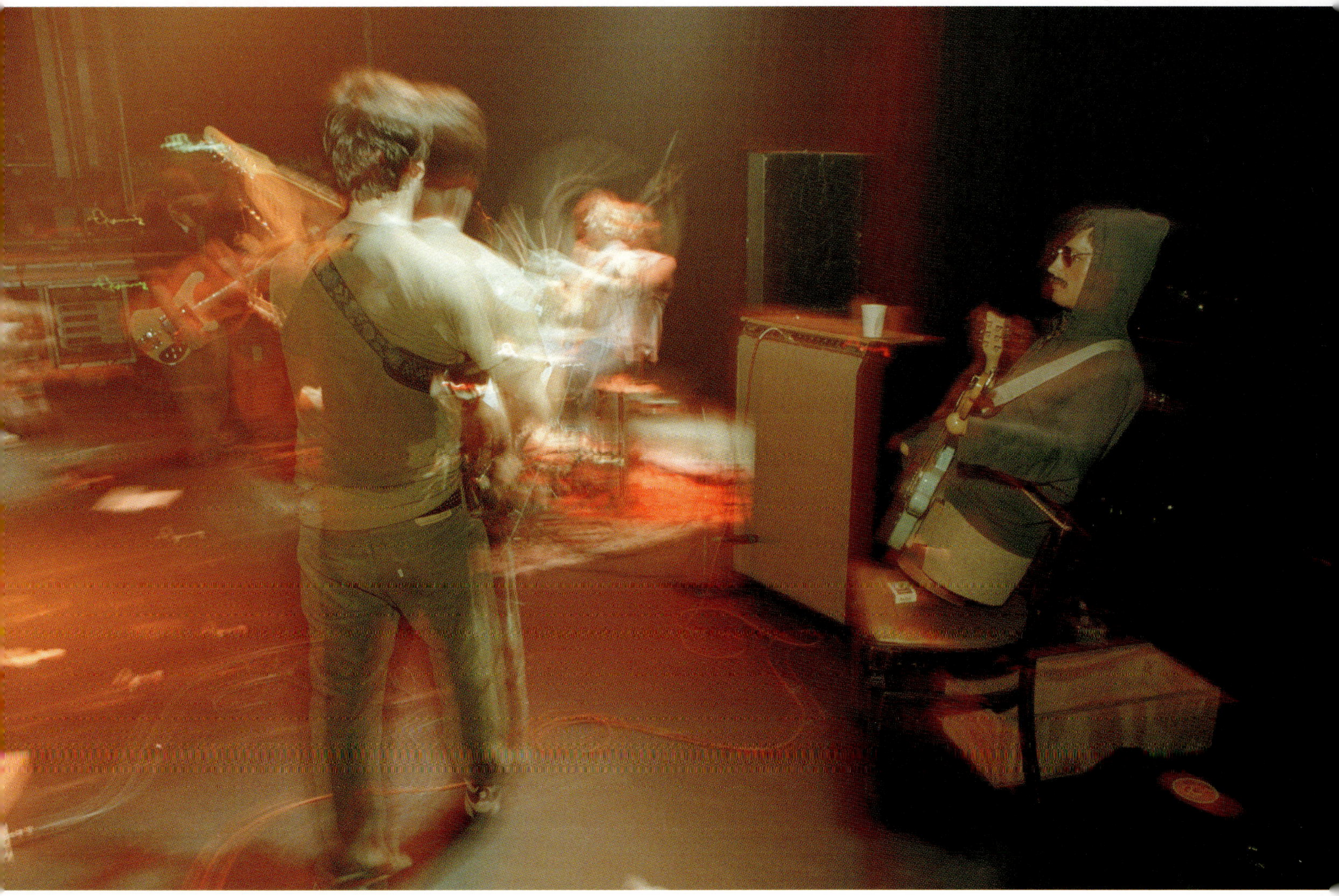

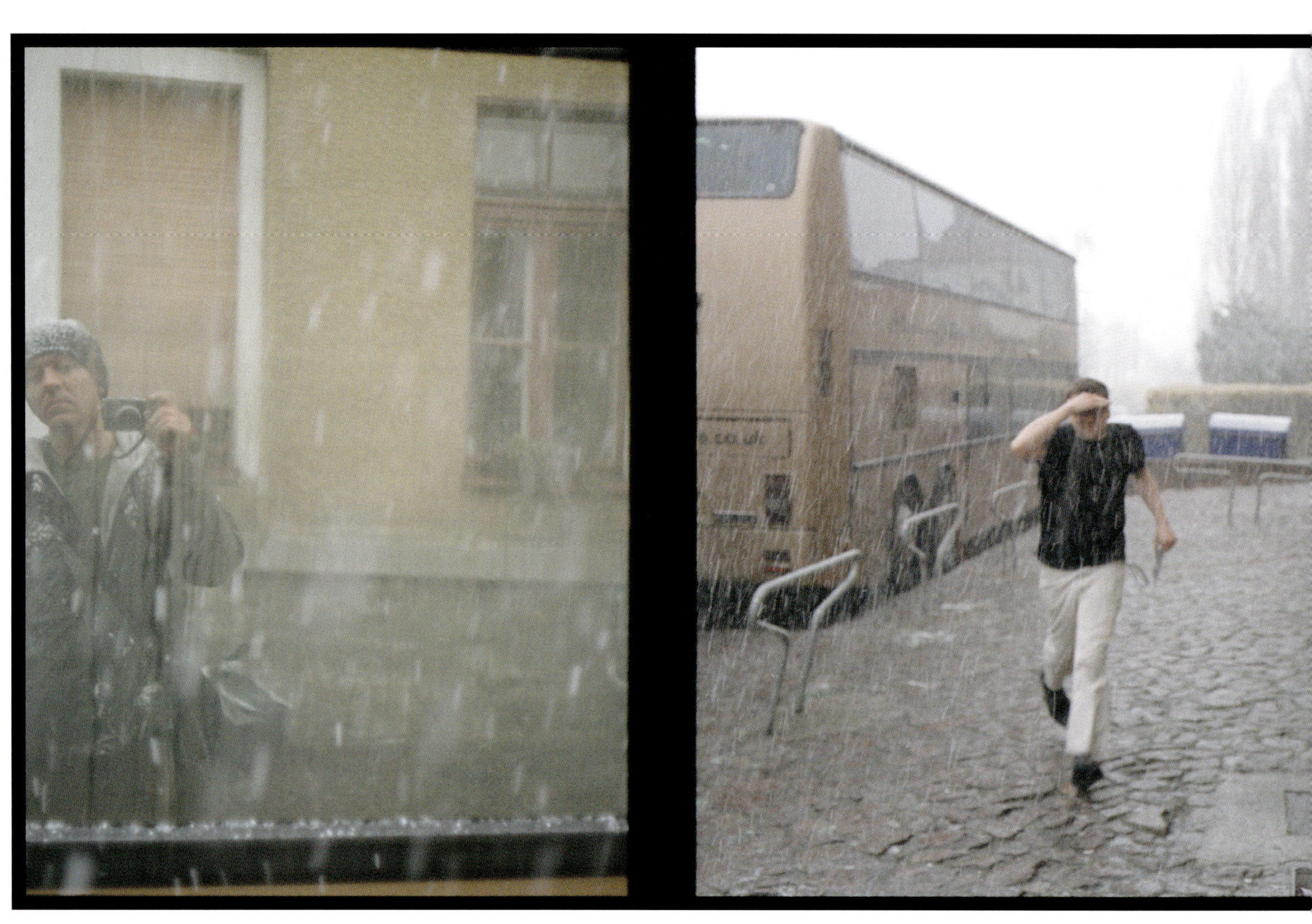

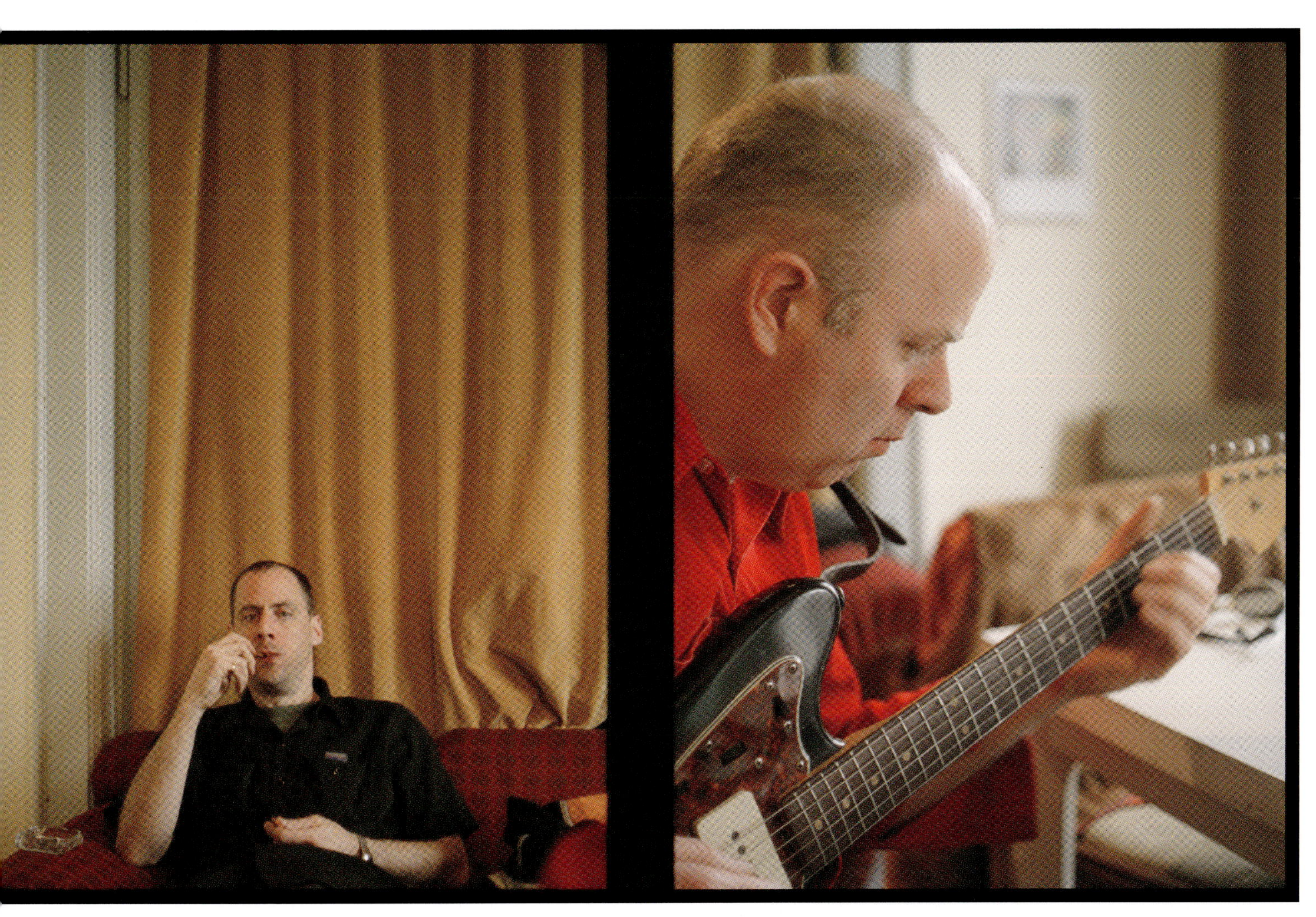

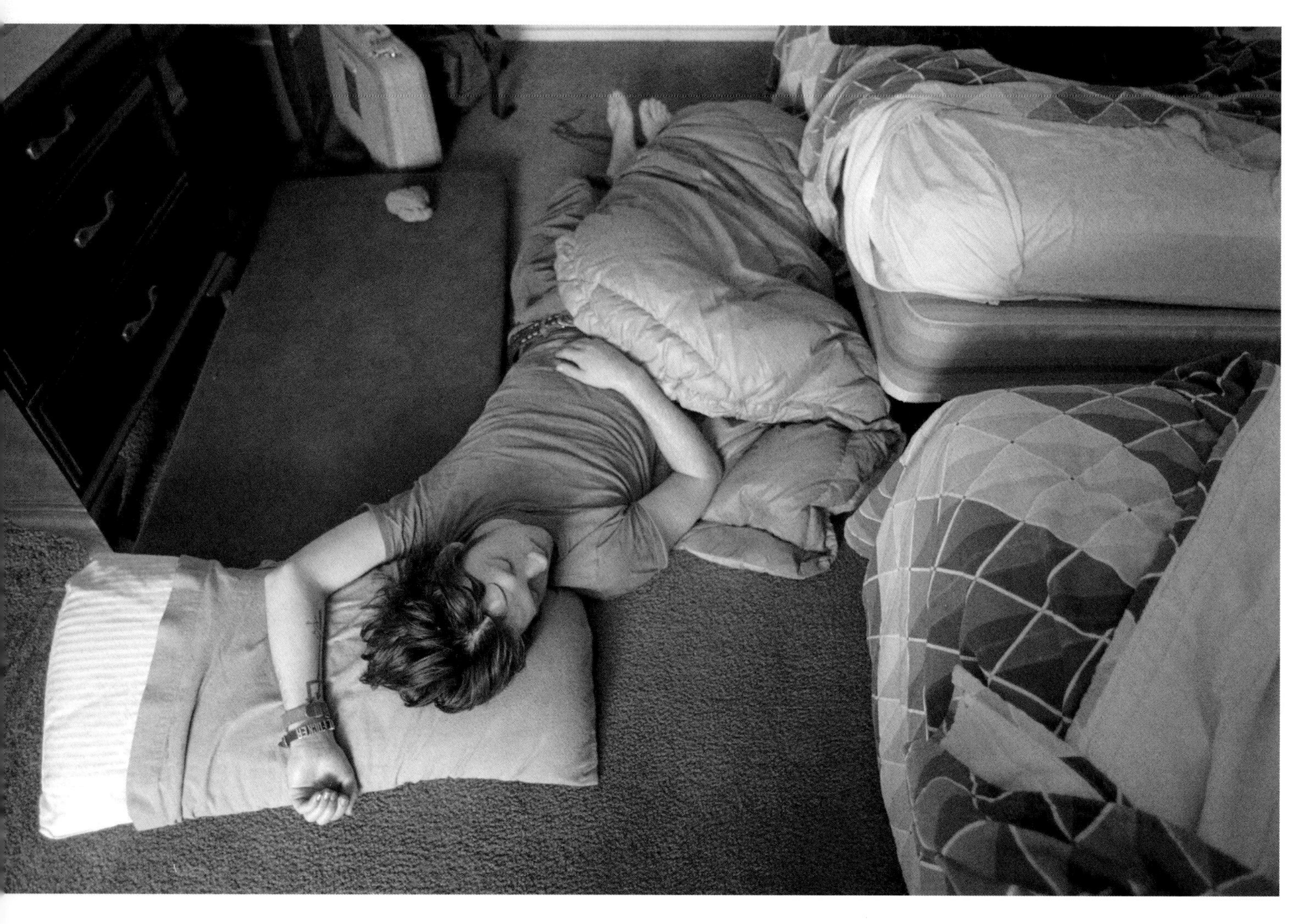

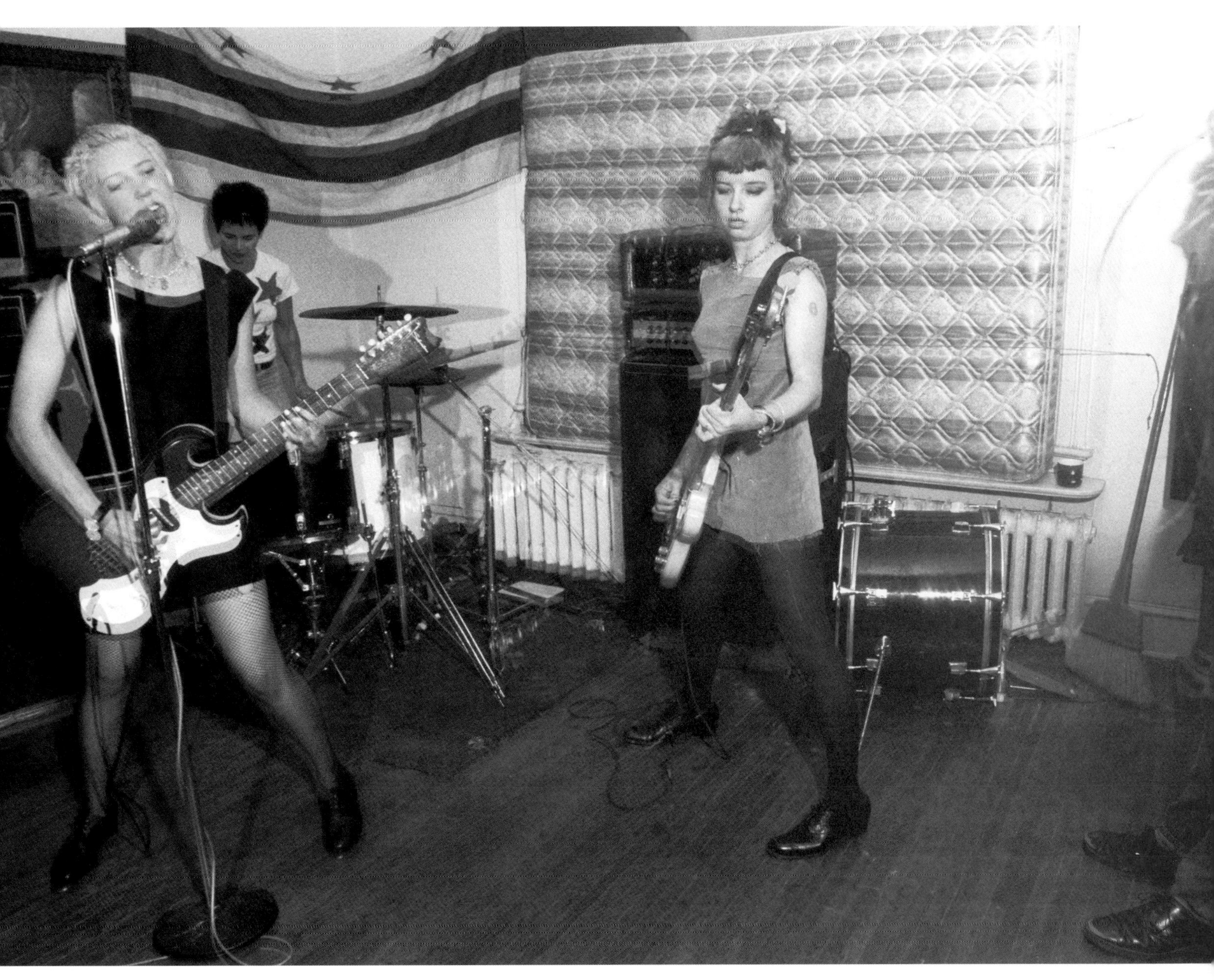

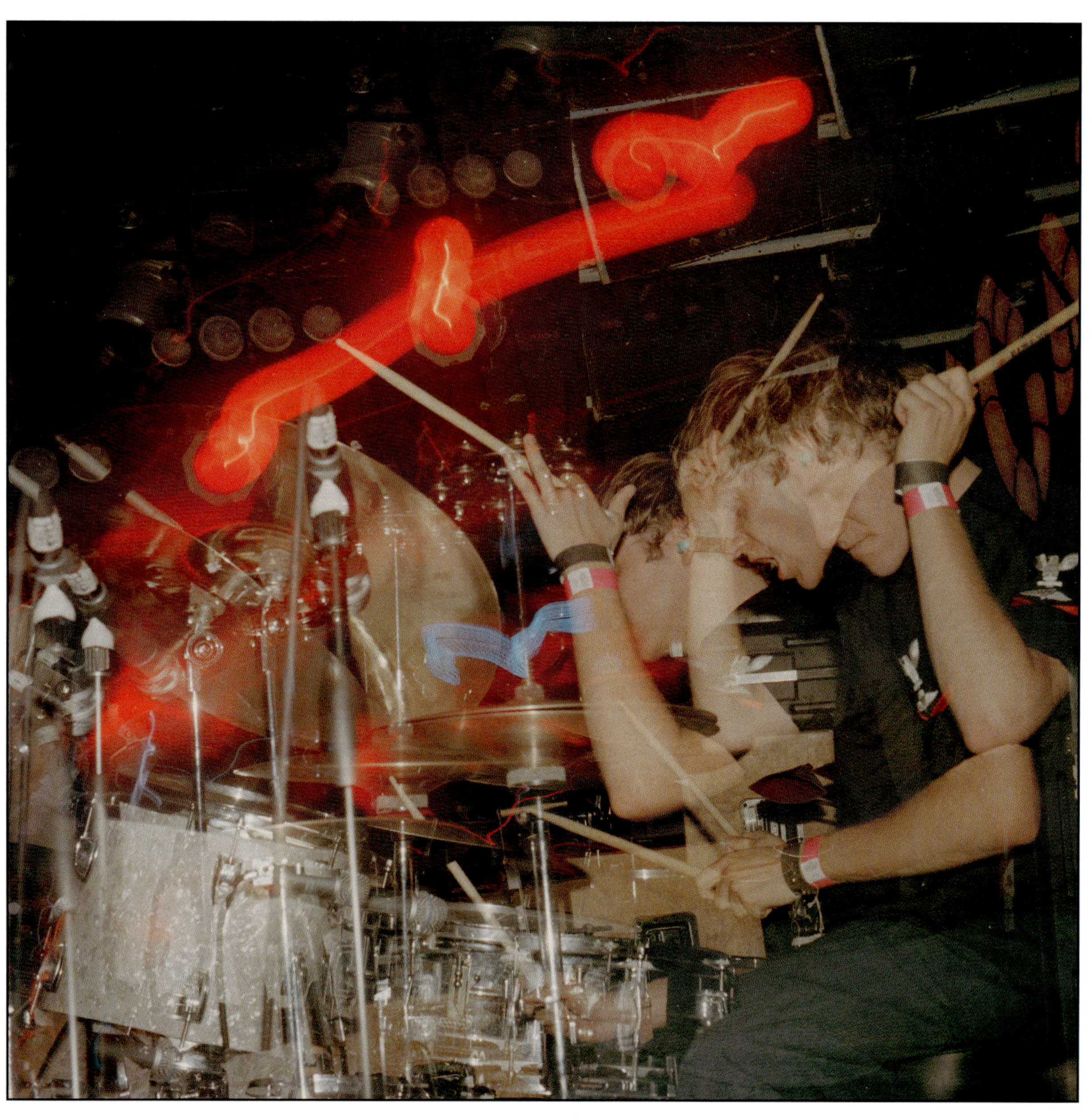

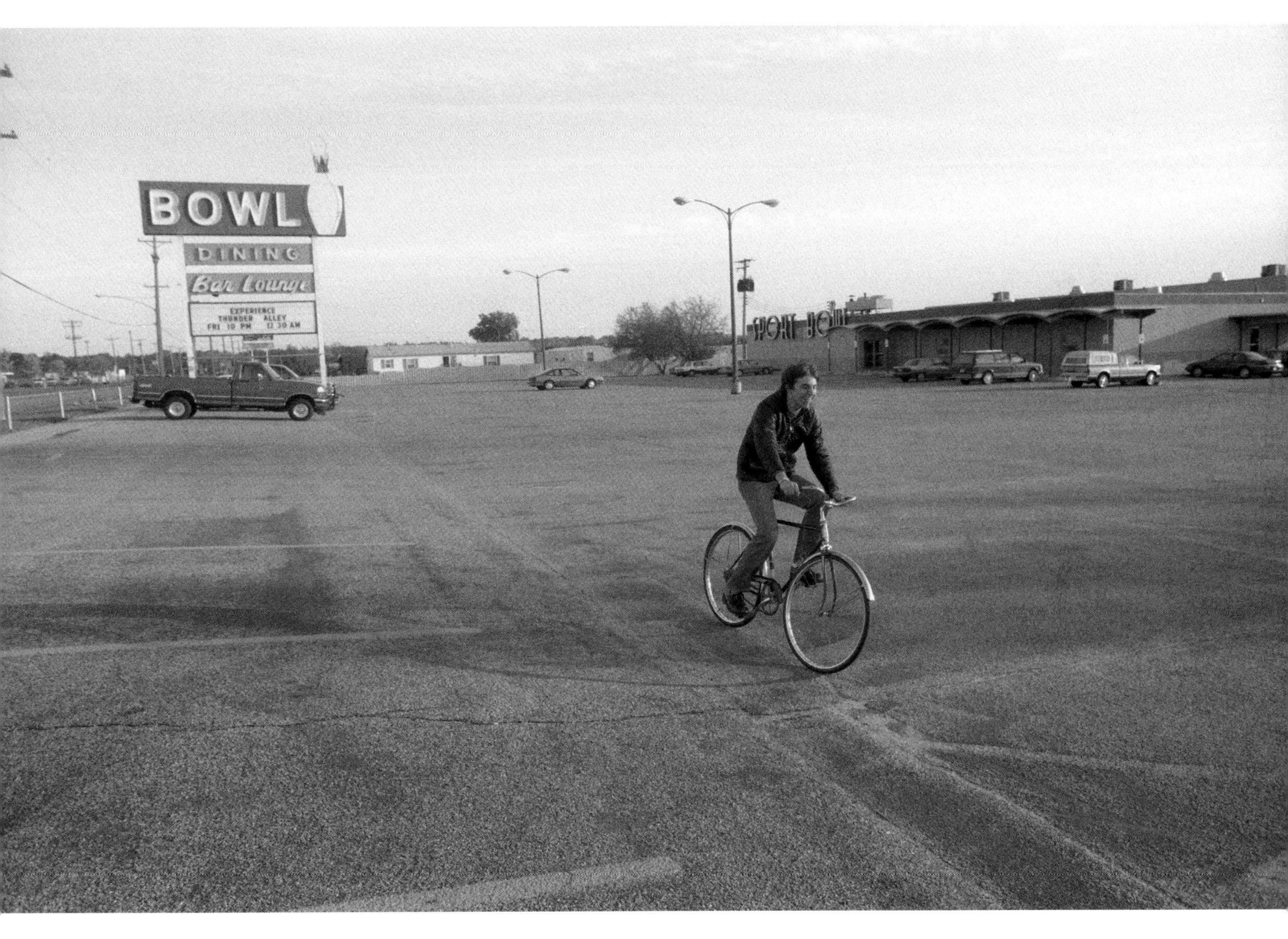
BOWL
DINING
Bar Lounge
EXPERIENCE
THUNDER ALLEY
FRI 10 PM 12 30 AM

by Cynthia Connolly

The punk music scene in Washington, DC from the early 1980s forward was a close-knit group of people who learned that the media, both print and radio, would never understand the energy and the drive that we had, both as individuals and as a group. From that experience, without resentment, we created our own true network of underground communication, using flyers and just simply talking.

This network and the people involved formed its own community, many living in group houses in DC, Maryland, and Virginia. It was all about how much living you could get out of the littlest amount of money, so you could do what you truly wanted to do (music, art, traveling, creating).

In 1981, musicians Ian MacKaye and Jeff Nelson, along with a handful of friends, rented one of these houses in Arlington, Virginia for $500 a month. It was close to DC and had a basement where Ian and Jeff's band, Minor Threat, could practice. This was also where their punk record label, Dischord, was based. Every bit of the house was used as a living space, and as a source of industry—for band rehearsals and the record label, and later for silk-screening, and even later, when I moved in, for letterpressing and yet more art.

Dischord Records underwent a series of office expansions in different locations as it grew in size. In 1996, the label consolidated mail order and wholesale business into one location and moved across the street. The house remained as a place to live, and also served as Ian's office and my letterpress studio. That spot on North 4th Street was, and still is, a beehive of activity: people running the label on one side of the street, and people on the other side living and working in the house. The hubbub came to an apex during the time that Fugazi—a Dischord band that Ian and several others formed in the late '80s—got very popular. It was during this time that Pat Graham showed up at Dischord House. I can't remember how or why. I think Ian invited him over, as he was always excited about new creative people who moved to DC.

Pat was exploring photography every which way, and was taking photo classes at an area community college. The two of us moved on our own paths, but we watched what each other was doing. He seemed to know all the tricks in photography that I couldn't be bothered with, but that's what made Pat Pat.

He moved in this slow, consistent, methodical, unassuming way. He didn't step loudly and never got in the way. Watching him take photos was always fun. I could never shoot a live band like he could. I just couldn't, and I admired him for it. He had this way with his flash with some paper taped on it, and he'd hold it up in some strange direction and point it—and for some reason, the photo would not only turn out, but would be an amazing shot. If I used the same method, the photos I shot would not express the moment half as good as Pat's.

Certain people "have it," and most people do not. I have it for black-and-white American landscapes, for portraits, and for street shots with my half-frame, and I know how to set that nearly pinhole thing up to get what I want under any light condition. Pat has it in many more ways, including for live bands, for Polaroid shots of his friends, for "hanging out" photos in 35mm color and black-and-white, and for his half-frame shots too. He is sincere and he always gets that back.

The Indie Rock Flea Market in Arlington, Virginia became a culmination of the fervor that was happening with the whole indie music scene in the early '90s. It started a little after Nirvana got huge and the Internet had not yet broken open. People would come far and wide to meet and see cool things that were happening in music scenes in different cities. (Now, you can just go to eBay or someone's website.)

The first Flea Market was so successful that it was done in a larger location the following year. Pat and I shared a table, where we sold our photos side by side. While hanging out that day, we came up with the idea to tour my photo show of musicians with their cars and his photos of the same people performing live with their bands. He found the first venue—Fuel Café in Milwaukee, Wisconsin—and then I booked a full tour in which the nearly thirty photos traveled to the West Coast and back, showing at cafés, clubs, stores, and galleries. The tour went on for nearly three years, with one of the final shows at the Institute of Contemporary Art in London, where Pat met his future wife, Melanie.

Pat became the man-about-town to hire to take your band photo. His style was consistently creative and each photo was different from the last. I remember one time driving home late at night and spotting Pat in front of this thrift/junk store in Arlington, taking a photo of local musician Jenny Toomey. There was Pat with the famous flash setup—lifting it out with his left hand and holding the camera with his right and releasing the shutter. It was cold out and late . . . and there was Pat getting the shot. It made me so happy to see, and I knew it was going to be great. The photo style went with the music style. It was all really really good and sincere.

A lot has happened since then, as Pat toured with Modest Mouse a billion times, continued to do more photography, and wound up living in London and getting married. In the winter of 2004, Pat and Melanie asked if I could come out and do a show in their gallery as a sort of "start-up" event and help them finish renovating the space. They even supported me with a stipend. There in London, I learned to print color photos with Pat and Melanie's equipment. They taught me what I used to call the "Pat" way—now it's the "Pat and Melanie" way.

Pat was always the nice guy. He was constantly helping people out, taking photos, giving photography advice to people like me. When he started getting all these jobs shooting photos for bigger magazines, he had problems, as do most photographers, with getting paid and receiving credit for his work. One year, for a gift, I letterpressed him some business cards with big words that said, PHOTO CREDIT: PAT GRAHAM.

Finally, Pat gets to put out the book we've all been waiting for, with his photo credit on the cover.

Plates

4/5 Ian Svenonius . The Nation of Ulysses
The Embassy, Washington, DC, Fall 1992

6/7 Sam McPheeters . Born Against
St. Stephen's Church, Washington, DC, 5/15/92

8 Tobi Vail . Bikini Kill
Rock for Choice, Sanctuary Theatre, Washington, DC, 4/4/92

9 Isaac Brock . Modest Mouse
Nita's Hideaway, Tempe, AZ, 6/6/00

10 Burning Truck (Modest Mouse tour)
Mojave Desert, CA, 9/11/01

11 Isaac Brock . Modest Mouse
40 Watt Club, Athens, GA, 5/27/00

12 Vice Cooler aka Chris Touchton . Hawnay Troof
Spitz, London, UK, 2002

13 Shelby Cinca . Frodus
Brighton, UK, 5/18/97

14/15 Guy Picciotto . Fugazi
Wilson Center, Washington, DC, 9/3/97

16 Chris Thompson . Circus Lupus
Club Asylum, Washington, DC, 6/28/92

17 Chris Majerus with Califone
Emo's, Austin, TX, 5/17/98

18 Quixotic
Black Cat, Washington, DC, 1999

19 Bill Callahan . Smog
Black Cat, Washington, DC, 1997

20/21 Brooklyn Bridge (Modest Mouse tour)
NYC, 2000

22/23 Blonde Redhead
Black Cat, Washington, DC, 1997

24 The Make-Up
European tour, Spring 1998

25 Myra Power . Slant 6
Vertigo Books, Washington, DC, 6/18/93

26 Ida
Woodstock, NY, 1998

27 Modest Mouse & 764-HERO
Outside the Side Door, St. Louis, MO, 11/10/97

28 Page Hamilton . Helmet
9:30 Club, Washington, DC, 1992

29 Dead Meadow
Upstairs at the Garage, London, UK, 2004

30 Ian Svenonius . The Nation of Ulysses
Madison, WI, 1990

31 Sarah Stolfa . The Delta 72
Black Cat, Washington, DC, 1990s

32 Sean Meadows . June of 44
South Eden St., Baltimore, MD, 1995

33 Didjits
The Unicorn, Milwaukee, WI, 1989

34 The Black Heart Procession
The Casbah, San Diego, CA, 9/16/01

35 Girls Against Boys
Lollapalooza, Charles Town, WV, 8/8/94

36 Modest Mouse
Olympia, WA, 1996

37 Dischord Records
Ian MacKaye's office door, Arlington, VA, 1994

38 Modest Mouse (crowd)
El Rey Theatre, LA, CA, 6/8/00

39 Ted Leo
Brooklyn studio, 9/11/02

40 Shelby Cinca . Frodus
Sweden, 1998

41 Eric Judy . Modest Mouse
Airport, Austin, TX, 2000

42-45 Fugazi
Sylvan Theater, Washington, DC, 8/7/93

46 Lou Barlow . Sebadoh
15 Minute Club, Washington, DC, 5/3/93

47 Dan Littleton & Jenny Toomey . Liquorice
GO Records, Arlington, VA, 9/13/95

48 Sam Prekop . The Sea and Cake
Silk City, Philadelphia, PA, 1997

49 Bikini Kill
Club Asylum, Washington, DC, 1992

50 Tortoise (drum)
Nita's Hideaway, Tempe, AZ, 6/10/01

51 Cass McCoombs
ICA, London, UK, 10/28/04

52 Jodi Buonanno & Geoff Farina . Secret Stars
Black Cat, Washington, DC, 4/16/95

53 Nobukazu Takemura & Aki Tsuyuko
Florida, 2001

54 "The Vansion" (tour van) . Modest Mouse
New Mexico, Spring 1998

55 Unrest
Bethesda, MD, Fall 1993

56 Jeff Mueller . June of 44
Ferry, Irish Sea, European tour, 1999

57 Rachel's
South Eden St., Baltimore, MD, 1995

58 Jennifer Finch . L7
Sanctuary Theatre, Washington, DC, 4/4/92

59 Modest Mouse (van)
Montana, April 1997

60 Ian MacKaye . Fugazi
St. Stephen's Church, Washington, DC, 1992

Ian Svenonius . The Cupid Car Club
Black Cat, Washington, DC, 1993

61 Carrie Brownstein . Excuse 17
San Francisco, CA, 1994

62/63 Daniel Higgs . Lungfish
Black Cat, Washington, DC, May 1996

64 Modest Mouse
Taco Bell parking lot, CA, 1997

65 The Jesus Lizard
O'Cayz Corral, Madison, WI, 1989

66 Doug Martsch . Built to Spill
Black Cat, Washington, DC, 1996

67 Ian MacKaye . Fugazi (guitar)
Arlington, VA, December 2001

68 Hoover
Gurr's house party, Alexandria, VA, 8/5/92

69 Sarah Stolfa . The Delta 72
The Embassy, Washington, DC, 10/28/95

70 Dirty . Rocket from the Crypt
Khyber Pass, Philadelphia, PA, 1994

71 The Make-Up
WPA, Washington, DC, 1996

72 Ian MacKaye . Fugazi
St. Stephen's Church, Washington, DC, 1992

73 James Bertram . Built to Spill
Black Cat, Washington, DC, 1994

74 Guy Picciotto . Fugazi
Malcom X Park, Washington, DC, 9/29/96

75 Donita Sparks . L7
O'Cayz Corral, Madison, WI, 1989

76 Regulator Watts
South Arlington basement, 1990s

77 Polly Johnson . 764-HERO
The Big Fish Pub, Tempe, AZ, 11/14/97

78/79 Sean Meadows . June of 44
Croation border crossing, Fall 1999

80/81 Eric Judy . Modest Mouse
Gas station, USA, Summer 1998

82 Mark Robinson . Air Miami
Basement studio, Arlington, VA, 1995

83 Montana (Modest Mouse tour)
April 1997

84/85 Tortoise (soundcheck)
Christiania, Denmark, 2001

86/87 Les Savy Fav
Pontiac Grille, Philadelphia, PA, October 1998

88 Beat Happening
Attic space, East Side, Milwaukee, WI, 1990

89 Erin Smith . Bratmobile
Peace Center, Washington, DC, 7/31/92

90/91 June of 44
Black Cat, Washington, DC, March 1998

92 Jennifer Herrema . Royal Trux
Black Cat, Washington, DC, 9/23/98

Elliott Smith
Black Cat, Washington, DC, 10/1/98

93 At the Drive-In
Black Cat, Washington, DC, Winter 1999

94/95 The Cupid Car Club
Black Cat, Washington, DC, 1993

96 David Yow . The Jesus Lizard
9:30 Club, Washington, DC, 1992

97 Jawbox
The 8x10, Baltimore, MD, November 1990

98 Allison Wolfe . Cold Cold Hearts
The Embassy, Washington, DC, 10/28/95

99 godheadSilo
Fireside Bowl, Chicago, IL, 1997

100 The Make-Up (crowd)
Munich, Germany, 1998

101 Marty Crandall with Modest Mouse
A Marty Party, Nita's Hideaway, Tempe, AZ, 6/6/00

102/03 Fugazi
George Mason University, Fairfax, VA, 12/4/98

104 Trevor Kampmann . hollAnd
WHFS, Landover, MD, 1996

105 Joanna Virello
Black Cat, Washington, DC, 9/6/98

Steve Gamboa
Diksmuide, Belgium, 1998

Rob Garza . Thievery Corporation
Felix Lounge, Washington, DC, 1998

106 Girls Against Boys
9:30 Club, Washington, DC, 1992

107 Cass McCoombs
ICA, London, UK, 10/28/04

107 Isaac Brock . Modest Mouse
Brownies, NYC, November 1997

108/09 The Warmers
Church, Washington, DC, 1996

110/11 Rodan
Lounge Ax, Chicago, IL, Summer 1993

112/13 Bikini Kill (detail)
Rock for Choice, Sanctuary Theatre, Washington, DC, 4/4/92

114/15 Lungfish
Maryland Institute College of Art, Baltimore, MD, 3/1/96

116 Tortoise (marquee)
Lawrence, KS, 2001

117 Jenny Toomey & Kristin Thomson
Simple Machines office, November 1991

118 Juan Carrera
Germany, 10/21/99

Modest Mouse
Desert in Arizona, 5/20/98

119 The Dismemberment Plan
Masonic Temple, Washington, DC, 9/14/98

Trans Am
Studio, Washington, DC, 1999

120/1 The Make-Up
Dom's Café, London, UK, Winter 1997

122 Andre 3000 . Outkast
Dressing room, DAR Hall, Washington, DC, 1998

123 Marty Crandall . The Shins
Outside Cane's, San Diego, CA 6/7/00

124/25 Ted Leo
New Jersey, September 2002

126 Rocket from the Crypt
Black Cat, Washington, DC, 1995

Superchunk
Simple Machines Working Holidays Weekend, Black Cat, Washington, DC, 1/9/94

127 Hoover
Univ. of Mary Washington, Fredericksburg, VA, 1992

128 Fugazi
London, UK, 11/4/02

129 Jason Farrell . Bluetip
Black Cat, Washington, DC, 1995

130 Blonde Redhead (guitar)
Black Cat, Washington, DC, 1998

131 Modest Mouse
Theatre of Living Arts, Philadelphia, PA, 5/22/00

132/33 Tortoise
Dresden, Germany, Winter 2001

134 Isaac Brock . Modest Mouse
Hotel in Albuquerque, NM, 1998

135 Slant 6
The Embassy, Washington, DC, Summer 1992

136 Jeremiah Green . Modest Mouse
Cane's, San Diego, CA, 6/7/00

137 Jeremiah Green . Modest Mouse
Fargo, ND, 10/21/97

Acknowledgments

Design Melanie Standage
Photo editing Melanie Standage and Lely Constantinople
Captions & archival resources Don Irwin, *Punk Life*
Production Jon Resh
Scans Photofusion, London, UK

Many thanks Johnny Temple & Akashic Books, Ian MacKaye, Lely Constantinople, Jon Resh, Gus White (Photofusion), Stevie Chick, Don Irwin, Cynthia Connolly, Sue & Bill Graham, Angela & Kevin Standage, Jason Farrell, Glen E. Friedman, Kristin Thomson, Jenny Toomey, Juan Carrera, Rich Jacobs, Jodi Buonanno, Geoff Farina, Scott Johnson, Vasillios Alexiou & Karsten Schneider at Less Rain, Ritu Gorczyca. And to the bands/musicians who have played, inspired, and supported my efforts, especially those I toured with: Modest Mouse, The Make-Up, June of 44, Tortoise, The Sea and Cake.

Pat Graham is the photographer who best captured the live performances of America's most loved and influential independent musicians during the 1990s & early '00s. His photos represent not just the bands, but the scenes—the venues, audiences, and instruments. He shows not only the public perfomances, but also behind-the-scenes: backstages, tour vans, hotel rooms, studios, and record labels, bringing a very intimate perspective to his work.

Graham began shooting in high school in Milwaukee, WI, but soon relocated to Washington, DC, where he worked extensively in and around the local and national music industry for over ten years. During this period he toured numerous times with bands such as Modest Mouse, The Make-Up, Tortoise, and June of 44 across the USA and Europe.

His photos have been published in magazines including *Rolling Stone*, *SPIN*, *ArtForum*, *NME*, *Dazed & Confused*, *VICE*, *Tokion*, *Swindle*, *Raygun*, the *Village Voice*, the *Washington Post*, *Washington City Paper*, the *Guardian*, *Punk Life*, *Punk Planet*, *Copper Press*, *Time Out*, *Guitar World*, and the *Chicago Reader*; as well as in books including *Dance of Days*, *Cinderella's Big Score*, Fodor's *Rock & Roll Travel Guide*, and the Dischord Records illustrated catalogue.

In 2000 he moved his base to London, England. He cofounded the contemporary art gallery, 96 Gillespie; a not-for-profit gallery dedicated to exhibiting American artists alongside their English counterparts in the UK. He works and exhibits internationally, frequently in collaboration with his wife, photographer/designer Melanie Standage.

His photos can be found in the Experience Music Project Museum in Seattle, WA, the Arlington Municipal Art Collection in Virginia, and in private collections around the world.

Select exhibitions

- Retrospect (with Standage)

  Space 1026, Philadelphia, PA, Jan 2007
  Cultuur Centrum Luchtbal, Antwerp, BE, Nov/Dec 2005

- Everyone Sees the Sun (group show curated by Rich Jacobs), Galleri Loyal, Stockholm, SWE, Dec 2005

- Past Perfect (with Standage)

  Transformer Gallery, Washington, DC, Oct/Nov 2005
  96 Gillespie, London, UK, Jul/Aug 2004

- The Wildebeest (with Standage), 96 Gillespie, London, UK, July/Aug 2005

- Move 3, 5, 8, 11, 12, 13 (group shows curated by Rich Jacobs)

  Clementine Gallery, NYC, Jan/Feb 2005
  New Image Art, LA, CA, Jan/Feb 1999, Feb 2000, Jan 2005
  96 Gillespie, London, UK, Nov/Dec 2004

- Hot Girls, Cool Guys & Other Stories (with Standage)

  New Space Gallery, Portland, OR, Jul 2004
  Mission Space, Baltimore, MD, Sep/Oct 2003
  Comet, Milwaukee, WI, 2002

- The Ascent of Civilization, Threadwaxing Space, NYC, 1997

- Cynthia Connolly & Pat Graham's Touring Photoshow

  Across the USA, 1996-1998
  Institute of Contemporary Art, London, UK, 1997

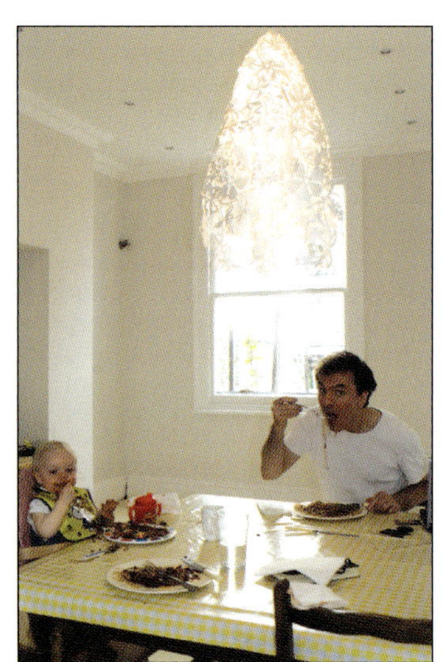
PHOTO: M. STANDAGE

Honor, Pat, Prue (under the table)

Published by Akashic Books
Printed in Singapore

www. patgraham.org www.96gillespie.com

ISBN-13: 978-1-933354-42-2
Library of Congress Control Number: 2007926134

First printing

Akashic Books
PO Box 1456, New York, NY 10009
info@akashicbooks.com www.akashicbooks.com